Jessica Balfour

Jessica Balfour

The Scented Garden

Rosemary Verey

MICHAEL JOSEPH
LONDON

A Marshall Edition

Editor Ethne Reuss Clarke
Editorial Assistants Helen Armstrong
Gwen Rigby
Art Director Barry Moscrop
Art Editor Simon Blacker
Picture Editor Zilda Tandy
Picture Researcher Mary Corcoran
Production Hugh Stancliffe

The Scented Garden was edited and designed by
Marshall Editions Limited,
71 Eccleston Square,
London SW1V 1PJ

First Published in Great Britain by
Michael Joseph Limited
44 Bedford Square,
London WC1

ISBN 0 7181 2050 7

Printed and bound in Spain by
Printer industria gráfica sa
Sant Vicenç dels Horts,
Barcelona D.L.B. 21438–1981

Contents

'And because the breath of flowers is far sweeter in the air (where it comes and goes like the warbling of music) than in the hand, therefore nothing is more fit for that delight than to know what be the flowers and plants that do best perfume the air.'

Francis Bacon

There are several people whom I wish to thank for particular help: Dick Balfour for his generous assistance with the rose chapter; Mr. Stageman and Dr. Brent Elliot of the Royal Horticultural Society Lindley Library for their knowledge so constantly called upon, and Anthony Lord, Acting Assistant Gardens Advisor for the National Trust, for so carefully checking my text.

I am grateful to all my friends who have so readily contributed their knowledge and opinions on scented plants and I would especially thank John Buxton, Peter Coats, Ruth Duthie, Joe Elliot, Ruth Henderson, Allen Paterson, Curator of the Chelsea Physic Garden, John and Lynn Sales, Sir David and Lady Scott, R.E. Stockley, Gordon Taylor, William Taylor, Graham Stuart Thomas, Lady Anne Tree and Helen Young. Of my friends in the United States, Fred McGourty of the Brooklyn Botanic Garden and Ellen Samuels of the Cloisters Museum, New York have been most helpful, advising me on scented plants in that country.

My sincerest thanks to my editor Ethne Clarke, who dreamed up the idea for this book. Finally, a special thank you to my husband for his patience, encouragement and assistance.

Dedicated to our seven grandchildren who have accompanied me on many walks round the garden, freely extending their opinions on matters olfactory.

Rosemary Verey 1981

Introduction

'Life is commensurate with the number of beautiful impressions that can be squeezed into it. Let us have as many as we can.' These words were written in 1907 by the architect Ernest Gimson to a client for whom he was building a large country house. I wholeheartedly agree with him, and would add, let us have as many fragrant plants in our gardens as we can.

A man who cannot see is blind, one who cannot hear is deaf, yet there is no everyday word to describe the man who has lost his sense of smell. Perhaps this is because a sense of smell, although it adds much to the enjoyment and appreciation of life, is not as necessary as the other senses. The moment you decide to explore the world of scents around you, you will be amazed by its diversity. I do not believe that you can increase your ability to smell, but you can certainly become increasingly aware of scent. Some scents have truly to be discovered, as some plants are 'fast' of their scent, in other words, they hold it until touched or even squeezed, while other plants are free with their scent, wafting it upon the air.

Words to describe scent are totally inadequate. Theophrastus wrote, 'Some things have a good, some an evil odour. But the various kinds of good or evil odour, although they exhibit considerable differences, have not received further distinguishing names, we speak of an odour as pungent, powerful, faint, sweet or heavy.'

Two thousand years later the 18th-century Swedish naturalist Carl Linnaeus does scarcely any better, saying simply that plants are either aromatic, fragrant, ambrosiac (food of the gods), alliaceous (garlic-like), hircine (goat-like), foul or nauseous.

Colours are described through the rainbow, a note of music by its name and octave, but there is no such commonly agreed scale by which one lay-man can convey to another the quality of a scent, except in very general terms.

The scent of all flowers and most leaves is due to an essential oil; that of flowers is known as an attar. In these essential oils there are various scented substances, but it is not possible to group them chemically as the relationship between their smell and chemical composition is not clear.

The delicacy and subtlety of a flower scent is due to a mixture of chemical compounds which make up the essential oil. The commonest of these compounds are the esters, formed from a combination of an acid and an

Wall paintings from Egyptian tombs, such as this fresco, c. 1400 BC, from the tomb of Nebamun in Thebes, provide us with a visual history of the nature of the earliest gardens.

Contained within mud walls, these private oases were shaded with scented trees and date palms, and irrigated from central pools planted with fragrant water-lilies, and the sacred lotus.

alcohol, and it is the type of alcohol contained in the essential oil which gives a flower its characteristic scent. In the rose it is geraniol which, when mixed with different chemicals, gives attar of roses with either a sweet, fruity, honey or spicy scent.

Benzyl acetate is present in attar of jasmine and creates the typically heavy scent; in daphne and lily of the valley it is mixed with other substances which make the fragrance lighter. When smelling mimosa you can discover two principal blends, those of violet and hawthorn. Yet the scent of hawthorn, if it is too strong, is not always pleasant, and violets themselves have a single delicate scent. Wallflowers have a mixture of scents reminding one of roses, orange blossom and primroses.

These five flowers, rose, jasmine, mimosa, violet and wallflower, all have a strong and distinctive fragrance, and you will find traces of them in many other flowers. But to try to define their fragrance is almost impossible. One flower smells like another and can be compared or contrasted with it: *Mahonia japonica* smells like lily of the valley.

Leaf scents too, are difficult to define, but often their essential oil is composed of only one substance. Eucalyptol gives the herby scent to santolina, yarrow and eucalyptus leaves. Many conifers and rosemary contain borneol acetate.

Lemon scent when it occurs is due to citral; lemon thyme, lemon-scented verbena and the leaves of citrus fruits all have this scent.

It is not necessary to study the make-up of the scented compounds in order to plant a scented garden. You can simply be aware of their presence, and enjoy them. Remember that sometimes it is the flowers which smell, at other times the leaves, and sometimes both.

In the evolution of plants, the scent substances are thought to have developed from the waste products of the plants' metabolism. The theory of why this should ever have happened is fascinating. Scent attracts the bees and butterflies that feed off and, in turn, fertilize, the plants they visit. Were it not for this symbiotic relationship, flowers might have evolved without scent.

Honey-bees, butterflies and moths have their organs of smell in their antennae, while ticks have odour-sensitive feet. All these insects, therefore, have the advantage of direct contact with the object they are smelling. But most vertebrates, including man, have the organ of smell in the nose, just above the mouth, so that we are aware of the odour of food before eating it. If the food smells bad our noses send a warning message to our brains; if the scent is delicious it helps us to appreciate the taste and adds to our enjoyment of the meal.

During the Middle Ages, the Persian influence extended beyond the Middle East into India and southern Europe and affected many aspects of life. This influence can be seen, not only in the artistic style of the early 18th century Indian miniature, *left*, but in the design of the garden portrayed: raised formal beds within a walled enclosure. The highly stylized flowerbeds may well have been planted with roses, which were valued throughout the Persian empire for their perfume.

However, at the same time in northern Europe, gardens were mainly to be found in monasteries. Also contained within high walls, these gardens were devoted to the cultivation of herbs and flowers for practical rather than aesthetic purposes. The 15th-century manuscript illumination, *right*, shows a garden typical of the period.

The shape of the nose acts as a distinguishing feature but our real nose, the one that matters to our aesthetic sense, is hidden away in the upper nostrils. It is a remarkable but relatively simple mechanism, and very delicate. In the upper nostrils there are two small areas of mucous membrane, consisting of spindle-shaped cells covered with olfactory hairs. As we breathe in, odorous molecules, when present, come into contact with these hairs and immediately send a message to the brain. The substances containing the molecules must be volatile enough to reach the nose in vapour form. What happens to these molecules after they have been inhaled and reached the olfactory cells is not yet determined.

Odour molecules, compared to other molecules floating about in the air, are heavy and tend to be found near the ground. This may be part of the reason why animals which live at 'ground-level' have a better range of scent than birds and other animals, such as squirrels, which live in trees. Over the centuries these animals have developed their sense of sight at the expense of their sense of smell. Have you ever wondered why a squirrel is stupid enough to lose its buried hoard of nuts?

Human beings are, as it were, halfway between, and our sense of smell, though not as keen as a dog's or as feeble as a squirrel's, is developed enough to assist in providing pleasure, as when sniffing a rose, or induce displeasure, as when inhaling noxious exhaust fumes on a busy city street.

This is a book to encourage you to be aware, to observe, enjoy and indulge in the odours of wood and garden that are a part of the 'fresh air' of the countryside. You will discover that among the best odours is the smell of the earth immediately after rain; as William Coles, the 17th-century herbalist observed, 'If a man want an Appetite to his Victuals the smell of the Earth new turned up by digging with a spade will procure it.'

Sweet smells and heady perfumes have always been important to man and they have been used for at least two thousand years for either personal adornment or religious purposes.

We can create scents around us in our gardens just as the ancient Egyptians did on the

scent, it appears that its primary connection was religious. In the Muslim faith great store was set by scent: musk was frequently added to the mortar used in the construction of mosques. But it is the private gardens of the Middle East that received the most acclaim, for they were certainly the most fragrant of early history. This is hardly surprising considering that some of the most highly scented plants are native to Persia.

The Greeks believed that the breath was the soul and escaped only at death, then to rejoin and merge with the universe, and that the soul, like sweet fragrance, entered the body through the nose. (Hundreds of years later Maeterlink was to describe scent as the soul of the flower.) The early Romans, apparently, were not aware of the delight to be had from perfumes and spices. It was not until their culture overtook the Greek and absorbed what were the best attributes of the conquered civilization, that the Romans began to appreciate and prize fragrant flowers and expensive perfumes.

The amazingly beautiful series of tapestries, 'The Lady with the Unicorn', hanging in the Musée de Cluny in Paris, is an allegorical representation of the senses and the tapestry devoted to the sense of smell is shown here. The set of tapestries at the Cloisters Museum, New York, entitled 'The Hunting of the Unicorn', was also designed and woven around 1500. This type of tapestry has been given the name *millefleurs*, meaning 'a thousand flowers', and in these particular hangings more than one hundred different plants are represented, woven so accurately that eighty-five of them have been identified. Many of the flowers shown are sweetly scented: violets, *Rosa centifolia*, wallflower, pansy, primrose, and forget-me-not. There are also herbs and fruit trees, and all are shown growing in a flowery mead, never in flower beds.

In 1577 a book was published called *The Gardener's Labyrinth* by Didymus Montaine, the pseudonym of Thomas Hyll. This is a manual of instruction, and the illustrations are most informative, showing what a small garden of the period would have been like. It was enclosed either by a wall or 'quickset' hedge, with raised beds set in square formation. This is a relic of the influence of eastern garden design, where irrigation was all-important and channels divided the garden into four squares, with beds raised to retain the carefully cultivated and manured soil. Remember, the

banks of the Nile. They imported sweet-smelling plants and spices like frankincense and myrrh. From these they made unguents, to scent and soothe their bodies while they lived, and to embalm them when they died. It is said that the royal barge of the Pharoahs was washed with flower-scented water before it set sail, and that Cleopatra had the sails of her barge drenched in exotic and seductive perfumes when she embarked to meet Mark Anthony.

The word perfume is derived from the Latin word *per*, meaning through, and the verb *fumare*, to smoke, literally, to perfuse with smoke. This recalls the ancient religious custom of making burnt offerings of scented wood.

The Egyptians, Greeks and Romans embraced this custom and it is still a practice of

In the 16th century pleasure came back to the garden and 'herbers', or arbours, cloaked in fragrant climbers were a popular feature. From them, the delights of a colourful and scent-filled garden could be enjoyed in shaded comfort.

some religions of the Far East, namely Buddhism and Hinduism. In the West, Christian churches are perfumed with incense on high holy days and for special services; which brings to mind the Jewish tradition of Moses and the instructions he received to erect an altar on which to burn offerings of incense.

The Song of Solomon proclaims the virtue of fragrance in the garden for which he longs: 'an orchard of pomegranate with pleasant fruits, camphire and spikenard, saffron, calamus and cinnamon, with trees of frankincense, myrrh and aloes with all the chief spices.'

Looking back over the historical province of

This engraving by Nicholas de Larmessin caricatures the group of gardeners known as Florists who, during the 16th and 17th centuries, did much to advance the appreciation of simple scented flowers, at a time when Europe was being buried under an avalanche of more flamboyant horticultural discoveries.

Garden of Eden was popularly believed to be divided by the four rivers of life.

There were beehives, an arbour or covered alleyway and a rather sparse planting of herbs and scented plants. The growing of fragrant lilies and gilloflowers in pots to stand on the beds was indicated. In the illustrations the sun seems always to shine and, charmingly, there are always people about, gardeners as well as the master and mistress. In the text there are careful instructions for the wife in 'the gathering and preserving of the greater number of kitchen herbs and roots.'

On a much more personal scale another group of people was helping to nurture and increase the love of beautiful and scented flowers. It is generally believed that the Huguenots, French Protestants fleeing from religious persecution in the late 16th and 17th centuries, carried with them into exile their precious hyacinth and tulip bulbs, ranunculus roots and seeds of auriculas and carnations, as well as their proven skill in growing them. Some of these people travelled to England and settled in small communities in East Anglia, Lancashire and London. They were not ordinary gardeners, but specialists, who cultivated the flowers for the sake of their beauty and scent. They became known as 'Florists' and were, in many ways, like any other group of people pursuing a common interest.

Florists' flowers were grown to be seen at close quarters and as individual plants. The eight special 'Florists' flowers' were the auricula, polyanthus, hyacinth, tulip, anemone, ranunculus, carnation and the pink. There are certain important features common to all these plants. They are essentially perennial and completely hardy; each bloom is of regular formation so that the Florist could select the most perfectly shaped flower. Endless opportunities for altering colour and form were made possible by careful culture and crossing of varieties, and scent was also considered important.

We are indebted to the Florists for the great diversity of auriculas and polyanthus, carnations and pinks which are to be found in old gardens and, occasionally, in plant nurseries. To lovers of old-fashioned flowers it is an exciting moment when an old variety is rediscovered, and recently there has been much renewed interest in them.

The 16th and 17th centuries were an unsettled but stimulating time. As the world expanded with voyages of discovery, so the sciences advanced to keep pace with the sudden flood of new and unfamiliar objects reaching the Old World from the New.

And no science was more overwhelmed than that of botany. Imagine the excitement that the first new species must have caused when unveiled, and the deep pleasure that was felt when a previously unknown plant, carefully propagated and cultivated, began to thrive in its new home.

During the 17th century two great botanical gardens were created in England and there were some very fine private plant collections on great estates. It was to these gardens that many of the new plants were first introduced from the wild, where they were subsequently propagated, and from which they were eventually distributed for general cultivation. One garden was at Oxford and the other at Chelsea, and both were called 'Physic Gardens', as was the garden at Kew, made in 1760 by the Princess Dowager of Wales, where the collection was arranged in the new Linnaean system of classification. Kew and Oxford became botanic gardens, but Chelsea retained the title of Physic Garden, and its history is fascinating.

An apothecary was one who mixed and administered drugs, and apprentices had to go through a strict training, learning the value and identity of many plants. The apothecaries were very proud of their skills, as is evident when reading their charter, and in 1617 they broke away from the great Company of Grocers to whom they were affiliated. The charter explains why: 'Unskillful and ignorant men . . . do abide in our city . . . which are not well instructed in the Art and Mystery of Apothecaries, but do compound many unwholesome and dangerous medicines and the same do sell . . . and daily transmit . . . to the peril and hazard of the lives of our subjects.'

So the Apothecaries created a teaching garden, first at Cobham House, destroyed in the great fire of London in 1666, and then at Chelsea, when in 1673 a plot of land was leased from Charles Cheyne. Later Sir Hans Sloane purchased the Manor of Chelsea and for £5 a year the Apothecaries were able to rent the

Of all the early flower portraits, those woven in the sets of tapestries known as 'The Lady with the Unicorn' and 'The Hunting of the Unicorn', are the most fascinating. The tapestry on the *left* is from 'The Lady and the Unicorn' series, which is an allegory of the senses. This particular panel represents the sense of smell and in it the lady and her handmaiden are shown fashioning a crown of clove-scented carnations. These flowers were extremely popular with medieval gardeners, artists and writers and were singled out because of their strong, spicy fragrance.

Many of the plants shown in these tapestries have been identified, and a garden at the Cloisters Museum in New York has been made using these flowers.

garden. In return they were obliged to demonstrate how useful plants may be distinguished from hurtful ones, and for the first forty years of their lease, fifty plant specimens from the garden were to be carefully dried, named and sent to the Royal Society annually. The agreement was honoured and these specimens are now preserved in the Natural History Museum, London.

In 1722 Philip Miller was appointed curator and remained at the Physic Garden for forty-nine prosperous years until he died aged 80. He was the author of the famous *Gardener's Dictionary* which first appeared in 1731, and was the most important and influential work for gardeners of the century.

Many of the plants grown in gardens today were introduced through the auspices and industry of John Bartram, a farmer and gar-

dener from Philadelphia, and America's first botanist of merit. I refer to him many times throughout this book as he, in partnership with a Londoner, Peter Collinson, did more than any other man to alter the 18th-century gardening scene, and that alteration had lasting effects. In England Collinson had a list of subscribers who, for £5 per year, were to receive one hundred packets of seed, and Bartram supplied the seed. As well as introducing American plants to Europe in this manner, he travelled extensively bringing hitherto unknown specimens back to his farm for cultivation and propagation.

Gardens in each century have their own distinctive fashion and my favourites are the intimate Tudor and Stuart gardens, bedecked with honeysuckles and herbs, with flowers planted to perfume the air. But two un-

fortunate trends, in my view, which temporarily pushed scented plants into the background, especially in fashionable gardens, were the 18th-century landscape movement, and the 19th-century Victorian vogue for bedding out and carpet bedding. The first caused the homely, scented blooms to be banished from beside the house to a concealed plot some distance away, so that they did not intrude upon the sweeping lawns and stately trees creating the carefully structured vista. The second did bring flowers back to the vicinity of the house, but garden owners attached far more importance to bright colours than to perfume, for the success of carpet bedding depended upon appearance.

This was a moment when many new flowers were being introduced, but greenhouses were full of cuttings and seedlings all grown for their effect, not their scent. Search as I may in early and mid-19th-century books and magazines I can find but few references to scented gardens, and it was not until William Robinson and Gertrude Jekyll, eminent Edwardian gardeners, that garden owners were once more encouraged to fill their plots with hardy, sweetly scented plants.

Today the pendulum has swung right back, and more and more people desire their gardens to be useful but beautiful, growing and using herbs and surrounding themselves with fragrant plants. In these pages you will find some plants to serve this purpose and I have attemp-

The fact that beautiful flowers are an inspiration to the senses is illustrated by the delightful print, *above*, by Frances Palmer, which was executed in 1862 for the American firm of Currier and Ives. It shows a mass of scented blooms against a landscape of the Hudson River Valley and is a refreshing adaptation of the classical flower-pieces of the 17th- and 18th-century Dutch artists, such as Jan Henrik Fredriks, whose painting, *right*, dated 1778, is typical of the genre.

ted to present some of the more unusual and exclude some of the already familiar. It is only a peep through the door of the scented garden; you must walk there yourself to discover its wealth, not only of scents but of all the pleasures and associations which go with them. Scents evoke memory, arouse our emotions, cause us to pause and wonder at the good things, which are there if only we look.

My ideal scented garden is surrounded by a wall or hedge, for scent is never still, indeed it is best when carried on the breeze, and a wall will help to contain it. If you have no wall then put the fragrant plants close to the house, so that when you walk outside you will easily catch their scent. Plant narrow beds and make many

paths, to allow you to walk close to the scented leaves and brush against and squeeze them. Make low hedges of lavender and southernwood. Have some raised beds for flowers which are fast with their scent so they may be enjoyed without bending low. Plants that release their perfume easily should be planted so the prevailing wind will bring the scent to you. Study the preferences of each plant and try to provide the soil and situation it likes best. Remember that every plant is an individual and appreciates personal attention.

The prophet Mohammed, when asked what gave him most pleasure in life, answered, 'Three things of the world which I love the most are women, perfume and prayer.'

Roses

The history of the Rose is not as well recorded as the lives and loves of the kings and queens, emperors and presidents and their ladies after whom many roses are named. While we know the date of introduction of most of the roses of the last two centuries and usually their parentage as well, there are many uncertainties and mysteries about the early history of roses.

The story probably started millions of years ago with the growth of wild species roses in the northern hemisphere. From these species roses, of which there are at least 150 and which normally come true from seed, have eventually come all the roses of today, either by sports or mutations, or by crosses with other roses.

The rose which had the greatest influence on the development of the genus in Europe, until the arrival of China roses at the end of the 18th century, was *Rosa gallica*, sometimes called *R. rubra* or the Red Rose. This rose was cultivated by the Medes and the Persians as early as the 12th century BC and was revered by them as a religious emblem. It was grown by the ancient Greeks at Miletus in Asia Minor in the 4th and 3rd centuries BC, from where the Romans later imported it. Since *R. gallica* is native from Persia to France, I sometimes wonder whether hybrids had already been produced and it was these which the Romans imported or whether it was the method of cultivation rather than the rose bushes which were taken to Rome.

Rosa gallica not only produced *R. gallica officinalis*, the Apothecary's Rose and many other hybrids, but was also one of the parents of the Damask roses. It was long thought that *R. damascena*, the 'Summer Damask', was a cross between *R. gallica* and *R. moschata*, the musk rose, and that the 'Autumn Damask' (*R. damascena semperflorens* or *bifera*) was a sport from it. But it is now believed that, while *R. gallica* is the parent of both, *R. damascena* arose from a cross with *R. phoenicea*, and the 'Autumn Damask' from one with *R. moschata*.

Whatever its origin, the importance of the 'Autumn Damask', also known as 'Quatre Saisons', is that it flowers in summer and again in autumn, unlike the other roses known in ancient times, which were only summer flowering. Although the Damasks may have originated in Damascus, it seems likely that their arrival in western Europe preceded that of the returning Crusaders, to whom credit is sometimes given for the rose's introduction.

A cross between *R. damascena* and *R. canina*, the wild rose found in hedgerows in most

'The Lover finds the Rose' from the *Roman de la Rose*. Written in the 13th century by Guillaume de Lorris, this is the tale of a would-be lover who receives instruction in the art of love by finding his way through a beautiful garden, and attains his goal when he uncovers the perfect rose.

countries of Europe, is thought to have produced *R. alba*. Its name, the Dog rose, is said to derive from the Roman belief that its roots helped in the treatment of hydrophobia. *R. canina* has played little further part in the breeding of modern roses, but has been the main root-stock on which they have since been budded.

It is not clear how old are the Alba roses (some of which, incidentally, have pink flowers). Yet it is thought that they are the white roses which became the emblem of the Virgin during the Middle Ages. In spite of its early pagan connections, the rose was later accepted by the Christian Church, which helped to increase the flower's popularity during the Middle Ages. It became the heavenly crown for martyrs, and Christian mystics saw the five wounds of Christ in the five petals of the red rose, presumably *R. gallica*. But the increased cultivation of the rose in medieval Europe was due mostly to its medicinal properties; the love of its beautiful flowers, though against the austere Christian ethics of the time, was allowable because of their practical uses.

It was once a popular theory that *R. centifolia*, the old Cabbage Rose also known as the Provence Rose, dated back to the days of ancient Greece and Rome, and that it was the hundred-petalled rose described by Theophrastus and Pliny. It is now accepted that this rose is a much later hybrid, probably between *R. alba* and the 'Autumn Damask', or is at least the result of a combination involving these roses and their parents. We owe a great debt to those Dutch rose breeders through whose genius and perseverance, from about 1580 until 1710, the Centifolia roses were developed.

From *R. centifolia* the Moss roses 'Muscosa' came as bud-sports, and for a time this line of rose development largely ceased until, very recently, Ralph Moore began breeding the moss characteristic into miniature roses.

Roses seem to have lost some of their popularity during the 17th and early 18th centuries, and much of the credit for their return to popular favour must be given to the Empress Josephine, who not only assembled at Malmaison an enormous collection of roses, but also did so much to encourage the breeding of new varieties. A great boost to such breeding was given by the arrival in Europe and America, from about 1790 onward, of China roses, not in the form of *R. chinensis* itself, but of what the eminent rosarian. Dr. C.C. Hurst calls the 'four stud Chinas', each of which had a different influence on rose breeding.

The honour for the first successful hybridization with one of these China stud roses goes to John Champneys, a rice planter from Charleston, South Carolina. By crossing *R. moschata* 'Miller' ('Miller's White Musk') with 'Parson's Pink China' he produced, in 1802, 'Champney's Pink Cluster'. This rose combined the climbing habit and scent of the Musk rose with the repeat flowering quality of the China roses. From seeds of this rose, Philippe Noisette, produced the first Noisette rose, described later in the chapter.

From crosses between Noisette roses and another of the stud China roses, 'Park's Yellow Tea-scented China', came the first yellow Noisettes and Tea roses.

Continuing the story of 'Parson's Pink China', we find that from it arose the 'Dwarf Pink China' at Coleville's nursery in England in 1805. This miniature rose was known in England as the 'Fairy Rose' (not to be confused with the much later 'The Fairy') or *R. lawranciana*. In France it was called 'Bengale

The sweetest things
    have fleetest end,
Their scent survives
    their close.
But the rose's scent
    is bitterness
To him that loved
    the rose.

A mass of deliciously
fragrant old-fashioned
roses embodies the
beauty and pleasure to be
found in a scented
garden, where each plant
grown is much more
than just a feast for the
eye.

Pompom' and became a grandparent of the first Poly-Poms also known as Polyantha roses.

In 1833 a cross between a Bourbon and another of the stud China roses, 'Hume's Blush China', produced the first of the pink Tea roses, called 'Adam'. But the greatest influence of the Bourbons was on the breeding of Hybrid Perpetuals.

The fourth of the stud China roses was 'Slater's Crimson China', which reached Europe in 1792. It was, apparently, widely cultivated in Italy where it is thought to have been one of the parents of the 'Portland Rose' from a cross with the 'Autumn Damask'. The 'Portland Rose' is named after the Duchess of Portland, who is thought to have found it in Italy around 1800 and brought it back to England, where it was also known as *R. paestana* or 'Scarlet Four Seasons' that bloomed in autumn as well as summer.

From the 'Portland Rose' was bred 'Rose du Roi', also called 'Crimson Perpetual', although it was first named 'Rose Lelieur' after Count Lelieur the superintendent of the Garden of St. Cloud, where it was raised in 1812. Unfortunately for him, a member of the King's household was so captivated by its beauty that he was determined that it should bear the King's name and, in spite of the strong views of the Count, its name was changed.

This was the first of what were then called the Damask Perpetuals, but it is now described as the first Hybrid Perpetual. It was the delicious fragrance, rather than the size or beauty of its flowers, which made it so popular until the arrival of the larger Hybrid Perpetuals in about 1837. To quote from William Paul's *The Rose Garden*, published in 1848, 'How delightful it is to wander through a plantation of Damask Perpetuals on a still moist morning in autumn, when the flowers are just expanding! It is not necessary to pluck them to inhale the perfume they inherit, for the very air is laden with their fragrance.'

Early in the 19th century the term Hybrid Chinas was used to describe the many hybrids bred from crosses between the repeat flowering Chinas, Noisettes and Bourbons and the summer-flowering Gallicas, Centifolias, and Damasks. These Hybrid Chinas, crossed with Portlands, Bourbons and Damask Perpetuals, produced the larger flowered Hybrid Perpetuals, which are, therefore, of very mixed parentage. Most of the early large-flowered Hybrid Perpetuals, starting with 'Princesse

Hélène' in 1837, were produced by M. Laffay at Auteuil. His most important success must be accounted 'La Reine' in 1842, with its large flowers of lilac-rose and its strong scent.

Very soon other growers started breeding Hybrid Perpetuals, and by 1848 William Paul was able to list 106, plus 80 Damask Perpetuals. Among them was 'General Jacqueminot', introduced in 1852, raised by an amateur, M.A. Roussel of Montpelier. Sadly, he died unaware of his success, and it was his gardener M. Rousselet, who found it after his employer's death. This rose, called 'The General' or 'General Jack', was not only widely grown for the florist trade, but was also to be the ancestor of so many of today's red roses.

For many years the Hybrid Perpetuals were the most popular roses, especially with exhibitors who valued their large flowers and their long-lasting qualities, but many were not really ideal as garden flowers, and too many were only suitable for the show bench.

I have already briefly mentioned Tea roses, which are believed to have been developed from crosses between *R. chinensis* and *R. gigantea*. There are many theories about the origin of the name 'Tea'; some said that the roses had a scent resembling the smell of a newly-opened tea chest, and some declared that their only link with tea was that they were imported on ships carrying tea. Sadly, they were lacking in hardiness, though a few are still grown outside as climbers. Nevertheless, they had their devoted admirers; the rose grower Jack Harkness quotes his grandfather John, who in 1890 wrote: 'If the Rose be the queen of flowers, the Tea-scented Rose may be regarded the queen of queens, for undoubtedly they are in refinement and delicate beauty superior to their robust and more highly coloured relatives.'

Their importance in the history of roses lies not in themselves, but in the qualities they passed on, through crosses with Hybrid Perpetuals, to Hybrid Teas. The first of these, 'La

France', was bred by M. Guillot in France and was introduced in 1867; it is still available. For many years the roses which preceded them, and most of the Hybrid Teas themselves, were limited to crimson, purple, dark red, pink and white and shades of these colours. The Tea Roses had introduced pale yellow to the colour range, but it was not until 1900 that a deep yellow was achieved. 'Soleil d'Or', a cross between a Hybrid Perpetual and *R. foetida persiana*, the 'Persian Yellow' was followed in 1910 by 'Rayon d'Or', the first deep yellow Hybrid Tea; both these roses were bred by the venerable French rose grower, Joseph Pernet, of the Pernet-Ducher nursery.

Over the following 70 years were developed all the deep yellows, golds, flames, oranges, and vermilions of so many modern roses.

To complete the outline of the history of roses, we need to go back to 1860 when seeds of *R. multiflora* were sent to France from Japan. This led to the production in 1875, by M. Guillot, of 'Paquerette', a dwarf white, repeat flowering rose, the first of the pretty Poly-Poms, from which, in the 1920's, Svend Poulsen in Denmark produced the first Hybrid Polyanthas by crossing Poly-Poms with Hybrid Teas. From this, through cross-fertilization with Hybrid Teas, evolved the Floribunda roses now more appropriately called Cluster-flowered roses. Although for a long time Floribundas had no scent, it is to the credit of rose breeders that the scent of the Hybrid Teas has been bred into them.

Although there is much romance in the story of modern roses such as 'Crimson Glory', 'Peach', 'Ena Harkness' and 'Silver Jubilee', I shall concentrate on old-fashioned roses and some of the other species from which they were developed.

Among these other species is *R. pimpinellifolia* (syn *R. spinosissima*), the Scotch rose, a tough plant with hooked thorns and blackish hips that suckers freely. Many hybrids were produced in the 19th century, especially in Scotland, and more recently Wilhelm Kordes has bred some modern shrubs from the Scotch rose. Although 'Nevada' and its pink sport 'Marguerite Hilling' are usually said to be hybrids of *R. moyesii*, their characteristics link them with the Scotch rose.

R. moyesii, from China, was named after the Rev. J. Moyes of the China Inland Mission in recognition of his help to the actual finder E.H. Wilson. These single roses have small flagon-

shaped red or orange hips after flowering.

The contribution of *R. wichuraiana* has been mainly in the production of strong-growing ramblers and climbers. *R. foetida* and its sports 'Austrian Copper' and 'Persian Yellow' have contributed colour rather than growth. *R. eglanteria* (syn *R. rubiginosa*) has given the sweet smell of its foliage to the Hybrid Sweet briers. The scent of the Hybrid Musks seems to have come not from *R. moschata*, the Musk Rose, but from *R. multiflora*, especially through 'Trier' and through the careful choice by the Rev. Pemberton, who bred so many Hybrid Musks in the 1920s. It comes also from other parents which were strongly scented, like the early Hybrid Tea 'Ophelia', the most sporting of roses. *R. sempervirens* has passed on to its progeny its almost evergreen foliage.

Between 1799 and 1807, Robert John Thornton published the *New Illustration of the Sexual System of Linnaeus*, and the third book of this work, called the *Temple of Flora*, is one of the most famous volumes of flower illustrations ever produced. It contains twenty-eight colour engravings which are the work of several artists, but the plate 'Roses', shown here, is the work of Thornton himself.

According to Dr. William Stearn, who in 1951 attributed the modern names to the roses, they are chiefly varieties of *Rosa centifolia*, the yellow *R. hemisphaerica* 'Herrmann' and an unidentified red rose and single rose.

The most famous flower painter is probably Henri Fantin-Latour, who 'studied each flower, each petal . . . as if it were a human face. . . .' His name is most closely associated with roses and there is a Centifolia rose named for him. The painting of the basket of roses, *far left*, is an excellent example of his skill. Curiously, his real love was music, particularly the works of Wagner, and he painted to live rather than lived to paint.

The plants to grow

The history of *Rosa alba*, the white rose, goes far back over the centuries to the days of ancient Greece, and the fact that it has been grown so successfully ever since is a sure sign of its hardiness and adaptability. The 13th-century writer Albertus Magnus aptly describes it as, 'the white garden rose which has often fifty or sixty petals, is very bushy and the branches are long and thin'. Although it is not a native of that country, John Parkinson calls it the English White Rose, probably because it was associated with the House of York during the Wars of the Roses.

R. alba semi-plena is one of the roses (the other being *R. damascena trigintipetala*) especially grown at Kazanlik in Bulgaria for distilling attar of roses. This is adequate testimony to the flower's strong perfume, emanating from clusters of milk-white, nearly single blooms with conspicuous hearts of golden anthers. This rose will grow to 1.5–1.8m/5–6ft and,

with its fine fragrance, grey-green foliage and colourful red hips in autumn, makes a valuable addition to a border of old roses.

R. alba maxima, variously known as the Great Double White and the Jacobite rose, is a rose of great antiquity. The double white flowers are flushed at their centres with cream and appear quite early, followed by an abundance of oval hips in the autumn. This is a very vigorous rose and will easily reach a height of 2.4m/8ft.

The 15th-century 'Great Maiden's Blush' has wonderfully fragrant blooms, blush pink as they open, changing to a warm cream at the edges as the flowers fade. The grey-green leaves are characteristic of *R. alba*, and make a great contribution to the whole display, showing off the flowers to perfection. This feature is especially evident in the 18th-century 'Celestial' which has sweetly scented, semi-double, soft pink flowers bedded in pewter-coloured foliage. To see this rose at the peak of its beauty you must catch it when the buds are just half open. It is a rose for the traditional garden and should be one of the first chosen by anyone starting a collection of old-fashioned roses.

'Köenigin von Dänemarck' is perhaps better known as the 'Queen of Denmark', and has no equal in perfection among the Alba roses, but may be compared in beauty to the Damask

'Madame Hardy'. The leaves are elegant, the buds perfect, and by the time these are fully open, the flower becomes a galaxy of blush-pink petals. This is an ideal rose to use as a tall (1.5m/5ft) specimen, placed where you can walk close enough to appreciate the glorious scent and voluptuous beauty.

'Belle Amour' is an Alba-Damask hybrid, similar in height and spread to 'Köenigin von Dänemarck', but much richer in colour; the coral-pink double blooms, set off by many golden stamens, have a spicy fragrance unusual in roses.

The Banksian rose is a vigorous climber needing a sunny wall to prosper. When it is happy, as I have seen it growing in the warmth of the south of France, it will climb to 12m/40ft.

Rosa alba semi-plena

'Celestial'

Then it is a wonderful sight, bearing many pendulous trusses of small, fragrant flowers on lateral shoots throughout the spring. This climber of Chinese origin is certainly well-travelled! Named in honour of Lady Banks, wife of the famous 18th-century naturalist Sir Joseph Banks, who travelled with Captain Cook in the 'Endeavour' on his first expedition to Australia, the Banksian rose was introduced to Europe in 1796 as a small-flowered white variety. Eleven years later the double white form was sent to The Royal Botanic Gardens at Kew by the plantsman William Kerr. Eventually in 1817, a double yellow was imported into France, where several seedlings were subsequently raised.

These early varieties, including a pink which must have had great charm, now appear to have been lost. Today we have available the single white, the single yellow 'Lutescens' and a double, buttercup-yellow called *Rosa banksiae* 'Lutea'. This is the most hardy, and consequently the most commonly seen, Banksian grown in gardens. But 'Lutescens' has a far stronger scent and should be chosen for a garden in a warm climate. An important point to remember when you are pruning Banksian roses is that the flowers are not carried on laterals from the previous year's growth as is usual with common ramblers, but on shoots growing from these laterals. In fact you need wood several years old to give a full display, so this rose requires very little pruning except for the removal of the oldest branches to make way for younger growth.

The sweet-smelling brier or dog rose, *Rosa canina*, has become naturalized in parts of North America and is found in most of the cooler parts of Europe. The delicately scented, pale pink to whitish flowers are followed at summer's end by egg-shaped or round hips; they are an excellent source of vitamin C and during World War II were used for making rosehip syrup. Most garden roses are budded on to the root stock of *R. canina* or *R. laxa*, but the dog rose itself is most at home in the hedgerows surrounding pastureland, where its vicious thorns prevent grazing animals from eating their way through its branches. When you are next on a country walk with children, if you should happen upon a dog rose in flower, point out the curious formation of the five green sepals, and teach the children the rhyme:

Five brothers in one house are we,
All in one little family,
Two have beards and two have none,
While only half a beard has one.

'Köenigin von Dänemarck'

Rosa banksiae 'Lutea'

Rosa canina

The history of *Rosa centifolia*, the rose of a hundred petals, goes back to late 16th-century Holland where it made its first appearance. The Dutch and Flemish painters immortalized it in the overly realistic flower pieces so popular during the 17th century, preferring the Centifolia to the Albas and Gallicas of Renaissance paintings. Sometimes known as the Cabbage or Provence rose, John Gerard mentioned it in the catalogue of plants he grew in his Holborn garden in 1595, and then explained in his *Herball* how it 'came first out of Holland but by all likelihood it came from the Damask rose'. In 1629 John Parkinson called it 'the Great Damask, Province or Holland Rose.' It is typically pink-flowered with large, drooping, sweetly scented blossoms that are completely double.

Then about 1800, a single-flowered form appeared; although this could well have occurred before but passed unnoticed. We know of this rose's existence because it is portrayed by Redouté. From it came *R. centifolia* 'Cristata', the Crested Moss or 'Chapeau de Napoléon'. It is identical to its parent except that the flowers are less full and round. But the special attraction, which gives the rose its common name, is the sepals that stand up like a cockade around the bud, framing it with a green frill and giving a shape reminiscent of the tricorn hat worn by Napoleon. It has the same sweet fragrance, some think it more intense, as *R. centifolia* and is often chosen as the rose for a scented garden.

'Fantin Latour' is another of the best Centifolia roses for scent and performance. It makes a strong bush with attractive foliage and is worthy of a place in any collection of old roses. It is historically interesting too, being named after the celebrated 19th-century French painter Henri Fantin-Latour.

Another vigorous Centifolia, needing support for its lax habit, is 'Tour de Malakoff'. The eminent rosarian Graham Thomas says, 'there is nothing like it in horticulture,' and that it has 'flowers that take one's breath away'. What more do you want in the scented garden? It will grow to 1.8m/6ft, and appreciates support in order to show off its vivid magenta – or are they pink? – blooms. The colour is as elusive as the perfume is pronounced. Mr. Thomas continues: 'Eventually before falling, a cool lilac grey assumes predominance over the five-inch blooms, and a bunch of flowers of all tones is a startling revelation of what a rose can do.' With space to spare, as well as the height to accommodate this magnificent variety, it should definitely be given a place in your scented garden.

If the size of 'Tour de Malakoff' is daunting, do not despair; the Centifolia has a rose for every garden. The mossy 'de Meaux', *R. centifolia pomponia*, is a small, charming plant,

'General Kléber'

'Fantin Latour'

flowering much earlier than the typical Provence varieties. Its flowers are clear pink and scarcely 2.5cm/1in across, but you seldom see it in private gardens today. You are far more likely to find 'Petite de Hollande', a bush up to 1.2m/4ft tall, with graceful arching branches bearing rose-pink flowers, or 'Village Maid', a robust bush that has milky white flowers clearly striped with pure pink.

The Moss rose, *R. centifolia* 'Muscosa', is very like a Cabbage rose in all its characteristics except for one distinguishing feature. This is the moss-like growth on the backs and edges of the sepals. The stems, stipules and calyx-tubes are also densely covered with glandular bristles. Squeeze or bruise these and you will release a resinous scent. This moss is sometimes rich green, sometimes wine-red, and is one of nature's most seductive devices, turning these roses into perfumed enchantresses.

Over two hundred and fifty years ago, at the Botanic Garden in Leyden, the Moss rose was discovered as a sport of *R. centifolia*. This lovely, clear pink rose is at first shaped like a goblet then, as it opens, it becomes flat with a 'button' centre; its fragrance is wonderful, causing some to compare it to perfectly ripe fruit.

'Old Pink Moss' – a misnomer as it is only fifty years old – has an exquisite perfume. It is a tall rose with lovely arching stems and pale pink flowers. 'Blanche Moreau' has perfectly formed buds opening to paper-white flowers which sometimes have a stray pink stripe or even a whole pink petal. One of its charms is its dark red moss, a perfect counterpoint to the delicacy of the flowers.

'General Kléber', named after one of Napoleon's generals, is one of the loveliest Moss roses, with double flowers of the same soft pink as the Alba 'Celestial'. It has a rich scent and fresh green moss.

Perhaps 'Henri Martin' could be considered the best of the red-flowered Moss varieties. It makes a vigorous bush 1.5–1.8m/5–6ft tall with a tremendous profusion of richly perfumed flowers, elegantly borne in full clusters.

'William Lobb', a favourite perhaps because of its easy name, has crimson buds. When these open the petal edges are dark purple and the centres a soft lilac-grey, hence its other name 'Old Velvet Moss'. It is an irresistible rose and very fragrant. But it needs a space all of 1.8m/6ft in height and spread to accommodate its vigorous growth.

My last choice of Moss rose is 'Mousseline', sometimes called 'Alfred de Dalmas'. Only 1.2m/4ft tall, it is a good choice for a small garden. The large, double flowers, which open from midsummer until autumn, are blush-pink and highly scented.

'Chapeau de Napoléon'

'Mousseline'

'William Lobb'

The arrival of *Rosa chinensis* in Europe, during the late 18th century, had a tremendous impact upon rose breeding, for it passed on to many of the modern recurrent flowering roses its ability to flower continuously from early summer to the end of the season and, given mild weather, until Christmas. Although the scent of these newer roses may not be as strong as that of old-fashioned charmers, which flower only once, they make up for this with a generous quantity of bloom.

The 'Common Blush China' or the 'Old Blush' rose, as it is sometimes called, makes a 90–110cm/36–38in bush and will grow even taller if you give it wall protection. The crimson-tinted buds open to rose-pink flowers carried in graceful clusters, and the rose is highly recommended for use as a low hedge.

'Hermosa' is a hybrid that is mostly China in character, being very like 'Old Blush', but growing to only 90cm/36in. Another favourite is 'Bloomfield Abundance'. It has miniature buds that are the shape of a perfect hybrid tea bud, and no larger than a thimble. It makes a

vigorous bush, up to 1.8m/6ft tall, with strong flower sprays from early summer onwards. This is the perfect buttonhole rose, for shape, scent and general allurement. The lobes of the green calyx around the bud have leafy extensions which add to the overall charm of this rose. The flowers of 'Cécile Brunner', the sweetheart rose, are the same size and shape, but lack the interestingly formed calyx. There is also a climbing 'Cécile Brunner', which is how many people prefer to grow this rose. It will reach 3m/10ft easily and is not fussy about its position. Personally, I think there is too much foliage on this rose, which obscures the diminutive flowerheads.

For fragrance and especially for performance, the free-flowering 'Natalie Nypels' is cherished by many old-rose lovers, although it was introduced in 1919. It is the ideal bedding rose and, with its clear pink, semi-double flowers, it was the favourite rose of that great horticulturalist H.H. Thomas.

The single *R. chinensis* 'Mutabilis' or 'Tipo Ideale', is one of the best repeat flowering China roses, and is a rose with great panache. The flame-coloured, pointed buds open to a copper-yellow and it is easy to see why it is sometimes called the butterfly rose. I have seen

it grown against a Cotswold house where the warmth and texture of the honey-coloured stone encourages the plant and shows off the flowers to perfection.

I must mention 'Cerise Bouquet' for its vivid crimson flowers and raspberry scent. It scarcely qualifies for this page but one parent is *R. multibracteata* from western China, a very thorny rose with a marvellous fragrance.

Until the advent of the China rose, the Autumn Damask produced one of the few recurrent flowering varieties in 'Quatre Saisons', *Rosa damascena bifera*, which is thought to have been grown at Pompeii. The double pink flowers are sweetly scented but, sadly, of poor quality. I must mention the famous *R. damascena trigintipetala*. Used in the production of attar of roses, this rose, also known as 'Kazanlik', is exceptionally fragrant. The flowers are deep pink and the dried petals are excellent for making pot pourri. 'Kazanlik' makes a vigorous shrub, up to 1.8m/6ft tall.

I have chosen five varieties of *R. damascena* for the scented garden; the first was among

'Cécile Brunner'

'Mme Hardy'

three perfect roses given to me by a friend ten years ago. The white 'Mme Hardy' is a strong shrub with the most exquisite white flowers, made of wonderfully folded petals surrounding green button eyes. The pleasing scent has a whiff of lemon. The second has a name that rings with romance and history: 'Ispahan' is a wonderful pink damask with richly fragrant double blooms, and grows to 1.5m/5ft. Alvilde Lees-Milne, one of the best contemporary gardeners, used this rose at the four corners of a herb garden in a particularly successful design and tells me that it is the perfect rose for this 'structural' purpose.

The third, 'Celsiana', has clusters of heavily perfumed, semi-double pink flowers with yellow stamens, set off by grey foliage. 'Marie Louise' is another perfect rose. It has increased splendidly in my garden and revealed its true

Rosa chinensis 'Tipo Ideale'

beauty, displaying enormous, deliciously fragrant pink flowers every season. This rose was a favourite at Malmaison as early as 1813, and now, as I walk around my garden on a July evening, I feel that my floral sentiments have been shared with others for more than a century.

'Omar Khayyam' is a subtle rose with rosy pink flowers and a delicious fragrance. In 1884, seeds from the rose growing on the grave of the Persian poet Omar Khayyam at Nishapur were brought to the Royal Botanic Gardens at Kew, and from the seedlings raised, a cutting was taken and planted on the grave of Edward Fitzgerald, who had translated the *Rubaiyat* of Omar Khayyam into English.

We must now consider the sweet brier, *Rosa eglanteria* (syn. *R. rubiginosa*). The wild plant has soft pink, deliciously scented flowers and similarly fragrant foliage. The graceful, arching branches, up to 2.4m/8ft long, are covered with prickles, and in the autumn and early

'Quatre Saisons'

winter the rose-red hips are a cheerful sight. 'Manning's Blush' with blush-pink flowers makes a 1.5m/5ft shrub and carries a special brier scent in its leaves.

'Janet's Pride' has bright cherry-pink flowers, and was probably the rose which influenced Lord Penzance to start breeding from the sweet briers in 1894–5. The hybrid 'Lady Penzance', a cross between *R. eglanteria* and *R. foetida bicolor*, is a coppery yellow with a bright yellow centre. Both this rose and 'Lord Penzance' grow into shrubs 1.8m/6ft tall with fragrant flowers and foliage, and make admirable hedges. 'Meg Merrilies' is another sweet brier hybrid, which has lovely crimson flowers followed by scarlet hips. One of the tallest-growing roses is 'Amy Robsart', which will reach 2.4/8ft and bears rich pink flowers in midsummer.

'Lady Penzance'

Rosa farreri persetosa, also known as the 'Threepenny Bit Rose', a reference to the flower's size being roughly the same as the old English coin, is a vigorous, thorny bush 1.8m/6ft high and just as wide. The foliage is small and fernlike, colouring nicely in the autumn. When in flower, the bush is covered with tiny, bright pink single flowers, with vibrant yellow stamens, which are followed by orange hips.

Rosa foetida, sometimes called *R. lutea* or 'Austrian Brier', has striking sulphur-yellow single flowers that are richly, almost over-poweringly, fragrant.

This is a rose with a long history, and was the only yellow rose besides *R. hemisphaerica* to be cultivated in the West. It is uncertain exactly when *R. foetida* was introduced, but it is described by the 13th-century Persian scholar Ibn-al-Awm, and was certainly growing in European gardens in the first quarter of the 17th century. The history in Europe of the double-flowered and sweetly scented *R. hemisphaerica* is at least one hundred years older than that of *R. foetida*.

For many years gardeners had dreamed of breeding yellow and orange roses. In 1629 John Parkinson was writing about the subject, but it was not until 1837 when *R. foetida persiana*, 'The Persian Yellow', was introduced that it became possible.

Brought from Iran by a returning British diplomat, this rose is a much stronger yellow than either *R. hemisphaerica* or *R. foetida* and is fully double and well formed. In the closing decade of the 19th century, Joseph Pernet, of the Pernet-Ducher nursery at Lyon in France, used this rose to develop the first successful orange and flame-coloured roses.

The flowers of the sport *R. foetida bicolor*, or 'Austrian Copper Brier' are very attractive; the insides of the petals are coppery red and the outsides brilliant yellow. Unfortunately, although the shrub in full bloom is a splendid sight, the flowers do not last more than two weeks and the rest of the time the bush looks rather uninteresting.

You can be sure that any plant with *officinalis* in its name was once used by antique apothecaries in unguents, potions or perfumes. *R. gallica officinalis*, the 'Apothecary's Rose', makes a wonderful garden shrub, with its large semi-double, richly fragrant, crimson flowers, opening wide and flat to show off the golden stamens. This 1.2m/4ft rose is almost thornless, a characteristic of the Gallicas and, in common with others in the species, it needs careful pruning to avoid overcrowding with short shoots which then bear only inferior blooms. After summer flowering cut out any weak growth and in spring reduce the strong shoots to two-thirds of their length.

'Rosa Mundi', a sport from the 'Apothecary's Rose', is a midsummer wonder. It is a lovely crimson rose, striped and splashed with blush pink and will form a beautiful hedge. The example *par excellence* of this is the famous twin hedges planted at Kiftsgate Court in Gloucestershire in 1928; they are still a striking feature of this garden. The rose was supposedly named after Fair Rosamund, the mistress of King Henry II, and may have been grown for her at Woodstock where she was secretly kept by her lover.

'Tuscany Superb'

'Camaieux'

Rosa gallica officinalis

A rose of which I have no personal experience, but one which introduces a different colour to the scented rose garden, is 'Président de Sèze'. In his manual of shrub roses compiled for the Sunningdale Nurseries in the 1960s, Graham Thomas describes it thus: 'The flowers are full-petalled somewhat quartered, and when fully open, with rolled petals, the intense purplish crimson of the centres remains in contrast to the lilac-white of the circumference. A most striking flower.'

The distinctive and very fragrant 'Belle de Crécy' is considered one of the best Gallicas. It has arching branches up to 1.2m/4ft long, covered with many mauve flowers that turn to a deep violet. For a small garden 'Belle Isis' is very suitable. The flesh-pink flowers have a strong scent of myrrh.

The striped 'Camaieux' is a lovely variety, prepared to stand alone or else in company with others. The flowers are white, heavily striped with crimson that slowly fades to pink. It has a distinctive sweet scent, and again is a good choice for the small garden as it only grows to 90cm/36in in height.

The 'Old Velvet' rose, or 'Tuscany', makes an admirable, tidy bush, about 1.2m/4ft tall, with neat foliage and dark red buds which open to maroon. It is one of my favourites and associates well with purple-leafed sage and with nepeta. 'Tuscany Superb', also deep maroon, is even more double. I believe these are among the best of the scented Gallicas.

Most Gallicas do not produce hips, the exceptions being 'Apothecary's Rose', 'Rosa Mundi' and 'St Nicholas'. The latter I have not yet described, but it is a lovely, clear pink rose which originated from the same garden in Yorkshire as the Musk rambler 'Bobbie James'.

The first Bourbon rose was a natural hybrid of *R. indica* × *R. gallica*, found in 1817 growing in a garden on the French island of Bourbon, or Réunion, among its parents 'Pink Autumn Damask' and 'Parson's Pink China'. Seeds were sent to Paris and the resulting seedlings distributed in France and later in England.

Many wonderful roses have resulted, vigorous and repeat flowering, ranging in colour from white to pink, crimson, purple and maroon. Most are fragrant and some penetratingly so.

'Boule de Neige' makes a sturdy 1.8m/6ft shrub and has creamy white flowers that look like camellias. These grow in small clusters set in dark, leathery foliage, and are richly fragrant.

The 1.5m/5ft shrub 'Commandant Beaurepaire' has a wonderful crop of striped blooms in midsummer, but only a few will appear later in the season. The flowers are spectacular: light carmine-pink splashed with purple and deep carmine, with random, breath-taking scarlet stripes. The long, pointed leaves are a fresh apple-green. Another variegated rose, 'Variegata di Bologna', illustrated on page 29, was only bred in 1909. It can be kept to a bush by pruning, but when you allow the stems to grow up a wall or round a pillar they will reach 2.5m/8ft, with spectacular blooms of white petals heavily striped with dark crimson. When the branches are pegged down it is a lovely sight but, sadly, since it has only one burst of flowers, I think it occupies too much space in all but the very large garden when treated in this way.

'Rosa Mundi'

Rosa foetida

'Souvenir de la Malmaison', named in honour of the Empress Josephine's famous garden in Paris, gives a succession of creamy, blush-pink blooms that are very flat, quartered and delicately scented. The quality of bloom in the late summer is often even better than the first flush. It makes a sturdy 1.2m/4ft tall bush.

The deep pink to crimson 'Mme Isaac Pereire' is as powerful in growth as it is sweetly scented of raspberries with beautiful full blooms and handsome foliage. It is best grown with support, for its branches can reach 4.5m/ 15ft; either a wall or pillar is suitable. For me this lovely rose is one of the best of the Bourbons, and with care and feeding will be a sensational sight, especially in late summer. The grandson of the Mme Pereire for whom the rose was named has a very beautiful garden near Chartres, and against the walls of his house there grows a fine specimen of 'Mme Isaac', planted by a previous owner.

Three free-flowering and well-scented Bourbons that should, if possible, be planted together are 'La Reine Victoria' and its sport 'Mme Pierre Oger' and 'Louise Odier'. The first, dating from 1872, has cup-shaped flowers coloured a delightful rose-pink, and an elegant

habit for a 1.5m/5ft bush. The second is very similar to 'La Reine Victoria', except that the flowers are pale pink, almost white. Finally, 'Louise Odier', which of all the Bourbons is one of the loveliest, has rich pink and perfectly cup-shaped flowers, every petal in just the right place. This 1.5m/5ft bush flowers continuously throughout the summer and has a strong and delicious scent.

A raspberry scent is not unusual with Bourbon roses and it is a quality that has been passed on from the older varieties to some of the more recent introductions. For example, the pink-flowered 'Adam Messerich', introduced in 1920 and one of the most beautiful modern shrub roses, is vigorous and bushy and has the characteristic fragrance, as does 'Kathleen Harrop' which is just one year older. This 2m/7ft tall bush is a pink-flowered sport of 'Zéphirine Drouhin' and has inherited the thornless branches as well as the delectable raspberry fragrance. 'Zéphirine Drouhin' is too well known to need a detailed description, but I

must sing its praises: thornless branches, recurrent flowering, rich scent and a long life; no younger rose has managed to end its reign as queen of the climbers.

Five years ago I was given a photograph, taken in 1900, of some previous owners of my house standing in front of the doorway that leads to the garden. It was clearly June, for there was 'Zéphirine Drouhin' in full bloom and looking magnificent. And so the rose continued, growing strongly until a very dry summer so weakened it that the only kind thing to do was to cut it to the ground, where the trunk had a diameter of 15cm/6in. Incredibly, a new shoot with the typical purplish leaves has since appeared – not bad for an eighty-year-old!

'Honorine de Brabant', another excellent hybrid Bourbon, is a finer, paler version of the striped 'Commandant Beaurepaire'. It has the same raspberry scent, and makes a vigorous 1.8m/6ft bush. Unfortunately I gave my speci-

Rosa 'Macrantha'

'Mme Pierre Oger'

men too little space the first time it was planted in my garden, and it had to be removed. Next time I will remember to allow plenty of well-deserved room for the rose to spread. Another lovely rose closely related to 'Commandant Beaurepaire' is 'Ferdinand Pichard'. It has the same pointed, light green leaves, and the pink flowers, striped with vivid crimson, fade gracefully with age. It makes a 1.2m/4ft bush and will flower the whole summer long.

A trailing rose that can be used effectively as a climber is *Rosa* 'Macrantha'. It is, perhaps, a trifle daunting to think of the correct place to plant it when you realize that it has a spread of at least 3m/10ft, but this rose is ideal for covering an old tree stump or unsightly outbuilding. Alternatively, it can be allowed to

The watercolour painting of roses, *left*, is part of a florilegium that contains over two hundred plates of various flowers including irises, foxgloves and primulas; the painting of carnations on page 48 is from the same book.

It is the work of Johann Walther who was commissioned by Count Johann of Nassau to record the many beautiful and unusual plants used in the reconstruction of the Count's garden and castle at Idstein in 1649.

Painted anthologies such as this were extremely popular during the 16th and 17th centuries, a time when renewed interest in gardening was inspiring creative work in many fields. Generally, the drawings were botanically fairly accurate, but they were, none the less, highly idealized, as they were intended to celebrate the beauty of the flowers and record the splendours of the gardens in which they were grown.

'Variegata di Bologna'

'Mme Isaac Pereire'

'Souvenir de la Malmaison'

ramble through a boundary hedge or over a bank. This is perhaps the best use for *R.* 'Macrantha' as it makes a wonderful ground-cover plant. Once you have found the right place for it, you will be grateful for its richly fragrant clusters of large, single, blush to clear pink flowers, which are followed by vibrant red hips in the autumn.

'Lady Curzon' is a hybrid of *R.* 'Macrantha' and *R. rugosa rubra*, and has enormous single, rose-pink flowers in summer. It forms a large rounded, prickly bush, quite unlike its sprawling Macrantha parent.

Rosa moschata, the sweetly fragrant Musk rose, is a true wild species that has been grown in gardens since Tudor times; it is an extremely vigorous climber of lax growth.

Graham Thomas explains that the Hybrid Musks are a mixed bag, but are mostly descended from a rose called 'Trier', raised in 1904, and various Hybrid Teas. The ancestors of 'Trier' are *R. moschata* and *R. multiflora*, both richly scented. Hybrid Musk roses make perfect summer-flowering shrubs for the scented garden, with their wonderful fragrance which travels easily on the breeze, and their free-flowering nature.

Most of the Hybrid Musks that are grown today were raised sixty years ago by the Rev.

Joseph Pemberton in his Essex garden. However, they did not achieve the popularity they so well deserve until the 1950s, when we suddenly began seeing such plants as 'Cornelia', 'Felicia' and 'Penelope'. These roses are all extremely useful for the mixed border or for dotting around the lawn in solitary splendour. They need the minimum of pruning – the routine removal of all dead flowerheads and some old wood in the spring. For the best blooms, it is as well to prune the side shoots back to two or three buds at the same time, but this is not essential.

'Cornelia' is the first to open its flowers, and the soft, coppery apricot blooms gradually

fade to pale pink. It is in flower for most of the summer but the autumn blooms are often the best of all. It has a delicious scent, fruity and sweet. 'Felicia' is the same colour in bud, but opens to a clear pink, and is almost recurrent, flowering evenly throughout the summer. The scent has subtle overtones of musk. 'Penelope' is creamy pink and also has the musk scent. It will form coral-red hips, so do not be too thorough when dead-heading.

'Buff Beauty' has the much-loved tea scent and creamy, fully double flowers. 'Pax' has the largest flowers of the Hybrid Musk group. They are semi-double, opening cream and turning to white, offset by golden stamens.

If you want one of these musk-scented roses for a wall, then 'Moonlight' can easily climb to 3m/10ft. The white flowers are carried in large trusses and show up wonderfully against the dark foliage. This rose is at its best in autumn and is, therefore, a most useful climber. 'Pax' will also climb, but not so enthusiastically. 'Prosperity', a soft ivory-white, and 'Pink

'Penelope'

'Cornelia'

Prosperity' have large trusses of small flowers. Both are strongly scented and make attractive bushes about 1.5–1.8m/5–6ft tall, but can be kept lower by judicious clipping if the situation demands.

There is a clear and unquestionable history of the Noisette roses, the first of which was a cross between *R. chinensis* and *R. moschata* produced in the early 19th century by John Champneys of Charleston, South Carolina. The flowers of this climbing rose were pink and grew in clusters. The local florist Philippe Noisette was given cuttings and began propagating extensively from the plants he raised. In 1817 he sent seeds from the original rose to his brother in Paris, who then named the best seedling 'Le Rosier de Philippe Noisette'.

'Blush Noisette', another variety raised from the original plant, has good foliage, and the mauve-pink flowers have a clove-like scent. More crosses were made from the original Noisettes, and Tea roses were also introduced into the breeding chain. The varieties now available are all of high quality. 'Desprez à Fleur Jaune' is a cross between 'Blush Noisette' and 'Park's Yellow Tea-scented China'. The warm-yellow flowers are flushed with peach,

open flat with a button eye and have a fruity scent. Given a warm wall, this rose will reach 4.5m/15ft.

One of the most famous Noisette roses, especially popular with our Victorian forbears on both sides of the Atlantic, is 'Maréchal Niel', another Tea-Noisette cross with soft yellow flowers and a most beautiful tea scent. In cool climates, it is a somewhat difficult rose to care for, preferring the warmth and shelter of a greenhouse or conservatory – the Maréchal must long for the sunshine of South Carolina. 'Gloire de Dijon', bred in 1853, is a very popular climber and rightly so, for it has a rich tea scent and very large buff-yellow flowers. It may be grown as a tall bush or climber.

The deliciously scented 'Mme Alfred Carrière' is a vigorous noisette climber that can reach as high as 7.5m/25ft and will do well on a north-facing wall. It has a burst of pink-white bloom in midsummer and then usually carries a few flowers right through until autumn.

'Céline Forestier' is not the most easy rose,

but very beautiful. Having been with us since 1842, it is still available at a few nurseries and should be kept in cultivation. The large yellow flowers have button eyes and a strong, spicy scent. Given a rich soil and a warm wall this rose will reach 2.4m/8ft and will produce a succession of blooms throughout the summer.

'Mme Plantier' is sometimes classed with the Noisettes and sometimes with the Albas, such is the occasional confusion over the classification of roses. It is undoubtedly one of the finest among the white old roses. The double blooms open with a creamy, almost yellow tinge and become pure white with a green button eye. It has a clear scent which carries on the air. It may be grown as a climber or a rather lax and sprawling shrub, and either way it is beautiful. However, for the small garden do remember that it has only one flowering, and that in midsummer.

'Céline Forestier'

'Buff Beauty'

'Prosperity'

Once you have experienced the scent of the young, fern-like leaves of *Rosa primula* after a shower of rain, you will understand why it is essential to have this rose in the scented garden: its common name 'Incense Rose' expresses the quality of its perfume. The pale, primrose-yellow flowers are single and open in May, followed by reddish hips. Another of its attractions is the startling red thorns, especially when seen with the sun shining on them. The leaves are thin and narrow; sometimes there are up to fifteen leaflets on a stem. The ideal place to plant this rose is beside your front door to give visitors a highly aromatic welcome. If I had it growing there I feel sure I would go out and spray it with water before my guests arrived! Thinking back, I recall that the two people whose gardens I loved, and which had an influence on my own patch, both had *R. primula* growing by their front doors.

One of the joys of my garden, from early summer right through autumn, is a hedge of *Rosa rugosa rubra*. The plants were raised from seed many years ago. The sweet spicy scent is especially strong and telling in the evening, and although the flowers are not exceptional – they last, at most, for two days – you know that you have the large oval, bright red and orange hips to come. I love the leaves, too, with their crinkled look and fresh apple-green colour in summer. As the months pass the leaves darken and the hips appear, making a splendid autumn colour display. During the winter my hedge is clipped to about 90cm/36in which keeps it at an admirable height both for smelling the flowers and as a protection for the garden from the prevailing west wind.

Perhaps you are wondering if this is the only Rugosa. Certainly not. There are other, more sophisticated varieties, just as attractive and as pleasantly scented. 'Blanc Double de Coubert' is a white Rugosa raised in 1892. It has papery, semi-double flowers and few hips. 'Frau Dagmar Hastrup' is an exquisite single pink with creamy stamens and many crimson hips. I have admired both these roses in other people's gardens, as well as 'Roseraie de l'Hay', which does not have the colourful hips, but does have the most marvellous velvety crimson, almond-scented blooms throughout the summer.

There are many Rugosas which have resulted from crosses with roses of other groups, producing varied fragrances, colours and forms. 'Max Graf' has a rich and lingering scent of unripe apples, single pink flowers and a trailing habit that makes it suitable for ground cover. 'Sarah van Fleet', a tall, repeat-flowering shrub, has clear pink flowers with pale yellow stamens and a rich, warm scent, while the recurrent 'Agnes', raised in Canada and an

Rosa primula

'Blanc Double de Coubert'

'Rosaraie de l'Hay'

early starter, has strongly scented, double yellow flowers.

Rosa sempervirens, the 'Evergreen Rose', is a hardy, vigorous rambler, smelling prettily of primroses. It is especially useful since the leaves remain throughout winter, just as the name implies. The best-known variety is 'Félicité et Perpétue, a beautiful rose to grow through a tree or over a high wall. Left alone, it will form a network of branches that in midsummer will be covered with a mass of ruby-tinted buds, opening to white and smelling of primroses. This rose creates the kind of display that makes me wish it was always summer. 'Adelaïde d'Orléans', named in 1826 after the daughter of the Duc d'Orléans, has pale blush semi-double blooms in clusters, likened by Graham Thomas to Japanese cherry blossom. This is a good rose

for archways or pergolas as the leaves remain well in winter.

Although I will be stepping out of my self-imposed alphabetical order, I do want to write about the rambling roses as a group, which brings me to *Rosa multiflora*. This species came to the west from the gardens of the Orient, and is responsible for the striking colours of some modern roses. The Polyantha varieties developed from this species are small-flowered, nicely scented and, as one might expect, unusually tinted. The variety 'Goldfinch' has a powerful scent, with clusters of yellow flowers touched with gold, fading to cream in midsummer. Left unpruned, this rose will form a dense bush as it is strong-growing like others in this group.

The so-called 'blue rambler', 'Veilchenblau', has a rich orange scent and a typical Multiflora habit of growth. The flowers open a dark magenta and fade to lilac-blue. I have seen this rose growing against a shady wall where the blueness of the flowers is far more noticeable

than when it is grown in full sun. The gloriously fragrant 'Rambling Rector' always reminds me of the exuberant garden belonging to a neighbour in Gloucestershire, where the rose is grown over a tall framework shaped like a bandstand. In early July this is literally smothered with the most fragrant white blooms, quite breath-taking in their quantity and quality. The other name of the rose is 'Shakespeare's Musk', but it is unlikely to be as old as that name implies. Of the Musk ramblers. 'Bobbie James' is a vigorous cream coloured rose that will reach 7.5m/25ft; the small flowers in large clusters have a pervading scent. The Himalayan Musk *R. brunonii* more widely known as the form 'La Mortola', is a vigorous rambler with large single white flowers. There is a lovely specimen growing in a garden on the Italian Riviera, where the generous warmth of the Mediterranean sun enhances the glorious musk perfume of this splendid rose.

'Frau Dagmar Hastrup'

'Félicité et Perpétue'

But the rambling rose which most thoroughly deserves its popularity is *R. filipes* 'Kiftsgate'. It arrived as a seedling in the beautiful and famous garden of Kiftsgate Court in Gloucestershire, and there joined forces with the tree behind it; now by early July, the tree is festooned with creamy white garlands of roses brushed with golden yellow stamens. This marvellous vigour, combined with the powerfully sweet fragrance of the roses, make this a most glorious show.

The wild rose *Rosa pimpinellifolia*, the Burnet or Scotch Brier, has tiny leaves and many thorns, but wonderfully fragrant, creamy white, single flowers in midsummer, followed by small black hips. This rose suckers freely and may become invasive, so take this into consideration when planting it in your garden. At a farmhouse near my home, this rose is grown as a hedge against a low garden wall, and I have often felt pangs of jealousy when it is in bloom and sweetly perfuming the air. There are other colours and forms of this rose which also have the delicious scent and valuable qualities of hardiness and self-sufficiency.

You should be able to find the double white form that has a lily of the valley scent and also 'Lutea Maxima', a vigorous 1.5m/5ft shrub

with black hips, or 'William III', a 60cm/24in rose with crimson-purple flowers and pretty grey-green leaves.

Two popular Pimpinellifolia hybrids, 'Frühlingsgold' and 'Frülingsmorgen', are very free flowering and have a rich and lovely scent. A group of 'Frülingsgold', flowering at the gardens of the Royal Horticultural Society, Wisley, in June 1960, made such an impact on me that I still remember the fragrance of the single, golden yellow flowers with gratitude. I came home and planted three together in an area of the garden, now called 'The Wilderness', that consists of specially chosen trees and shrubs growing in unmown grass. The three original roses make a great contribution to the summer garden each year, but in their old age they have become leggy, so seven new plants

have recently been put in, this time along a boundary fence. I hope that their strong thorns will deter the cattle from eating them through the fence. 'Frühlingsmorgen' has large, single, rich pink flowers, fading to white at the centres, and followed by hips in the autumn.

Perhaps the best known, though, is 'Stanwell Perpetual' with shell-pink flowers and a wonderfully rich fragrance. This rose is a Damask and Scotch Brier cross and has inherited repeat flowering from its Damask parent. It makes a 1.5m/5ft shrub and looks well grown as a hedge or in a group in the wild garden. In either case you will never regret the space you have allowed it.

Many of the Wichuraiana ramblers have the distinct fruity scent of ripe or unripe apples, and exceptionally attractive glossy leaves. The creamy yellow, double-flowered 'Alberic Barbier' roses, twining through an old iron fence in my garden, were planted three years ago as cuttings from autumn pruning.

'Stanwell Perpetual'

'New Dawn'

The two-toned flowers of 'Albertine' open with tremendous éclat in early summer. The buds are salmon-pink and then open to reveal a light, clear pink. The lovely fragrance, which perfumes the garden for many yards around, is especially satisfying. This rose is a truly vigorous grower and will sprawl over a garden shed, or with more careful treatment will be equally happy grown against a wall. Personally, I like to have it growing low enough to be able to remove all the dead flowerheads – but only for tidiness, because the dead petals do not fall. Sadly, 'Albertine' is not repeat flowering, so you must be content with the one flamboyant burst each summer. The Hybrid Tea-shaped 'New Dawn' is a soft pink, repeat-flowering climber with a sweet scent.

The China rose, as we know, was used with various other old roses, to develop a recurrent flowering rose. By the early 1800s this had been achieved and there were many such plants, varying widely in colour and form. These became known as Perpetuals and eventually evolved, with the aid of Bourbons and sundry other roses, into the class known as Hybrid Perpetuals. The size of their blooms, which were large compared to what was available when they were introduced, the rich fragrance

unsurpassed by most roses, and the deep maroon to light crimson colour range were considered great attributes. These roses created quite a stir in rosarian circles and laid the foundations for the Hybrid Tea roses so popular today.

'Baron Girod de l'Ain' has crimson flowers edged with white, and a rich scent, as does 'Roger Lamberlin', which is a somewhat less accomodating rose. There are several roses with maroon to purple flowers which should be grown by the enthusiast: 'Souvenir du Docteur Jamain', a port-wine-coloured rose that can either be grown as a bush or up a wall, and 'Souvenir d'Alphonse Lavallée' which has no purple shading in the maroon blooms.

These roses may be used to good advantage by pegging down the long branches. Each branch will then bear up-turned blooms all along its branches. There is 'Empereur du Maroc' with maroon flowers, opening flat and very fragrant – this rose is said to have the darkest complexion of any. Another dark rose 'Rose du Roi à Fleurs Pourpres', whose blooms turn to crimson as they fade, can also be used as a climber.

Until 1900 the colours of Hybrid Perpetuals (and of Hybrid Teas, of which they were one of the parents) were confined to white, pink, crimson, violet, maroon and purple. Then 'Soleil d'Or' was introduced, with its striking orange and yellow flowers. It is strongly fragrant, repeat flowering and only 90cm/36in tall, so fits into the front of the border quite nicely. It has an interesting history: Joseph Pernet successfully raised some seedlings from a cross between the Persian yellow rose and a red Hybrid Perpetual. One of them produced seed and the surprising result was the important rose 'Soleil d'Or': the original rose from which all the yellow, orange, vermilion and brightly coloured modern roses have developed.

'Rose du Roi à Fleurs Pourpres'

'Souvenir du Dr. Jamain'

'Albertine'

Roses all the way

A gazebo, such as the wooden structure shown above, was a popular feature of the Victorian garden. The trellis-work sides provided the support necessary for the favourite climbing roses of the period: 'Gloire de Dijon' and 'Souvenir de Docteur Jamain'.

In a large garden the seating provided by a small gazebo makes the perfect setting for enjoying the perfumes of old-fashioned shrub roses, planted as a hedge either side, or trained to cover the framework.

There are scented roses suitable for almost any site in a garden, except deep shade, and for gardens of every size. But it is wise, before planting them, to make certain that they really are suitable for the particular position in the garden for which they have been selected. Try to see them in a mature garden where they will have reached their normal height and shape. An excellent place to do this in the United States is at the National Herb Garden, part of the U.S. National Arboretum, Washington, D.C. and in Britain, at the Royal National Rose Society's gardens near St. Albans in Hertfordshire.

Some people will choose their roses before deciding on the site, perhaps because of a glowing description in a catalogue or book or because the roses were favourites in a former garden. Others will be looking for roses for a particular site. Whether it is the roses or the site which is selected first, it is vital to measure the area to ensure that there will be room for each rose to reach its full size. It is better to fill empty spaces around your roses with other plants for the first year or two than to have to move the roses later because of overcrowding.

Remember that you will want to be able to smell the blooms of your scented roses and also pick a few, so choose positions where you can reach the plants without too much difficulty. If roses which bloom only in the summer are being planted, try to visualize how they will look for the rest of the year and add other plants to create interest. In fact most old-fashioned roses look best in association with other plants.

It is most important to buy roses from reputable rose growers, and to order early because stocks of old-fashioned roses are limited. If possible, prepare the soil well in advance of planting time and add plenty of humus. Ensure that the roses have adequate water in their first season and give them an annual mulch of manure, peat or bark fibre to conserve moisture and reduce weeds. If you are planting where roses have previously been growing, it is wise to change the soil as it will have been depleted of nourishment essential to roses. Do not plant climbing roses too close to house walls, they will lack moisture.

While it is important that bush roses should be pruned hard in the first spring after planting, shrub and climbing roses do not need such severe treatment, nor in subsequent years do most of them need much pruning, except for the removal of dead and diseased wood and crossing branches. Bear in mind that the object of pruning is to encourage the plant to form the shape which will be best for its own health, to provide an abundance of bloom and in due time to fill the site for which it was chosen. While the usual advice is to prune to outward pointing buds, it may sometimes be necessary, especially with horizontally trained climbers and trailing roses, to prune to an upward pointing bud. Shrub roses do not need hard pruning but they can be cut back hard if they have become too rampant and straggly; new shoots will soon grow.

Climbing roses and some shrub roses welcome summer training: a pleasant task for a summer evening in the scented garden. The climbers and ramblers should have their new shoots trained horizontally, fan-wise or spirally, according to the site and support, and carefully tied so that they will not be broken in strong winds. Some shrub roses with lax and straggly growth will benefit from support and training. Other varieties, such as the Hybrid Perpetuals, are best pegged down or tied to plastic-covered wires stretched a few inches above the ground.

Among the old-fashioned roses which I have described are varieties suitable for most positions in the garden, from rampant climbers ideal for growing into tall trees, to a few for

When Hybrid Perpetual roses appeared on the gardening scene in the mid-19th century their extremely large flowers guaranteed them instant popularity. Nowadays, some gardeners might think the flowers vulgar, but a rose such as 'Penelope', *left*, with its vast creamy flowers and golden yellow centres, would make an impressive display throughout the summer and be an invaluable addition to a garden of old roses, which bloom once only in early summer.

Hybrid Perpetuals grown as half-standards in pots would be ideal for the balcony garden. Treat them as you would any other container-grown shrub, paying close attention to regular feeding and watering.

patios and pots. It is probably true that they are less suitable for formal gardens than the modern bush roses, so many of which are also strongly scented.

Although in a large garden a most striking effect could be achieved by planting groups of three or more of one variety, there will not be space in most gardens for more than one of each, except for the shorter more compact varieties. Fortunately the colours of the old roses blend well together and with the colours of other flowers, with the exception of oranges and vermilions.

In choosing varieties it is important to bear in mind that many bloom only once and that the foliage of some is rather drab after flower-ing, while others have attractive leaves and hips in the autumn. It is wise, therefore, as in garden planning generally, to have other features nearby to attract the eye away from plants which are past their best, toward a different focal point. Sometimes it is possible to provide a succession of interest throughout the year using bulbs, plants with foliage of varying colours and autumn berries.

A rose which is particularly suitable for small gardens is the Alba 'Great Maiden's Blush'. It blends well with lilies, sweet rocket and other plants, and will help to make the garden a mosaic of colour for much of the year.

But it is also suitable for larger gardens, as illustrated on the left, where it is used with

Roses all the way 2

other old roses to flank a gazebo, dividing a formal area of beds of modern scented roses and lilies from the rest of the garden. The repeat flowering Hybrid Musks could be used to provide a somewhat taller division, preferably with ground cover plants at their base.

For a more formal hedge the best old roses are the Rugosas, which not only provide a succession of flowers, but also autumn colour with their large hips and dense foliage. They make excellent boundary hedges, being sufficiently thorny to discourage most intruders. For an even more impenetrable barrier, the Penzance Briers could be used, compensating for their single show of flowers by the sweet scent of their leaves.

Another way of using roses as a form of hedge is to plant scented roses to cover a fence 1.2–1.5m/4–5ft high. This will enable you to look after the plants without excessive stooping or stretching. An open wooden fence is probably ideal although the roses can be trained along wires or over wire netting.

By using some of the less vigorous old climbers or ramblers like 'Albéric Barbier', 'Emily Gray' or 'Albertine', combined with modern, repeat flowering climbing roses, the fence would provide a colourful display for many months each year. In some situations it might even be possible to plant on both sides of the fence, alternating the roses at about 1.8m/6ft apart.

On taller fences some of the climbing sports of the older, very strongly scented Hybrid Teas like 'Crimson Glory', 'Étoile de Hollande', 'Ophelia', 'Madame Butterfly' and 'Shot Silk' could be used. As for all climbing roses, it is most important that whenever possible these should be trained horizontally or fan-wise to encourage flowering shoots to break all along the branches.

The season of scent and flower on the fence can be prolonged by including a few honeysuckles or other scented climbers, and by underplanting with scented bulbs.

I know a bank whereon the wild thyme blows . . .
Quite over-canopied with luscious woodbine,
With sweet musk roses, and with eglantine:
There sleeps Titania . . .

Although it was once the fashion to have formal beds of roses planted with an almost military precision, they are much happier, and look far prettier, if treated in a more relaxed manner. But of all flowers, the rose seems to be the one most comfortable with man-made structures, which seem to lose their solidity in the presence of this marvellous flower.

All the climbing roses I have suggested for the scented fence are also suitable for walls, pergolas, archways and trellises and the shorter ones can be trained spirally around pillars.

Generally the more vigorous the climber, the more attention it will need and the stronger its support must be, except for those grown to climb into old trees.

Many evergreen shrubs provide the ideal foil for old roses, which can be allowed to grow into them, and the corner of two hedges would provide a good site for the taller shrub roses. Buddleia, pruned hard each spring, gives late summer flowers to follow a once-flowering shrub rose and, for a prelude to the roses, try *Viburnum carlesii* and *burkwoodii*.

You may like to produce an all-white border, which would be especially sweet-smelling in the evening and attract moths at night. In such a bed the white Albas, 'Madame Hardy', 'Nevada' or 'Moonlight' could be used at the back, with Floribunda roses 'Iceberg' and 'Margaret Merril', one of the most strongly scented modern roses. The front of the border could be planted with white-flowered sweet rocket, stocks, white narcissi and, as an edging, white violas, muscari and snowdrops.

In a large garden it would be possible to devise an historical rose bed, starting with examples of the Gallicas, the 'Autumn Damask', an Alba, a Centifolia, a Moss rose and a China; leading on to a Bourbon and a Portland; followed by a Hybrid Perpetual and a Tea (which would probably have to be a climber on a tripod), and on again to the first Hybrid Tea, 'La France'. Examples of other shrub roses could be added, such as the Scotch rose, Rugosas, Moyesii, Hybrid Musks, Penzance Briers, and a modern shrub rose. A similar bed of species roses could also be planted and, if the picture was to be completed, a bed showing the development of modern bush roses from 'La France', and the introduction of strong yellows and oranges through 'Soleil d'Or'.

One way to grow roses which I have not yet mentioned is as standards. Unfortunately few of the old roses are available as standards so it may be necessary to bud them yourself. A standard's value is to raise the height of a bed and I prefer to plant a standard of the same variety as the bush roses planted below. Such roses as 'Ballerina', 'The Fairy' and 'Little White Pet' are particularly suitable for growing in this way, and a bed devoted to only one of them, with a standard of the same rose in the centre, would make a lovely feature in any garden. Half-standards of these varieties could even be grown in large pots for a patio.

Some of the smaller old roses, such as those I have just mentioned and 'Natalie Nypels', as well as the China roses, could be planted successfully in this way.

These interesting ways to grow roses are taken from *The Rose Garden* by William Paul, a respected Victorian rosarian.

Above. By pegging and pruning new growth into a pyramid shape, a compact container-grown plant can be formed.

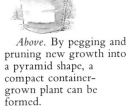

Right. a 'wigwam' structure of chains, stretched to the ground from a central pole and firmly secured with pegs, provides just the right kind of support for a variety of climbing roses. For a maypole ribbon effect, a different coloured rose can be grown up each of the chains.

Another suitable method of training a climbing rose is to stretch large-mesh nylon netting over pillars or other architectural features and then to tie the rose to this.

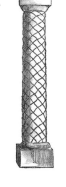

The pleasure of pot pourri

When plague was a fact of life, lice and fleas man's constant companions, and waste disposal meant throwing the rubbish out of the nearest open window, scented flowers, shrubs and herbs were greatly used for it was realized that, as well as masking bad odours, the fragrant oils which were present in many plants had antiseptic qualities. Bundles of dried herbs were burned indoors to fumigate rooms against plague, and one of the most common devices to sweeten the air was to cover the floors with strewing herbs. These included branches of lavender, rosemary and sage and leaves of sweet flag.

It was not a big step to the transference of fragrant leaves and petals from floor to bowl, and so the first pot pourri was created.

Ladies took great pride in the blending of these floral comforts, and some went so far as to create mixes for each room of the house. Many books were published on the subject, among the best of which are Sir Hugh Platt's *Delight for Ladies* first published in 1594, Gervase Markham's *The English Huswife*, in 1623 and Ram's *Little Dodoen* of 1606.

From the apple-scented Wichurianas to the raspberry-scented Bourbons, the rose has the widest range of scents in the floral kingdom, and the flower petals, whether dried or fresh, retain their scent well. One of the first perfumes used was made from rose petals crushed and blended with olive oil.

The rose itself, and the scent it produced were especially prized by the ancient Romans, and in the frescoe, right, a Roman lady is seen filling a small scent bottle with perfumed oil.

Your garden can easily provide nearly all the ingredients necessary to make a deliciously fragrant mixture. The one ingredient you may have to buy is the fixative, added to preserve the flowers' scent, which is due to aromatic oils and resins present in the cells of the petals and leaves. In some this oil is very volatile, and in others it evaporates slowly, but evaporate it will, and you must do what you can to preserve the scent for as long as possible. Musk, civet and ambergris are the fixatives advised in the old recipes, as are coumarin and benzoin. These you cannot produce for yourself, and they can only be bought at great expense. But an entirely home-grown fixative can be made from powdered orris root, meadowsweet, melilot and sweet woodruff.

The time to start organizing pot pourri making is in the spring. You then have the

whole summer ahead of you to collect and dry a wide range of scented flowers and leaves so that you will be able to vary the mixtures, just as a master chef will blend fine ingredients for perfect dishes.

First decide upon the most convenient and least time-consuming way to dry the flowers. On page 43 you will find instructions for drying whole flowers in a box of sand. This method may also be used for drying petals and produces less wrinkled and better coloured results than any other method. The petals and leaves can be easily separated from the sand by using a sieve. Alternatively petals may be dried in a warm dark place that is well ventilated. I have found a good method is to lay them on sheets of newspaper spread over wire cake racks, and then to slide these under the beds or chests of drawers. There is always a current of air flowing at this level, it is dark and dry, and it is easy to reach the petals to turn them as they gradually dry.

Gather the flowers early in the morning after the dew has evaporated, but before the sun has heated the flowerheads. Pick only those flowers and leaves which are in the best condition; this is of utmost importance. You must carefully strip the petals or, in the case of flowers like lily of the valley and hyacinths, the individual flowerheads from the stems. Lay them carefully to dry, trying to keep each one separate, so that it may dry unimpeded by its neighbour. As you do this you will inevitably discover and enjoy the different formations of each flower.

When high summer arrives and roses are abundant you will be busy, but do not neglect to snip off the white piece at the base of each petal. This is a counsel of perfection, and well worth the trouble. If you have children in your household they will doubtless want to help you, and this is a job that will keep them happy and occupied on summer evenings, if you are prepared to encourage them and appreciate their efforts.

Now you must decide which method you will choose to make the pot pourri – the dry or the moist. In the moist method the flowers and petals are pickled in salt. This preserves the scent better, at the expense of the colour. A dry pot pourri is, as the name implies, a mixture of plain dried flowers, which is more colourful but not so scented. A dry pot pourri is better suited to centrally heated homes. Put the pot pourri into a large bowl and place it in a part of the room where there is a gentle current of air.

The dry method

Gather and put the flowers to dry. As soon as they are dry and brittle put them into individual storage jars with orris root or some other fixative in the proportion of 30g/1oz to eight handfuls of flowers.

When the gathering and drying is complete, blend the pot pourri in one large jar. Choose one fragrance to predominate – for example, roses – and add a blend of herbs and other plants such as rose geranium leaves and lavender flowers as the secondary scent. A few drops of an essential oil like sandalwood or vetiver may be added, or slivers of lemon and orange peel for a lighter perfume. Add more orris root or other fixative such as cinnamon or mace. Cover the jar tightly and store in the dark for six weeks to blend the fragrances, shaking the jar occasionally.

The moist method

Collect the leaves and flowers and put them to dry, but do not allow them to become brittle; they should only be 'leathery' and not crumble or break when you squeeze them. Then lay alternate layers of leaves and petals with a thin sprinkling of salt in a tall glass storage jar. Do not use iodized salt; sea salt is recommended. Continue doing this until the jar is full, pressing each layer down firmly. It may take several days to fill the jar, but it is advisable to stir the contents each day or before you add the next layer. When the jar is nearly full put it away in a dark place for a week, keeping the lid firmly screwed on. When you open the jar you may find that a firm crust has formed on top of the mixture. If so, break it up with your fingers and mix it in with a small sprinkling of salt. This will assimilate any outside moisture that might invade the jar and give a crumbly consistency to your sweet-smelling pot pourri. The finished pot pourri may be put out in an open bowl for all to enjoy, but you must then be prepared for the fragrance to dissipate. If you put it into a china jar with a perforated lid, especially designed for pot pourri, then the scent will remain pungent for years, being captive inside the jar.

Scented candles are easy to make with the help of kits sold in candle shops. Traditionally, scented candles are associated with religion. This dates back to Rome in classical times. All through the ages scented candles have been burned in houses to give a gentle and exciting fragrance.

The early settlers in North America made use of wax myrtle, *Myrica cerifera*, the berries of which have a waxy crust around them. These were scalded in hot water; the wax floating to the top could be skimmed off. This wax burns with a clear white light, giving a smokeless flame and a delicious aroma. The berries of sweet gale, *Myrica gale*, and of bayberry, *M. pensylvanica* also provide a fragrant wax which may be collected the same way.

If you are giving a party and find you have no scented candles, then try fixing a coloured candle at the bottom of a shallow bowl, half fill this with water and float roses to match the candle.

The following recipe from Ram's *Little Dodoen* of 1606, and quoted from Eleanour Sinclair Rohde's book, *Rose Recipes* (1939), captures the spirit of making pot pourri. In the same way the painting, *above*, by George Dunlop Leslie, entitled *Pot Pourri*, conveys the pleasure to be found in this most rewarding pursuit.

'Take drie Rose leaves, keep them close in a glasse which will keep them sweet, then take powder of Cloves. . . . Put the same to the rose leaves then put all these together in a bag, and take that to bed with you, and it will cause you to sleepe, and it is good to smell unto at other times.'

Tastes of roses

'Of the Red Roses are usually made
many compositions, all serving to
sundry good uses . . .'

This comment by Nicholas Culpeper serves as favourable testimony to the high esteem in which roses have long been held, as much for their medicinal properties and cosmetic qualities as for their beauty.

The earliest perfumed unguents were nothing more than rendered animal fat, blended with rose petals – not an appealing idea – and the scented oils of the mysterious orient were just a maceration of rose petals and olive oil.

Rose water, first prepared by Avicenna, the 10th-century Persian scholar and physician, is still manufactured today and used in soothing lotions for chapped and dry skin; it is also a standard flavouring ingredient in Persian cuisine. Rose hips are rich in vitamin C, and on both sides of the Atlantic during World War II, rose hip syrup was a valuable dietary supplement.

The stillroom and larder of the Victorian housewife provided the most delicious rose-based jellies, conserves and candy. Sugar was flavoured with rose petals, and powdered rose petals were used to scent candles. There were bags of sweet petals to scent linen, rose lozenges to sweeten the breath and musk rose snuff to clear the head. Whole rose buds were preserved to bring out as decorations at Christmas and on other festive occasions, when fresh roses were not available.

There are hundreds of rose recipes to be gleaned from old books: all are of great charm and many produce pleasurable results. But these recipes are often complicated and time consuming to follow, so I have concentrated on those which are most practical and useful.

Bear in mind that the rules for collecting flowers for use in pot pourri apply also to gathering them for cosmetic and culinary purposes. Naturally, roses that are to be used in these ways should not be sprayed with insecticides. (Well-tended roses will, in any case, be healthy roses, untroubled by pests and disease.) In all the following recipes, the only preparation of the flowers that is needed is to rinse and dry the petals carefully, and then to remove the white portion at the base of each petal. All quantities are given in metric and standard American measures; be sure to follow only one set of measurements through a recipe.

Rose water

Fresh rose water lasts only for about two days, but takes very little time to prepare, so it should be easy enough to keep a supply on hand.

Put 900g/2lb rose petals in a deep earthenware casserole and just cover them with cold rainwater. Tap water will do if it is soft, but domestic water supplies are usually hard and full of chemicals. Put the casserole into a hot oven (230°C/450°F) and bring to boiling point. Alternatively, use an enamel saucepan and bring the water very slowly to boiling point on top of the stove. (I prefer the oven method as it draws out more of the scent from the petals.) Simmer for ten to fifteen minutes.

If you are using red roses the water will become pink, but yellow or white blooms make the water a dirty brown colour, so add a few drops of cochineal to make it appear more attractive. Allow the liquid to cool and then strain it into a pretty bottle. Use the rose water to relieve sunburn or to soften chapped skin. It also makes a refreshing eyewash.

Dried rose petals may also be used so you can have freshly made rose water in the depths of winter; use half to three-quarters of the quantity given for fresh petals.

A variation on the recipe is to infuse the petals in milk instead of water. However, this lotion must be used before the milk sours as it then becomes astringent and drying, and not at all good for roughened skin.

Rose water syrup

This recipe is based on the sweet syrups used to flavour the water dispensed by water vendors in the Middle East.

Make a sugar syrup by boiling 300ml/1¼ cups water with 450g/2 cups sugar and the juice of one lemon until the syrup is thick enough to coat the back of a spoon. Remove from the heat, add a tablespoon of rose water and stir well. Use the syrup to make a cool drink by adding one teaspoon of syrup to a glass of iced water.

Rose petal vinegar

For each 300ml/1¼ cups white wine vinegar, pick a large cupful of rose petals. Prepare the petals and put them into a large enamel container with the vinegar and tightly cover

the container. Set to steep on a sunny window-sill for at least three weeks. Taste the vinegar; if you think you want a stronger rose flavour, repeat the process. Strain the vinegar into clean bottles and store in a dark cupboard.

Rose vinegar can be used to make dressings for summer salads or, as a soothing compress, to relieve headaches.

Rose petal wine

Bring 4.25L/1gal water to the boil in a large pan. Add 1.3kg/6 cups sugar; stir well and leave to cool. Put 2.25L/4 pints (dry volume) rose petals into a plastic bucket with the juice and rind of two lemons and pour in the sugar water. Stir well and add a white wine yeast according to the manufacturer's instructions.

Cover the bucket with a clean cloth and leave for six to seven days. Filter into a clean gallon jug, fit an air lock and leave until all signs of fermentation have stopped.

Rose petal honey

Prepare 25g/1oz rose petals. Put them in an enamel pan with 115g/$\frac{1}{2}$ cup honey. Boil for ten minutes and then strain the honey, while still warm, into a screw-top jar. Use to relieve sore throats, mouth ulcers and ticklish coughs.

Rose petal jam

Prepare 900g/2lb red rose petals and simmer in 1L/4$\frac{1}{2}$ cups water until the petals are tender. Add 900g/4 cups sugar and the juice of five lemons. Boil rapidly until the jam sets. Rose water may be added to enhance the flavour.

Rose petal ice cream

Put a large cupful of red rose petals, a table-spoon of fine white sugar and 175ml/$\frac{3}{4}$ cup rosé wine into an electric blender and blend to a smooth paste. Meanwhile put a large carton of vanilla ice cream to soften slightly in a warm place. Add the rose petal mixture to the softened ice cream and beat until well blended. Return the ice cream to the freezer and stir it once or twice as it refreezes. Serve the ice cream decorated with crystallized rose petals.

Crystallized rose petals

Pick four or five red roses in full bloom, and carefully remove the petals from each flower head. Discard any petals that tear. Wipe each petal individually with a piece of moist kitchen towel.

Beat the white of one large fresh egg until it is just beginning to stiffen. Put 225g/1$\frac{1}{3}$ cups fine white sugar into a clean bowl. Holding each petal lightly, dip it first into the egg white and then into the sugar, taking care to coat each one perfectly. Lay the petals on a baking sheet so that they do not touch each other and put them to dry in the sun or on the bottom shelf of a very cool oven. Store in an airtight container with sheets of greaseproof or waxed paper between the layers. Use to decorate cakes, and light desserts.

Rose petal beads

Prepare 900g/1lb red rose petals. Put them in an enamel saucepan and just cover with water. Heat gently for one hour, never allowing the water to boil. Cover and leave to cool over-night. Repeat this process three times more.

By the fourth day the petals and water should be reduced to a smooth paste which can easily be formed into little round beads 5mm/ $\frac{1}{4}$in in diameter, by rolling small amounts of the paste between the palms of the hands. Shape as many of these as possible, piercing each one with a darning needle. Dry the beads on a sheet of newspaper in a warm cupboard.

Thread the beads on to lengths of rose-coloured ribbon or silk thread to make a perfumed necklace. When worn, the warmth of your skin will release the beads' musky rose perfume.

Preserving whole roses in the Elizabethan manner

Pick the roses when they are just on the point of opening. Immerse the stems in deep cool water and give the flowers a long drink.

Put a 2.5cm/1in layer of fine dry sand in the bottom of a large flat box; keep back enough of the sand to cover the roses.

Take the roses from the water, dry them and strip off the leaves. Lay the flowers in an orderly manner on the sand so that they do not touch each other. Completely cover the roses with the remaining sand.

Cover the box and put it in a warm dry place such as an airing cupboard until the flowers are absolutely dry. The roses may then be removed from the sand and kept upright in jars, or hung upside down, in a warm dry place where moisture cannot reach them. These whole dried roses make a lovely addition to winter flower arrangements.

A decoction of rose hips

Gather at least 450g/1lb *Rosa rugosa* hips. Cut them in half and remove the seeds, stems and whiskers. Put the hips into an enamel pan and completely cover with cold water. Bring slow-ly to the boil and allow to simmer for ten minutes. Leave overnight, then strain the liquid into clean jars. Flavour with honey or sugar if desired.

This mixture is excellent to use instead of water when stewing apples or pears, or it can be used as a cool drink, with the addition of a slice of lemon or orange.

...by any other name

Would you appoint some flower to reign
In matchless beauty on the plain,
The Rose (mankind will all agree),
The Rose the Queen of Flowers should be.
So sang Sappho, the poetess of ancient Greece. Greek legend tells us that when Aphrodite was hurrying to the side of her dying lover Adonis, she was scratched by thorns as she pushed her way through a white rose hedge, and forever after the blooms have been tinted red with her blood. But the red rose, according to Roman myth, was a reflection of the blushing Venus when the prowling Jupiter surprised her when she was bathing.

In Roman tradition, roses signified success; the petals were torn off and threaded, overlapping, on brass wire, to form thick rolls which were then fashioned into wreaths and crowns – imagine the number of blooms required! So it is not surprising to read that the peasants, thinking they could earn more money for rose petals than for corn, planted rose trees.

Roses were of social significance as well as being a symbol of valour. The 8th legion, under Scipio, returning victorious from North Africa, was given the distinction of having a rose reproduced on each man's shield. But the honour of wearing the rose as a sign of success was not granted lightly. The prosperous money-changer, Lucius Flavius, was thrown

In classical times the rose was prized so far above all other flowers that one Roman, Heliogabulus, arranged to shower his dinner guests with rose petals. The quantity used was such that several of the guests suffocated, and their hapless end provided the inspiration for Alma Tadema's painting, *Roses of Heliogabulus.*

into prison for wearing a rose wreath as he stood outside his shop in the Forum.

A rose garden was called a *rosarium* to distinguish it from a *rosetum*, a rose nursery. If a Roman citizen was fortunate enough to raise a rose of distinction, the flower would be given a name and the family would henceforth be named after it, rather than the rose being named after the family.

Roses became indispensable for table and house decoration as well as for wreaths and crowns. Lovers exchanged roses; drinking cups were decked with rose garlands so that the petals could be torn off and put into the wine. And later, when roses in the summer were not enough and people demanded blossoms out of season, shiploads were brought to Rome from the warmer shores of North Africa. Then greenhouses were built in which to grow the roses so that they would bloom in the winter, and to help keep the soil warm, ditches around the buildings were filled twice a day with warm water.

According to Cicero, Verres, the governor of Sicily, had himself carried about in a litter, the cushions of which were stuffed with rose petals. Not content with this, he had rose wreaths on his head and around his neck.

Guests attending Nero's banquets had rose petals showered on them and the floor of his banqueting hall was reputed to be thick with petals for the guests to lie upon. This, perhaps, was done because the Romans thought that roses were protection against drunkeness. The rose was also the symbol of mystery and secrecy, and any meeting or conversation said to be held under a rose, or *sub rosa*, placed the participants under an oath of secrecy.

In 1187 the sultan Saladin conquered Jerusalem and gave orders for the Omar mosque to be cleansed. Five hundred camel-loads of rose water were brought to the holy city for the purpose.

From the time of Scipio's 8th legion the rose has been an important symbol, and in 15th-century England the flower represented the warring factions during the Wars of the Roses.

As the fame of the rose spread, and as admiration for its perfect beauty increased, the flower found its way into literature. Poems were composed lauding the myriad splendours of the rose and, at the same time, poets used the flower allegorically to represent the very virtues with which the rose was credited.

Sappho's poem, quoted above, and references to the rose in Homer's *Illiad* and *Odyssey* are the earliest representations of the flower in literary history, since both the well-known biblical references to the Rose of Jericho and the Rose of Sharon, are to different plants. The latter is thought to have been a narcissus, although today *hypericum calycinum*, also from the Near East, is called by this name.

The cult of the rose was denounced by the early Christians, who banned roses from churches and churchyards, believing that the flowers had an aura of paganism. But in time, this most alluring of all flowers became acceptable to the Christians, even becoming associated with the Virgin Mary: the red rose for her sorrow, the white rose for her purity. Generations of worshippers have been awestruck by the beauty of the great rose windows found in many of Europe's great cathedrals, notably at Chartres in Normandy, the design of the stone tracery, like the petals of a rose, framing jewel-like patterns of coloured glass.

Several American states have adopted the

rose as their floral emblem, for example New York, Iowa and Georgia, which has taken the white Cherokee rose.

No history of the rose, whether legendary or true, would be complete without mentioning the Empress Josephine. Born in June 1763 on the island of Martinique, she was christened Josephine Rose. Thirty-five years later, as the wife of Napoleon, she came to live at Malmaison, and there made a beautiful garden devoted to her special love, the rose. She then commissioned the great painter Redouté to portray all the roses she grew. Josephine died before the book was completed, but *Les Roses* is one of the most beautifully illustrated flower books ever published.

The prolific 19th-century author Shirley Hibberd extolled the virtues of the rose for floral decoration. *The Amateur's Rose Book* was first published in 1863, followed by a New Edition in 1874, which was dedicated to the great rosarian, the Rev. S. Reynolds Hole, Dean of Rochester and founder of the National Rose Show.

Hibberd wrote, 'To make the best use of roses in decorative works requires more than an ordinary degree of skill.' He explains how it is necessary to consider the kinds of material the flowers are to be associated with and, 'In dressing a dinner table with roses, it is important to suit the colouring to the kind of light under which the flowers are to be seen.'

Miss Hassard of Norwood and Mr Cypher of Cheltenham were the two best 'floral artists' he knew. No doubt they made use of Hibberd's advice: 'A simple but effective mode of displaying roses on the dinner table may be accomplished by bedding them in living lycopodiums.' These were arranged by lining zinc pans with lycopodium, a club moss. The roses were then placed in small tin tubes and inserted into the mossy bed.

In his delightful Victorian book *Rustic Adornments for Homes of Taste* (1856), Shirley Hibberd gave more recommendations on floral arrangement for the dinner table: 'A dinner table is intended for the enjoyment of those who sit at it and should never be made an occasion for ostentatious display of plate or cumbrous ornaments.' Remember, 'The chief adornments of a dinner table are the guests themselves.' Yet when one considers a Hibberd-inspired decoration, such as the one shown here, it is difficult to believe this dictum was closely adhered to.

The small table decorations, *right*, are made by floating rose heads and candles in shallow bowls of water. If you make your own candles then scent them with rose essence and colour the wax to match the colour of the flowers. You must use an oil-based perfume made specially for scenting candles which is available from hobby and craft supply shops. Add the perfume at the last moment, just before pouring the melted wax into the mould. Stir the mixture well to distribute the scent evenly. For candles that will be used at the dinner table, only a few drops of perfume are necessary, otherwise the smell could be overpowering. Do not use perfumed wax in rigid plastic candle moulds as the perfume will damage the mould.

Roses have always been favourite decorations on the dinner table and it is not necessary to go to the extremes achieved by Heliogabulus or undertake the master works of Mr Cypher of Cheltenham, who was described as one of the two best artists in the field with his 'dashing and precise hard style'. The centrepiece, *left*, was entered in the Birmingham Horticultural Society's show of 1870 and won first prize. Its composition is described by Shirley Hibberd in *The Amateur's Rose Book* (1872).

'The centrepiece had a base of silvered glass, with a margin of small flowers. The lowest tazza had circles of scarlet geranium, white eucharis and crimson roses relieved with sprays of astilbe, stipa, milium and maidenhair. The middle tazza was dressed with pink heaths and white and crimson roses, with grasses and ferns to soften the outlines. The trumpet top was filled with astilbe and scarlet geraniums, with grasses to give a feathery finish. The side vases (not shown) were modified repetitions of the centre.'

Annuals, biennials and perennials

The American novelist Edith Wharton wrote 'the Italian garden does not exist for its flowers, the flowers exist for it.' She was, indeed, right, but in America, Britain and other European countries the flower beds are often the essence of the garden, sweet smelling, colourful and full of contrasts, shapes and contours; as beautiful in detail as in the whole.

Every spring it fills me with wonder when I sow seeds of annuals, knowing full well that within the space of a few months these will produce an abundance of bright flowers which will, in turn, produce the seeds for the following year. And these flowers often provide a wonderful perfume as well as colour and shape – marvellous riches to give so freely in so short a space of time, and from such a tiny start.

A seed we may say is a simple thing,
The germ of a flower or a weed,
But all Earth's workmen, labouring
With all the help that wealth could bring,
Would never make a seed.

Annuals are wonderful infillers. Some are hardy enough for their seeds to be sown in the autumn, giving them a good start in life so that they will bloom early and well the following year. If the autumn is cold and they do not germinate before the winter sets in, do not worry, the seedlings will come up as the soil warms in the spring. As you tidy the borders in the autumn, always scatter a few hardy seeds such as limnanthes; you can afford to be lavish if you collect your own seeds, as gardeners had to do before the days of professional seedsmen.

Some annuals are best sown in trays indoors during spring, while others are the minimum of trouble and may be scattered in the place they will flower. These are the hardy annuals, such as night-scented stock and calendula.

With forethought it is also easy to keep yourself well supplied with biennials. Choose a small space in your vegetable garden and prepare a good seed bed; a little time spent on this is well worth while as it will later save you money. In midsummer, when it is time to sow wallflower seeds for the following year, buy also the seeds of other biennials – pansies, foxgloves, dianthus, and hollyhocks. Sow these in straight rows kept free of weeds. By the autumn when work starts in your herbaceous borders, the biennials will be ready for transplanting.

Two tips I would like to pass on. Always mix the seeds of annual plants with plenty of dry sand; make your drill and sow the mixture.

I have loved flowers that
    fade,
Within whose magic tents
Rich hues have marriage
    made
With rich unmemoried
    scents.

There are few devoted
gardeners who would not
sympathize with these
lines by Robert Bridges,
for the beauty of a
flower's scent frequently
outlives that of its
appearance.
   In his garden at
Giverny in northern
France, Monet planted
the flowers he dearly
loved and repeatedly
portrayed throughout his
creative life, trying to
capture the essence of
each one's colour. He
cannot have been
unaware of the
importance of scent in
the garden, for a
harmonious planting of
annuals, biennials and
perennials that sets forth
the colour and habit of
each flower, will
inevitably enrich the air
around with sweet
aromas and heady
perfumes, as many of
these plants are,
fortunately, fragrant.

The drill is clearly defined by the sand which consequently makes it much easier to distinguish the weed seedlings from the flower seedlings. Secondly, when you pull up the spent biennials – forget-me-nots and wallflowers – throw them into an unused corner in the garden, out of sight, out of mind; by autumn you will have a new crop of young plants, without any effort.

Try to imagine the following flower borders – they may give you inspiration or a new perspective on a time-honoured garden feature. The borders are quite narrow leading from the garden gate to the front door. Standard roses are generously underplanted with lavender bushes to provide permanent greenness. Plants such as primroses, violas, pansies, dianthus and fragrant bulbs are used to provide scent throughout the year. Old-fashioned sweet peas could clamber through shrubs such as philadelphus and lilac. There should be bergamot, night-scented stocks and tobacco plants. White madonna lilies are planted in fragrant clusters on either side of the door. Such a perfumed border provides all the senses require: the eye is pleased by the colour, the ear by the buzzing of bees and the nose by the sweetly mingled scents.

It is of the utmost interest to imagine how plants were first used in cultivation. The earliest were utilitarian; then someone with a taste for the beautiful must have decided to bring in flowers from the wild and 'cultivate' them in a special place near their house. This could be called the first flower border. But the word 'border' does not appear in use until the 16th century, and then it meant a bed bordering a well, or a decorative pattern of flowers around a knot garden.

In medieval days flowery meads were all the fashion. The medieval poets wrote most lyrically and ecstatically of the coming of spring, and of trees and flowers in full bloom. Pictures in old manuscripts often show the lady and her knight sitting happily on a bank surrounded by bright flowers growing in a grassy meadow.

An excellent example of the medieval love of flowers is the Unicorn Tapestries (commissioned by Philip, Duke of Burgundy in 1449) some of which now hang in the Cloisters Museum in New York. The background of each tapestry shows all of the most beautiful plants grown at the time. *Prunus cerasus* is predominant in four of the tapestries. The walnut, symbolizing durability is there; as are

The carnation, or gillofloure, has a long association with drinking. Chaucer recommended '. . . clove gilovre and nutmeg' to put in wine. The watercolour drawing *above* is by Johann Walther (1654).

sweet violets 'all too beautiful and periwinkle, fresh and new' as described in Chaucer's translation of *The Romance of The Rose*; also the precious violets that, according to Macer in his 16th-century herbal, have great power against 'wicked spirits'.

The English daisy appears, associated with The Virgin Mary and 'good women'. There are wild strawberries and *Rosa centifolia*: chaplets of roses were given by the ladies to their lovers. A 13th-century poem tells us that, 'He whose heart burns with love should wear a crown of roses.'

Salvia and marigolds, wallflowers and pansies are shown. Marigolds were associated with the festivities of marriage, and primroses were the keys to heaven – St Peter's keys. Feverfew, according to German tradition, should be ground to a powder, mixed with wine and 'it will make women fruitful and lighthearted'.

Forget-me-not was a healing herb; *Iris germanica*, a flower of nobility; wild orchids, scillas and carnations, with their clove-like fragrance, were emblems of betrothal and marriage. The meads are full of stocks, gilloflowers, and lilies.

These flowers are typical of those grown in Europe before the Age of Discovery, when the pioneering sailors brought plants from the New World back to the Old, and with much coming and going across the Atlantic, European gardens became far richer in flowers. Tradescantia, smilacina, dicentras, sedums and evening primroses were introduced, and monarda and phlox to scent the evening garden.

As John Winthrop wrote in his *Journal* as the ship approached the shore near Boston, after ten weeks at sea, 'We had now fair sunshine weather and so pleasant a sweet Aire as did much refresh us, and there came a smell off the shore like the smell of a garden.' What a moment of rejoicing this must have been, and he no doubt imagined how he would make a garden more grand than the one he had cultivated in England.

The 17th- and 18th-century garden writers for the most part content themselves with describing the plants that were grown, and unfortunately say little about how they were disposed in the beds. In the late 17th century, John Rea in *Flora, Ceres and Pomona* describes the flower beds in an ideal garden. This was a square surrounded by a wall and with a series of narrow beds, each edged with lattice rails, but his repertoire of plants had not increased much since Parkinson wrote in 1629.

In 1730 the first illustrated seedsman's catalogue was published. This was issued by Robert Furber who had coloured plates made of the flowers which his clients could expect to have blooming in their gardens in each month of the year: wallflowers in January; daphne in February; narcissi, hellebores, and cowslips in March. The April flowers were all bulbs or flowering trees, and there were peonies and spiderwort in May. In September bloomed the French and African marigolds, which despite their names had both been brought from Mexico in the late 16th century. For November, golden rod, a North American native, must have been a welcome introduction to European gardens. It was sent with other flowers, campanulas and asters, phlox and oenothera, from North Carolina.

Philip Miller's *Dictionary*, which appeared in many editions from 1735 onward, is a great help in discovering which flowers were growing in gardens of the period, and so is the later *Encyclopedia of Gardening* by John Loudon.

Through it all, the flower border had its ups and downs. The vogue for landscape gardening dispatched the borders to distant areas, as it was fashionable to surround the house with only trees and lawns.

Jane Loudon, the wife of John Claudius Loudon a much respected plantsman of the early 19th century, was a flower lover *sans pareille*. Their books and other writing (hers executed especially for ladies) had an enormous influence on gardens of that period. They advocated a lavish use of plants, especially unusual ones, but, at the same time, insisted that they be well trimmed and carefully groomed – not a leaf out of place. Then, the era of regimented bedding-out schemes came on as an irrespressible wave, with exotics arriving and greenhouses springing up everywhere like crystal mushrooms.

But as is always the case, a new school of thought emerged to contradict the old. In this case the central figures were William Robinson and Gertrude Jekyll. They were both flower lovers and, most importantly, lovers of the natural. Robinson's mission was to search for and find the special herbaceous plants which had made up the glory of the banished herbaceous borders, and once more to establish them in the gardens of the grand houses and town villas. It was a reaction against the artificial and Robinson, later helped by Gertrude Jekyll, was triumphant. His success was doubtless due to the intervention of years of war, when labour was scarce and fuel to keep the greenhouses heated was becoming expensive. Our present-day flower beds are a direct result of the influence of these two master gardeners, who made lavish use of old-fashioned flowers.

Immediately after World War II, Victoria Sackville West took up the cause at her garden at Sissinghurst Castle in Kent, together with the American plantsman, Lawrence Johnston, in his garden at Hidcote in Gloucestershire. They created between them the prototypes for what many gardeners today consider to be the ideal garden: borders full of colour, leaf texture, shapes and surprises. What I add is that they should also be full of scent, and that flower beds should include the sweet-smelling annuals, biennials, perennials and sweet shrubs.

Robert Furber, a nurseryman of Kensington, produced the first illustrated seed catalogue in English, with twelve hand-tinted engravings showing the flowers in bloom each month of the year; they included plants that were being introduced from North America.

1 Double Nasturtium.
2 Double white Maudlin.
3 Prince picoté July flower.
4 True Caper.
5 Virginian yellow Iasmine.
6 Painted Lady Carnation.
7 Double blew Throut-wort.
8 Scarlet Martagon.
9 White Lilly strip'd with purple.
10 Spanish Broom.
11 Carolina kidney bean tree.
12 Double strip'd female balsom.
13 True Olive tree.
14 Red Oleander.
15 Painted Lady pink.
16 White Lupin.
17 Princess picoté July flower.
18 Geranium noctu olens.
19 White Valerian.
20 Hop Horn beam.
21 Indian or china pink.
22 Double Pomegranate.
23 Double mouse ear.
24 Virginian Scarlet honey suckle.
25 Double white Throat-wort.
26 French Marigold.
27 Double scarlet Lychnis.
28 Double blew Larkspur.
29 Hungarian Climer.
30 Double Stock.
31 Bean Caper.
32 White Oleander.

JULY

Design'd by P. Casteels.

From the Collection of Rob. Furber Gardiner at Kensington 1730.

Engrav'd by H. Fletcher.

The plants to grow

Achillea filipendulina, a member of the yarrow genus, is a hardy perennial native to the Caucasus mountains in southwestern Soviet Union. The chief beauty of this genus is in its foliage, often grey and usually deep cut and richly pungent, especially when brushed against or squeezed.

Achillea thrives in a sunny position where the warmth will draw out the plant's aroma and enhance the colour of the beautiful foliage. Avoid planting it in heavy soils as the roots prefer the free run of a well-drained sandy site.

A. filipendulina makes a splendid border plant, 90–120cm/36–48in high with yellow corymbs of flowers carried on stiff stems that stand erect and need no staking. The scent of the leaves is strong yet refreshing and reminiscent of feverfew. If cut before they reach maturity, and dried in a cool, dark, moisture-free cupboard, the flowers may be used as a framework for a yellow-toned dried flower arrangement.

A. millefolium is a native of the British Isles and France where the juice from the leaves was once used to heal wounds made by carpenters' tools. Two popular cultivars are 'Cerise Queen' and 'Fire King' but beware of their roots which, if left untended for too long, can become invasive. My favourite is *A.* 'Moonshine' (*A. taygetea × A. clypeolata*) with soft lemon-coloured flowers appearing in late summer and lush fern-like foliage. It will grow to 60cm/24in high and is quite suitable for the front of the border, where the mat of attractive evergreen leaves can be best enjoyed.

Alyssum maritimum, with a distinctive scent of new-mown hay, relies on its many clusters of white or lilac-tinged flowers for its attraction. Botanists have now put sweet alyssum in the genus *Lobularia*, and so it may appear under this name in some catalogues.

It is a tidy little plant, only 15cm/6in high, tailor-made for the front of the border. 'Little Dorrit' is pure white and 'Lilac Queen' has pale lilac flowers. If you can find them, sow the seeds of a slightly taller white cultivar such as *A.* 'Sweet White'. It is very sweetly scented and would look quite at home growing between roses, the two scents vying with each other.

Sweet alyssum is a hardy annual so you can sow it *in situ* or else in pans ready to prick out later when the spring flowers are over. Plant them as edging or in good-sized groups between low-growing perennials in a sunny place. As it is an affable little plant you will

often find self-sown seedlings appearing as a bonus the following year.

Bees love sweet alyssum and will work them all day when the sun is shining and the nectar is at its peak.

Asperula odorata, the Elizabethan strewing herb sweet woodruff, is described with the herbs, but there is a pretty annual species of asperula with whorls of bristly leaves on 25cm/10in stems and sky-blue, scented flowers, which was introduced from the Caucasus in 1867. This is listed variously in catalogues as *A. azurea setosa* and *A. orientalis*. It is quite undemanding of space and likes a cool run for its roots, so is an ideal annual for the rock garden and to sow among paving stones, or to infill in the herb garden.

In early summer when biennials are being cleared from beds of bulbs, sow seeds of hardy annuals in their place, so that the fading leaves of the bulbs will give protection to the young seedlings. Choose the cottage garden pot marigold, *Calendula officinalis* or the new cultivar *C.* 'Mandarin'. This latter is only 30cm/12in tall and becomes smothered with rich orange flowers 7cm/3in across. Both leaf and flower have a sharp, tangy quality which I like as a contrast to sweet scents. I also enjoy the culinary properties of the plant, using the leaves to perk up stews (an age-old method of seasoning) and the flower petals to add colour and savour to green salads.

Many flowers have a place in the tradition of the early Christian church. Calendula is one flower traditionally associated with the Virgin Mary: its antique name was simply 'golds' and eventually the Mary was added to proclaim the association with the Mother of Christ. In 1629 John Parkinson recommended marigolds to be used in 'possets, broths and drinks as a comforter of the heart'. William Turner, the father of English botany, was more

Centaurea moschata

practical in his approach, and says how admirable the flowers are in helping to turn the hair yellow. It is tempting to imagine Queen Elizabeth I following his advice and using the juice from the marigold flowers to increase the lustre of her auburn hair. Another 16th-century writer who proclaimed the virtues of this flower was Thomas Hyll, who says, 'This Marigold is a singular kinde of herbe sowen in Gardens, as well for the pot, as for decking of Garlands, beautifying of nosegays, and to be worn in the bossome.'

Marigold seeds should be sown in early spring. They will then start flowering after two months have passed, and continue into winter. They will self-sow each year, so be careful where you make the first planting.

Cheiranthus cheiri

Calendula officinalis

Asperula orientalis

Alyssum maritimum

Plants with a history, particularly those which have been grown in domestic gardens for centuries, have a special appeal to me. The sultan flower, *Centaurea moschata* was referred to by John Parkinson as a 'stranger of much beauty, lately obtained from Constantinople, where the great Turke . . . liked it and wore it himself' – perhaps as a buttonhole? *C. moschata* is an annual, growing to 60cm/24in with white, yellow or purple flowers, and is very fragrant. It is good for cutting, bringing its scent indoors. If you can obtain the seeds, then a good type to try is the 120cm/48in tall *C. imperialis* with its large, sweetly perfumed

flowers. It is well worth growing these, if only for their musky exotic scent.

The familiar cornflower or bachelor's button is a relative but, pretty though it is, it has no perfume.

I like to use a mixture of annuals and biennials with my herbaceous plants; doing this helps to keep a steady flow of colour and interest in a border planting that might otherwise be dull and lifeless.

Cheiranthus cheiri, or wallflowers, have been with us for hundreds of years and are especially useful for interplanting. Parkinson described their use in nosegays – the genus name means

'handflower'. They are among the most pervasively scented plants: the fragrance, not unlike that of border pinks, reminding one of sweet spices.

Strictly speaking, wallflowers are perennials, but the most rewarding way to grow them is as biennials, sowing seed in spring ready for transplanting in the autumn. To be sure of success, do not postpone the seed sowing. Wallflowers have a wide and lovely range of colours, are all richly scented and lend themselves to interplanting with tulips and daffodils, the colours blending harmoniously and the habits complementing each other.

Corydalis lutea is a humble plant which, in my garden, has seeded itself into a limestone wall. Because of the glaucous, much-divided leaves the plant is pretty without flowers and makes a welcome carpet in an otherwise bare corner. But the flowers, which first appear in spring and continuously until autumn, have a delicious primrose scent which must be enjoyed individually, for they are fast with their scent and only reveal it to those who are prepared to seek it. The flower spur resembles the spur of a lark. *C. bulbosa* (syn. *C. cava*), also scented, has pale purple flowers early in the year and is a good plant for the wild garden.

Theophrastus, the Greek 'father of medicine' who lived in the 4th century BC, gave the name *Dianthus* to the plants we commonly call pinks or border carnations: *dios* meaning of Zeus and *anthos*, a flower – literally, flower of the gods.

The limestone regions of southern Europe are the native home of practically all dianthus, but some have naturalized themselves here and there. *D. caryophyllus*, from which hardy border carnations are derived, has for a long while been a popular garden flower in Britain. The early history of these plants is obscure, but it is thought that the Normans must have brought them from Europe after 1066, for they are naturalized at Rochester Castle in the county of Kent, one of the first Norman strongholds to be raised in England, as well as on the walls of William the Conqueror's castle at Falaise in Normandy. But this is supposition.

Clove gillofloures, gilly-flowers and sops-in-wine, are their antique names, the latter being a reference to the Tudor habit of spicing wine with the flowers. That most earthy gardener, William Lawson, wrote in *The Countrie Huswife's Garden* of 1618, 'Gilly-flowers, or Clove July flowers (I call them so because they flower in July) they have the name of Clove, of their scent. I may well call them the King of flowers except the Rose . . . I have of them nine or ten, several colours and divers of them as big as roses.' Master Tuggy of Westminster was famous in the 17th century for his gillofloures: he is mentioned by both Gerard and Parkinson. These writers note the difference between gillofloure and carnation, the latter being less hardy.

If you wish to make a collection of hardy border carnations for your scented garden, I suggest the following. 'Dicker Clove' has a strong clove scent and is white, edged and striped with crimson. Of self-colours, 'Bookham Perfume' is a rich crimson, reputed to have the strongest clove perfume of all available varieties; 'Cherry Clove' is a clear cherry rose; 'Lavender Clove' a grey lavender shade and 'Pamela Thain' is white with a superb habit of growth. 'Oaken Fragrance' is white 'ticked' with beetroot red as is 'Robin Thain', a vigorous strain with a fine clove scent. For the sake of conservation, all these varieties should be widely grown and so preserved for future plantsmen.

The pinks, largely derived from *D. plumarius*, are more hardy and thrive without special care. They can be grown from seed and produce a wonderful range of colours with single laciniated flowers and a sweet scent. *D. × allwoodii* is a hybrid race of hardy plants, a cross between the perpetual-flowering carnation and the hardy border pink, with single or double flowers and a fragrance that hangs upon the air.

Many of the hybrid garden pinks, some of recent breeding and others much older have a rich scent: 'Mrs. Sinkins', the well-known double white; 'Doris', a shrimp colour with a darker eye, and 'Charles Musgrave', a fringed white with a distinct green eye. The rockery pinks and dianthus have little scent.

To me, the ultimate in perfection in garden scents is *D.* 'Loveliness', a hybrid between *D. × allwoodii* and *D. superbus*. The flowers are single and have a delightful shaggy appearance. Raised by Montague Allwood, the flower is lauded by him as 'perhaps the most fragrant of all flowers'. The scent is elusive yet strong, best in the evening yet there in the morning. This 'come-hither' playfulness on the part of a plant

Corydalis lutea

Dictamnus alba (syn. *D. fraxinella*)

Dianthus barbatus

Dianthus 'Loveliness'

Dianthus caryophyllus 'Robin Thain'

appeals to everyone who visits my garden; they wish to be introduced and are not at all surprised by the name.

D. barbatus, sweet william, is a very old garden plant. The first description in the English language is in Henry Lyte's *Newe Herball*, of 1578, a translation of Dodoens' *Historie of Plants*. Of the flowers he says there are 'three or four togither at the toppe of the stalkes, sometimes nine or ten togither, like to a nosegay, or small bundell of floures, of colour sometimes red, and sometimes spotted with white, and sometimes (but very seldom) all white.'

The celebrated lady gardener of the 19th century, Mrs. Loudon, considered they were so

beautiful as almost to rank as Florists' flowers. They have many virtues in the garden today, making a grand show at a time when the main burst of summer flowers is over, lasting a long time in their prime and giving off their sweet spicy scent, especially in the evenings. In my garden I treat them as biennials and use them as infilling plants wherever a space arises.

I pray the reader to explore the world of dianthus; they have riches to offer to those who love scent upon the air, scent in the hand or scent in the house. Grow them from seed and if you find a plant with a fragrance new to you, never pass it by without asking for a cutting.

Dictamnus albus (syn. D. fraxinella) a native of

southern Europe, is a handsome herbaceous perennial which, given time, will form a bold clump, but it is a plant which requires patience. It does not transplant easily and is slow to flower from seed, but once established will be a special feature, not only for its beauty, for it is definitely a plant of distinction, but also for its scent. Rub the leaves and the scent they give off will remind you of lemon peel; strike a match on a still summer evening and hold this beside the flower stalk and for an instant it will burst into a blue flame! No harm will be done, for it is just the volatile inflammable oil secreted in glands on the stem igniting. Parkinson says 'the whole plant as well as leaves and flowers are a strong scent, not so pleasing for the smell, as the flowers are beautiful to the sight.'

Filipendula hexapetala

Lathyrus odoratus

Heliotropium peruvianum

Dracocephalum moldavicum, in spite of its impressive name, is an unassuming annual from Siberia which, surprisingly, has been in cultivation since 1596. I am tempted to believe that it was one of the plants brought to England by John Gerard. After finishing his apprenticeship as a barber-surgeon, he became a member of the Company of Merchant Adventurers and travelled with them as a ship's surgeon. Trade routes to Russia had recently been opened, and from reading his herbal we know that he visited Russia; so maybe it is not too fanciful to imagine him gathering seeds of *D. moldavicum*. The flowers are blue or white, growing in long racemes and the aromatic leaves are an added interest. The perennial species *D. sibiricum*, now classed under *Nepeta sibirica*, also from Russia, was a later introduction (1760) to Europe. It is easy to grow, with big spode-blue flowers in summer; perhaps not a collector's item, but most useful for colour and its catmint-like scent.

Filipendula hexapetala is a hardy perennial. Dig it up and you will see why its common name is dropwort, for tubers the size of a little finger hang on fibrous roots. The juice from these tubers was recommended by herbalists as helpful to 'women's complaints'. The panicles of white flowers, tinged slightly red, are very sweetly scented, reminding me of almonds or hawthorn. The ferny foliage is beautiful and, as Gerard said, is 'spread about like feathers', making an enticing rosette. The leaves are useful for making the charming little nosegays called tussie mussies.

The attractive heads of white flowers appear in summer when the plant will have reached a height of approximately 50cm/20in.

Many of the nymphs in the myths of ancient Greece and Rome who died for love were transformed into various flora and fauna. Clytie was no different. Her love for Apollo caused her death, and he (as thanks?) changed her into a heliotrope. For the scented garden, the species *Heliotropium peruvianum* is an essential plant. The French botanist de Jussieu sent seeds from Peru to the royal garden in Paris in 1757. Thirty years later, Thomas Jefferson sent seeds from Paris to his friend Francis Eppes in Virginia with the instructions, 'to be sown in the spring, a delicious flower, but I suspect must be planted in boxes and kept in the house in winter, the smell rewards the care.'

It was immensely popular during the Victorian era and was much used in bedding

The curiously shaped flowerheads of *Dracocephalum moldavicum* give the plant its genus name, which is a compound of the Greek words for dragon and head – a fierce description for a delicately lemon-scented plant, much loved by bees.

Hesperis
matronalis

DRACOCEPHALUM MOLDAVICA L.
Die Türkische Melisse

schemes or as edging for rose beds. There were many more cultivars to choose from then, but the delicious fragrance has earned it a special place in today's gardens and it is still grown for its almond scent; or perhaps, more accurately, the scent is of cherry pie.

Heliotrope is half-hardy and so must be nurtured, remembering that the paler mauve flowers often have the stronger scent. Grow it from seed as an annual and place it near the front of the summer border so the scent can easily reach you. Then save a plant or two to overwinter in the greenhouse.

Hesperis matronalis, a native of southern Europe and known to the ancient Greek writers, has been grown in gardens in Britain for generations. Known commonly as sweet rocket, it has, as Philip Miller wrote in his famous *Gardener's Dictionary*, a 'grateful scent' which is not unlike that of wallflowers. The single flowered variety makes a splendid plant for the wild garden, where you may walk on a warm summer evening, or at the back of the border – for it is more scented than handsome. Once you have it, you have it forever, but not aggressively so, with volunteers springing up in interesting places. The species *H. tristis* comes from Hungary and, I am told, has the best scent: ladies even grew it in pots to stand in their boudoirs for its evening perfume.

Lathyrus odoratus, the old-fashioned sweet pea, is my first choice for annuals. It is easy to grow and free with its scent: when a handful is brought indoors it will fill the room with fragrance. Grow sweet peas in your border to clamber through spring-flowering or evergreen shrubs, or allow them to loll over early perennials. An original idea is to put a few plants beside the tall *Crambe cordifolia*, and as this dies down its sturdy skeleton will make a natural support for the sweet peas.

The purples are the most fragrant of the old-fashioned cultivars, a quality they inherit from their ancestors, the wild Sicilian peas. In 1700 a monk sent seeds to England to Dr. Uvedale, who nurtured them for their fragrance. Twenty years later Thomas Fairchild recommended them as, 'flowers that will grow well in London, fit for adorning of squares, for the sweet scented pea makes a beautiful plant. The scent is something like honey, and a little tending to orange flower smell. These bloom a long time.'

The first sweet pea with frilled petals appeared in Countess Spencer's garden at Althorp Park at the beginning of the twentieth century. Since then many different cultivars have been bred, some fragrant and some good looking but scentless. If you wish to be sure of the scent then you must take care to choose the old-fashioned types. But do not let me put you off the new cultivars, for if you choose wisely you can have both scent and size. Whichever your choice may be, do remember that sweet peas revel in a rich soil: in fact, they are gross and greedy feeders. Dig a trench or hole and infill it with plenty of compost or manure. If you cannot get this then comfrey leaves, dug in generously, will give a good boost. Failing these, use a general fertilizer.

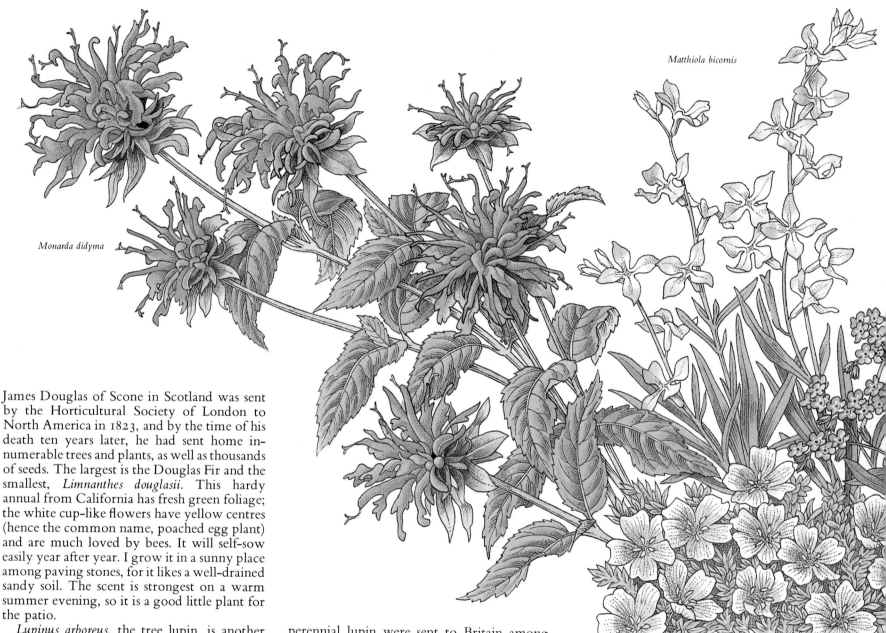

Monarda didyma

Matthiola bicornis

Limnanthes douglasii

James Douglas of Scone in Scotland was sent by the Horticultural Society of London to North America in 1823, and by the time of his death ten years later, he had sent home innumerable trees and plants, as well as thousands of seeds. The largest is the Douglas Fir and the smallest, *Limnanthes douglasii*. This hardy annual from California has fresh green foliage; the white cup-like flowers have yellow centres (hence the common name, poached egg plant) and are much loved by bees. It will self-sow easily year after year. I grow it in a sunny place among paving stones, for it likes a well-drained sandy soil. The scent is strongest on a warm summer evening, so it is a good little plant for the patio.

Lupinus arboreus, the tree lupin, is another native of California which had been introduced to Britain by 1793. It grows to more than 150cm/60in high in its natural surroundings, but to achieve this in a garden you must give it a sunny spot with sandy, or otherwise well-drained soil. It is not a long-lived plant so a few spares should be kept going. The honey-scented flowers are usually bright yellow, but you can get them in rather a faded blue or lilac. *L. polyphyllus*, one of the parents of the modern lupins (the other being *L. arboreus*), also comes from California and the seeds of this blue perennial lupin were sent to Britain among Douglas's discoveries.

All the lupins flower in early summer and should be placed in the border where their rather untidy appearance later in the season can be hidden by taller plants.

Matthiola, named after the famous 16th-century Italian botanist Mattioli, are among our most useful flowers for the scented garden. Sow seeds of the humble annual *M. bicornis*, the night-scented stock, tucked away behind taller plants, under your living room window, between shrubs or anywhere there is a small empty space with enough sun and light. By day they will be unnoticed, but on summer evenings the flowers will open and their scent will reach you, sweet and mysterious; one moment it will be with you and the next will have vanished. So elusive is it that you must move along the path to find it again.

In general, treat the Brompton stocks group as biennials; sow the seed in summer and plant

Lupinus arboreus

Myosotis alpestris

purple-tinged leaf bracts. It has various cultivars with lilac, pink or crimson flowers which are all aromatic, but none as intensely fragrant as the excellent *M. didyma*.

Seeds of this scarlet bergamot were sent by the dedicated collector John Bartram, a Virginian farmer, to the equally committed British plantsman Peter Collinson, in 1744. Collinson germinated the seeds that year and records that the plants flowered the next, and by 1760 there 'were plenty in Covent Garden Market'. I like John Hill's description of the plant, given in 1757: 'The flowers are very numerous, singular and elegant; they are long, tubulated and gaping, and in colour of a most elegant scarlet; a little paler or deeper, according to the degree of culture, but always beautiful.'

Although scarlet bergamot grows wild in North Carolina, the seeds Bartram collected came from Oswego on Lake Ontario, where the Indians used the leaves for an infusion which they drank, hence Oswego tea. When next you are making a wine cup in summer, add a few leaves to impart a delicious and refreshing flavour of oranges.

When you are siting *M. fistulosa*, remember that this plant will succeed on a drier soil than *M. didyma*.

The genus is named for Dr. Nicolas Monardes, the Spanish physician whose book, *Joyfull newes out of the newe founde worlde* caused quite a stir in the 16th century; the repercussion is still felt, for it is in this book that tobacco was first described and illustrated. The common name bergamot derives from the bergamot orange, a close relative of the Seville orange grown at Bergamo in Italy, whose fragrance was said to resemble that of the leaves of monarda. This raises an interesting point: it has often been noticed that plants with similar scents come from opposite sides of the world. Could this have been nature's aid to the insects which effect pollination, helping them to avoid confusion? If you give credence to this theory, it might be as well to separate similarly scented plants in the garden – you wouldn't want to bedevil the bees and butterflies!

Myosotis sylvatica, the much-loved forget-me-not, is more or less perennial. The flowers are azure-blue with a small yellow eye and the whole plant grows to about 20cm/8in. By 1870 *M. sylvatica*, *M. dissitiflora* and *M. alpestris* were being used as spring bedding plants, and some of the present day cultivars are hybrids between these species. The evening scent of

the seedlings out in autumn, ready for spring flowering. Given a sheltered spot, however, the plants can survive for several years, growing 80cm/30in tall and covered with scented flowers.

From a spring sowing the East Lothian group will flower in summer, and the Beauty of Nice strain can either be used in the garden or potted into good compost and brought into the greenhouse for winter flowering indoors. All the different sorts have a penetrating clove scent which 'is far sweeter in the air (where it comes and goes like the warbling of

music) than in the hand,' as Francis Bacon wrote in his 17th-century essay, 'Of Gardens'.

If I had to shortlist my favourite scented plants *Monarda didyma* would be included. Every part of this plant smells delicious – the flowers, the leaves and even the roots. In the border it is greedy, sending out next year's flower shoots all around. In so doing it tends to exhaust its centre, so you must either feed the clumps well with compost or manure, or else dig them up in the autumn or spring and very carefully pull off and replant each shoot. After doing this their scent will remain on your fingers until you next wash them. Monarda, bee balm, bergamot, call it by any name you will, was brought to England from the Virginia colonies. The wild bergamot *M. fistulosa*, then called 'the wild mint of America', was collected by John Tradescant the younger in 1637. I love it for its square stem and crown-like whorls of showy purple flowers and today's forget-me-nots is derived from *M. alpestris* and the other two provide the good deep blue, the bushiness and the height.

They are invaluable for interplanting with tulips and narcissi in spring bedding, as they stay fresh and attractive for several weeks. In light woodland, where they have been left undisturbed to regenerate themselves year after year, a blue carpet of forget-me-nots is a marvellous sight. It is said that in the year following Napoleon's defeat at Waterloo, the entire battlefield was smothered in an azure mantle of forget-me-nots – and so these tiny plants became the precursors of the scarlet poppies of Flanders Field.

The only member of the *Nemesia* genus which is scented, as far as I can discover, is *N. floribunda* which bears white and yellow flowers in graceful racemes. It is an annual, and if you wish to include it in a scented garden you will probably have to acquire the seeds from South Africa, its country of origin. The cultivars generally offered as bedding plants, bright as they are in colour, have no fragrance.

Nepeta mussinii, the catmint from the Caucasus arrived in England about 1800. Mrs. Loudon, writing soon after, described it as 'of no beauty', but many years later Gertrude Jekyll in *Colour in the Flower Garden* considered it a 'plant that can hardly be overpraised'. My sympathy is with Miss Jekyll, for to me it is an indispensable border plant. Perhaps the answer lies in the explanation that the plant we grow today and call *N. mussinii* is, in reality, an improved form, *N. × faassenii*, an accidental cross between *N. mussinii* and *N. nepetella*.

It is a favourite with bees and butterflies and makes an alluring blue-grey edging or an underplanting for roses. The pale lavender flowers last for weeks and are the perfect foil for pink flowers, or as a frill for delphiniums. All in all this 30cm/12in high plant has much to offer besides its keen, pungent aroma. When the first blooms are over, cut back the flower stalks and soon new lateral stems will appear, bearing a second crop of flowers. If you have trouble with your neighbour's cat rubbing itself on the leaves and then making a comfortable bed on the plant, a simple remedy is to put a few prickly stems, such as berberis or bramble, across it.

Nicotianas are annuals and perennials, mostly coming from South America, and they all love a deep, rich, moist soil. The well-known tobacco plant, *N. alata* (often listed in cata-

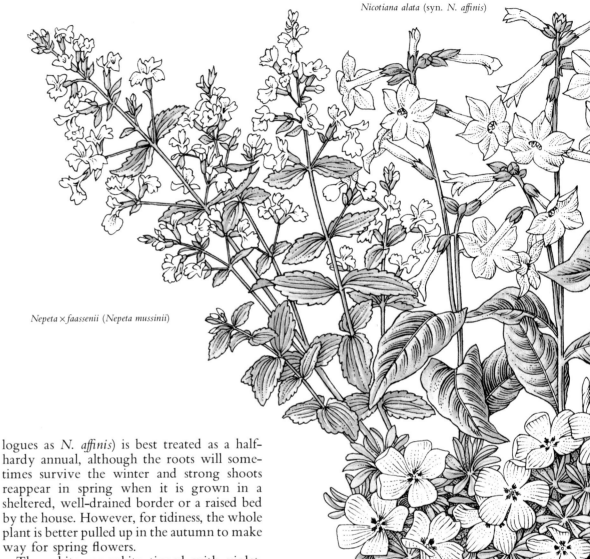

Nicotiana alata (syn. N. affinis)

Nepeta × faassenii (Nepeta mussinii)

logues as *N. affinis*) is best treated as a half-hardy annual, although the roots will sometimes survive the winter and strong shoots reappear in spring when it is grown in a sheltered, well-drained border or a raised bed by the house. However, for tidiness, the whole plant is better pulled up in the autumn to make way for spring flowers.

The white, or white tinged with violet, varieties have a stronger scent than the dark-flowered ones, and the now popular lime-green types are scentless. Plant them under your living room window or beside a path; their flowers are droopy and untidy by day but open up into bright stars in the evening, offering their wonderful rich perfume to you and to the moths which penetrate their long corolla tubes to collect the nectar, fertilizing them at the same time.

The flowers of *N. suaveolens*, from Australia, are smaller and pure white inside. It makes an excellent potted plant to stand out on a west-facing patio. Given favourable soil and growing conditions, the plant can reach a height of 60–100cm/24–40in.

My favourite of this genus is *N. sylvestris*, a fine, sweetly scented plant that is a native of the Andean foothills of northwestern Argentina. This is a 150cm/70in tall perennial, usually grown as an annual, with a stout stem and large leaves; perhaps it is a trifle coarse, but the white flowers in racemose panicles are wonderfully fragrant, becoming more so as the evening wears on. The corolla tube is long and narrow, so guarding its nectar especially for moths. Two or three plants in a large pot will help to scent the greenhouse, and if they are brought indoors for the evening, their scent

Nicotiana sylvestris

Oenothera biennis

Oxalis enneaphylla

only allowing the petals freedom to expand in the late afternoon. These are lovely plants for a special corner in the border or grown in the wild garden against dark foliage, so that they stand out in sharp contrast in the half-light of evening. Collect the seed and scatter it in odd corners and in two years time you will be rewarded by an effortless effect: one of those extras which make a garden exciting and worthwhile.

O. missouriensis is another superb plant, but it needs more attention than the evening primrose. It requires and deserves more space than I usually allow it, for it sends out long stems flat upon the ground, and if these are overgrown by their neighbours the flower buds will suffer. These are tawny red and open to 10cm/4in yellow blooms; the seedheads are pretty too.

It is gratifying to find a plant for the trough or rock garden which is as sweetly scented as *Oxalis enneaphylla*. It is a native of the Falkland Islands, from where it was sent to England in 1876. It was then apparently lost to cultivation, but early this century the renowned alpine expert Mr. Clarence Elliott went to the Falkland Islands to collect it once more. Not only did he recover the plants, but he discovered that the lovely waxy, white or pink flowers were deliciously almond scented. The glaucous blue leaves are fan shaped and finely folded on 7cm/3in stalks. Altogether it is a very desirable plant, flowering throughout the summer, and spreading gently by means of small tubers. Because its diminutive height makes it difficult to enjoy the fragrance, allow it a place in a raised bed or somewhere above ground level.

Some peonies are herbaceous, others shrubby, and many are highly fragrant, but all kinds have been important in China for centuries. They were of prime importance in the Imperial Gardens, Peking, and records of their cultivation and propagation date back to the 4th century AD. The Chinese word for peony *Shoyo* means 'the beautiful'.

Herbaceous varieties were causing quite a stir in Europe in the 16th and 17th centuries. Gerard talks of the double red, 'in fashion very like the great double rose of Provence, but greater and more double'. He must certainly have grown it for his patron Lord Burghley in his gardens in London and at Theobalds, for in writing of the double white form he says, 'we have likewise in our London gardens another sort bearing flowers of a pale whitish colour, very single'.

can pervade the house. They will seed themselves, but it is far safer to collect a few seeds on a dry autumn day. This way you will have seeds to give away as well as for your own use, and scented plants are always welcome gifts.

It is the leaves of *N. tabacum* that are used today for making cigars and cigarettes. Their first use in the mid-16th century was powdered, as snuff, but Gerard also described how: 'the dry leaves are used to be taken in a pipe and set on fire'.

Another genus of flowers that withhold their scent until evening is *Oenothera*. It is a large genus, mostly fragrant and indigenous to North and South America. Among them it is possible to find a species for the border, rock garden or wild garden. *O. caespitosa* is a handsome low-growing perennial from the Rocky Mountains of North America. It makes small tufts of grey-green leaves from which the flower buds appear. These open just before sunset, in time to unpleat the glowing white petals and give off their strong perfume, often described as a blend of lemon and jasmine. If you pick the buds when they are still closed then float them in water, you can watch them open, slowly but surely. *O. californica*, also perennial, but taller and so just right for the front of the border, has white flowers with a yellow centre.

The best biennial variety is *O. biennis*, the evening primrose. In good soil it will produce flower spikes at least 120cm/48in high, bearing buds which open in succession over many weeks in late summer. Examine a bud and you will find that the sepals cling together by day,

Paeonia officinalis 'Rubra Plena', the old-fashioned dark red double form, is not so scented as *P. lactiflora*. This species was introduced to England from Siberia and Mongolia in 1874, and from it many of today's cultivated varieties, known as Chinese peonies, have developed. Among the most popular are the spicy-scented 'Marie Crousse' with fully double blush-pink blooms, and the lovely white 'Duchesse de Nemours' and the pale pink 'Sarah Bernhardt', both sweetly scented.

The pure white flowers of *P. emodi* have ravishing golden stamens and a scent to match their beauty. *P. mlokosewitschii* has unrivalled lemon-yellow flowers in early summer; they are single with golden anthers. The foliage is attractive too – grey-green and downy.

Prepare the ground well before you plant the root divisions, feed them with leaf mould or compost each year, and remember not to disturb them. Early in the spring the shoots push resolutely through the cold soil. Young shoots are easy prey for slugs and snails, but a circle of charcoal or wood ash around the young plants protects them from such hungry garden pests. After the flowers have faded, in the early autumn months, the foliage often becomes richly tinted with red and golden shades.

The hardy border phlox are mostly hybrids of the perennial species *Phlox paniculata*, which is a native of the eastern seaboard of North America. These hybrids are the more showy varieties, with vibrant colours and enticing names like 'Brigadier', a bright orange-red, and 'Sweetheart', a lovely dark-eyed salmon-rose. They are all fragrant, make superb border plants flowering throughout late summer, and will even thrive in semi-shade. I believe that the white, pink and mauve cultivars have a stronger, sweeter and more heady scent than the bright reds and oranges.

Do not overlook *P. maculata*; the mauvy-pink flowers are carried on tall cylindrical heads. I think it is more graceful than the hybrids, and ·usually not so susceptible to eelworm troubles.

Root cuttings are the best method to increase your stock of these plants which are so well worth maintaining in every scented garden. They like a rich soil and appreciate watering during dry spells while they are flowering. Especially if troubled by mildew or eelworm, the lower leaves tend to look shabby by late summer, so hide them with a low-

Phlox maculata

Primula veris

grower such as lavender, santolina or heliotrope planted in front.

Phuopsis stylosa, the Caucasian crosswort, has attractive narrow, bright green leaves in whorls. On wet days, and as the dew falls in the evening, they give off a remarkably strong scent; some say it is delicious and others wonder where the fox is hiding. Crosswort makes a wonderful ground cover during the summer, but do keep it away from your more precious plants which it could smother, as the stems are floppy and long. The dusky-pink flowers on globular heads start in midsummer and continue for months. In autumn cut the spent stems to ground level and interplant with spring bulbs – the scented *Narcissus* 'Trevithian' would be a good choice.

Polyanthus are a cross between the primrose and the cowslip. Plants can be divided, but they do grow readily from seed and in this way you can achieve a good spring display. Generally, the paler flowers have the strongest scent.

Primula auricula is an alpine flower that has been in cultivation since the 16th century.

Spring and early summer gardens would be much the poorer without primroses, polyanthus and primulas. *P. vulgaris*, the common primrose of the British Isles, grows happily in woods and hedgerows. It has a sweet mossy scent, as I remember from my childhood picking of bunches of these simple flowers for Mother's Day. Given good moist soil and ample space in dappled shade they will spread and delight you every spring. These single-stemmed yellow primroses are native to many parts of Europe but now, thanks to the hybrids,

Paeonia emodi

Reseda odorata

Phuopsis stylosa

you can have a galaxy of colours, all sweet smelling and all from seed.

Cowslips, *P. veris*, will make fine 45cm/18in stems of flowers if grown in cultivated ground. They are softly fragrant when cut and brought indoors, and can be used to make a lovely wine, redolent of gentle spring mornings. I love cowslips, not only for their scent, but also for the admiration they always arouse.

The Asian primulas must have plenty of moisture and so are well suited to pond-side or bog gardens. There is *P. florindae*, the giant cowslip, brought to England from Sikkim in

1924 by Captain Kingdon-Ward, which has a strong, sweet scent, and *P. denticulata* with round lavender or white pompons and a faint smell of honey. *P. involucrata* from Tibet is my choice for the rock garden. The glossy white flowers have a conspicuous golden centre with a scent which on a sunny day reminds me of bees and honey.

Reseda odorata, the ever-popular mignonette, is an annual with a sophisticated musky scent. Philip Miller was the first to grow it in England, in the Chelsea Physic Garden. He says in his *Gardener's Dictionary*, 'The seeds of this were sent me by Dr. Royen, the late professor of botany at Leyden . . . . The flowers are of an herbaceous white colour, produced in long

spikes at the end of the branches, and smell very like fresh raspberries, which occasions its being much cultivated in the English gardens.' He also comments that it is very like *R. phyteuma*, whose flowers have no scent hence some 'have supposed the plant was degenerate'. My advice is to throw out any plants with no scent and gather seed from any fragrant ones you may have; it is well worth the extra trouble.

The Empress Josephine was sent seeds by Napoleon from Egypt and for a short while it became the fashion in Paris to grow mignonette in pots on balconies. If you choose to revive this fashion, bear in mind that mignonette's scent tends to fade when you bring it indoors or otherwise take it out of the sunlight.

For spring flowering indoors, sow seed in the autumn, for summer flowering outdoors, sow seed in the spring.

Salvia sclarea or clary sage is an old-fashioned biennial. The leaves were once used as a remedy for sore eyes, but now the oil extracted from them is used as a fixative for scent. Brush against the leaves and they produce an unpleasant odour, but the oil smells of grapes.

S. sclarea turkestanica qualifies for inclusion in the scented garden, not for its typical odour but for its good looks. It is a handsome biennial with large hairy leaves and a square stem bearing labiate flowers which are white with mauve bracts.

Two more salvias, which should be in the flower garden rather than the herb garden, are *S. microphylla* (syn. *S. grahamii*) whose crushed leaves smell of red currants and *S. rutilans*, the pineapple-scented sage. *S. microphylla* came from Mexico, and in a frost-free climate will grow into a 120cm/48in high shrub, but otherwise it behaves like a herbaceous plant. To ensure plants for the next year take cuttings in the autumn; they root easily. *S. rutilans* is winter flowering; in fact, it is best kept in a pot and brought indoors for its attractive carmine-red flowers. However, I like to have it in the border as well, just to be able to squeeze the leaves and indulge in their fruity scent.

Smilacina racemosa is a perennial native of woodlands in eastern North America and is a splendid plant for shady corners. The stems, up to 60cm/24in long, are angled in a zig-zag fashion from one set of leaves to the next. Because of its pretty, arching growth it is easily mistaken for Solomon's seal, but the flowers are quite different. They appear in fluffy white spikes at the ends of the stems, and have a delicious sweet scent.

We have talked of old-fashioned pot marigolds, but do not neglect the African and French Tagetes. The latter was held in high esteem by John Parkinson, but in both species the flower and leaf have an aromatic scent. Because of the flowers' strong yellows and oranges, keep them well away from soft pink colours in the border.

In springtime forget-me-not growing under cherry trees reminds me of my childhood and in summertime nasturtium, *Tropaeolum majus*, does so too. When I was ten I remember planting nasturtium seeds along the garden fence. My anticipation was intense and the resulting border of bloom was wonderful, living up to my expectation. They love the sunniest place you can give them, and will produce a greater abundance of flowers in poor soil, for given too much goodness they produce all leaves and no blooms. You can use every part of the plant; the flowers for decoration, the succulent leaves to eat in salads, and the seeds are good for pickling. Nasturtiums are not quite hardy in cool climates so do not sow them outside until the danger of frost is past. The 'Whirlybird' cultivars make inviting low mounds for the front of the border and the trailing ones will climb through low shrubs.

In 1629 John Parkinson wrote of nasturtiums, Indian Cress or Yellow Larkes Heels as he calls them. He says the seeds were sent from the West Indies to Spain and thence came to England where they 'are now very familiar in most gardens of any curiosity . . . . The leaves are smooth, green and as round as penni-

Verbena x hybrida

Tropaeolum majus

wort. . . . The flowers are of an excellent gold yellow colour. The whole flower hath a fine small scent, very pleasing, which being placed in the middle of some carnations or gilliflowers make a delicate tussie mussie . . . both for sight and scent.'

The common garden verbena *Verbena × hybrida*, whose parents came from South America, like many plants from this region, is only half-hardy in cool climates. Formerly, it was usually propagated from cuttings taken in the spring from plants which had been overwintered in a cold frame, but now there is a wide selection of seed available which comes true to colour and form. The best

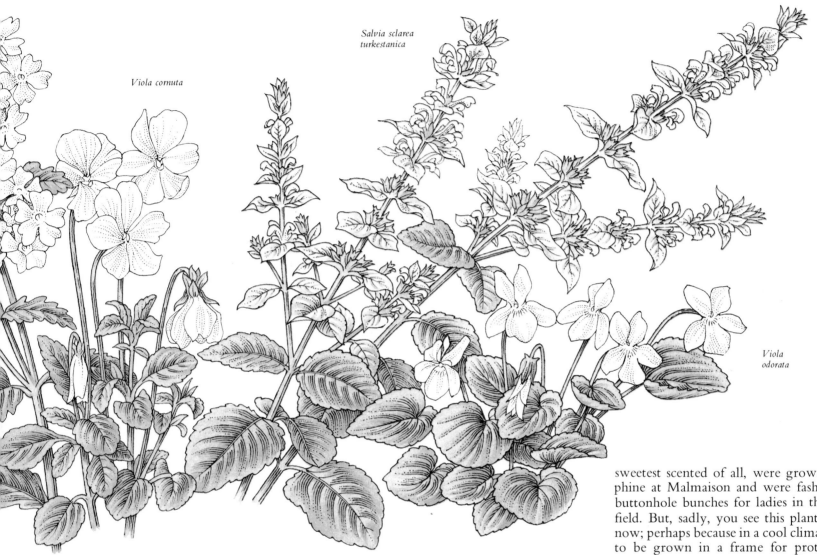

Viola cornuta

Salvia sclarea
turkestanica

Viola
odorata

way is to grow verbenas from seed sown early in the year, so that seedlings are ready to prick out when spring bedding is removed. They will flower continuously from midsummer until autumn frosts cut them back. As with many plants, the pale colours – pinks and, especially, white – have the strongest scent. Plant them in bold groups at the front of the border where tulips, daffodils and wallflowers have scented your garden in spring.

More has been written about the humble violet, *Viola odorata*, than almost any other flower, except possibly the rose and lily.

'Meadows of softest verdure purpled o'er with violets.' Do our violets have the same perfume as Homer's, I wonder? The Greeks

made chaplets and garlands of them on festive occasions. The Romans used them too, for violet wine and candied violets; they also fried them with slices of lemon and orange. Later the poet Fortunas, Bishop of Poitiers, sent violets to St Radegunda to decorate her church. The Empress Josephine had violets embroidered on her wedding dress and they were forever the signature of love between her and Napoleon.

Today we do not honour them as much as we should in our scented gardens. They are easy to cultivate, new plants that flower well growing readily from runners and division. Their main flush of flowers comes in spring and again in late autumn, but it is seldom you will not find one to pick. Parma violets, the

sweetest scented of all, were grown by Josephine at Malmaison and were fashionable as buttonhole bunches for ladies in the hunting field. But, sadly, you see this plant less often now; perhaps because in a cool climate it needs to be grown in a frame for protection, or because labour costs for picking the flowers are so high. Neither of these reasons, though, should stop you cultivating a small patch under cloches.

The lovely cultivar 'Coeur d'Alsace' has dusky-pink flowers and 'Nellie Britton' is a ravishing, pale warm mauve.

V. cornuta in its white and blue forms is also sweetly scented, and is useful anywhere near the front of the border, where it will climb through low-growing neighbours. It has been hybridized with the garden pansy, once known as heartsease, to give us tufted pansies, or violas, in many shades. I would hate to be without them in my garden, for their variety, their fragrance and their unexpected appearance in odd corners.

A sense of scent

Bees, butterflies and moths play such an important role in the life of the garden, fertilizing the plants and adding another kind of colour and interest, that we should do all we can to provide the tiny creatures with the food and habitat they need.

Pollen and nectar are the bees' two main sources of food. Pollen is rich in protein and, for three days early in the year, the bees feed it to the larvae being reared in the hive; most of them are afterwards fed on nectar converted into honey. The larvae in the queen-cells are fed with this protein for a longer time, to help them develop fully. The flow of nectar, which indirectly provides us with honey, increases as the spring turns to summer.

While bees are busy collecting pollen and nectar, they fertilize the plants they visit by carrying pollen from one flower to another on the hairs of their bodies, thus effecting cross-

Bees find members of labiate family, such as basil and golden marjoram, especially appealing. Although these will all be growing in the herb garden, some of them make a splendid show as border plants, thyme and purple sage in particular.

pollination which leads to cross-fertilization of the plants. This is an all-important factor in keeping plants productive of seed and fruit. With no bees about our fruit and vegetable crops would be very much poorer.

Scent serves as a guide for bees, but is secondary to colour in attracting them. However, the bees exploit the flower's scent for their own purpose. When a worker bee returns to the hive, after it has visited a flower with plenty of pollen or nectar, it will perform a kind of dance. This attracts the other workers who gather round and touch the scout with their antennae. Because bees can memorize the shape, colour and scent of flowers, as well as having a sense of direction, the other workers recognize the scent and immediately fly off to the appropriate flower. In early spring when food is scarce, there will always be more scout bees about than when the supply of pollen and nectar is flowing. Another useful function of scent is that it helps to keep the bee faithful to one species of flower at a time, ensuring its effective pollination and fertilization.

Many careful experiments have been made to assess the bees' ability to smell and to see colours, and it has been found that they have much the same sense of smell as humans have. But as scent is of less importance to them than colour, many of the flowers which are pollinated by bees are scentless. For instance, although the labiates such as sage, mint, balm, ballota and nepeta have aromatic leaves, it is the flowers that are designed to receive the bees, their lipped lower petals creating a landing site for alighting bees, and the flower's colour attracting them.

The colours that bees are most strongly attracted to are yellow, blue-green to blue, mauve and purple, and red containing ultra-violet. It has been discovered that bees are blind to any other kind of red. For instance, the red of a Flanders poppy has ultra-violet in it so that the poppy looks blue to the bees, but red without ultra-violet looks khaki or green to them, in much the same way that the colour would appear to a man who is 'colour blind'. Bees can confuse some shades of blue with violet and purple, and yellows with orange and green; but, on the whole, yellow is the most attractive colour to them.

Now that you understand the importance of colour and scent to bees, you must next think about planting accordingly. Bees seldom visit a solitary flower, as they like to carry as much as

For centuries, bee-keeping has been an essential labour for the sincere gardener, profiting him not only by the delicately flavoured honey produced by his colony of bees, but in the pleasure to be had from listening to and watching the apian workers. The 16th-century master gardener, Thomas Hyll, wrote, 'the fittest place for bees is that which is in a garden, not farre or rather neare to the owner's house, which by that means suffereth not the windes, nor accesse of thieves or beastes.'

As bees busily churn the fragrant breezes about the nectar- and pollen-producing flowers, the scented garden becomes more than decoration as its utilitarian aspect becomes evident. Bee-flowers, from the dainty white woodruff to the riotously colourful chieranthus, should be planted in bold clumps, as a bee will never linger on one flower. In the flower border, *right*, plantings of blue and white phlox are suitable companions for a mass of sweetly fragrant, vibrant red bee-balm, *Monarda didyma*, making a colourful and fragrant, yet purposeful, display.

While bees rely primarily on colour to find the flowers they seek, moths and butterflies respond to scent. As a consequence butterfly-flowers are often the most heavily perfumed but delicately coloured in the garden. This provides an appealing contrast to the elaborately beautiful wing markings of the insects themselves. Among the most showy butterflies common to the United States are the bright orange Monarchs and multicoloured Camberwell Beauties. Red Admirals and Painted Ladies and the small Tortoiseshells are a few of the butterflies most frequently seen in the gardens of Britain and northern Europe. All these are illustrated *far right*.

Camberwell Beauty

Painted Lady

Monarch

Red Admiral

Small Tortoiseshell

A sense of scent 2

they are able before returning to the hive. So arrange the plants in bold groups and drifts, choosing pollen and nectar flowers for different positions in the border, and bear in mind when selecting them that, as a general rule, single-petalled flowers are easier for bees to work than double-petalled. Bees will usually choose to work flowers in the sun, in preference to those in the shade, so select plants that like a sunny site.

Early pollen and nectar come from the early-flowering bulbs. These can be planted to grow through ground cover plants such as aubrieta arabis, lamium and forget-me-nots.

Another early flower, much loved by the bees, is hellebore. The Christmas rose, *Helleborus niger*, is too early, but by the time *H. corsicus* and *H. orientalis* open their flowers, there are sure to be bees about. I think hellebores are the jewels of spring and should be given the place of honour.

There are trees which provide forage early in the year, namely willows, hazels, elms and poplars. Then come the spring flowers: sweet violets, primroses and cowslips, which can all be planted under these deciduous trees. By late spring several varieties of fruit tree — pears, cherries, plums — begin to blossom, and these, and the apple blossom which opens a little later, provide the finest nectar for honey-bees.

Bees appear in their hundreds when the unusually scented flowers of the white cotoneaster open at the end of spring. At the same time, the raspberry and bean flowers in the vegetable garden are waiting to be fertilized. Then

summer arrives, and in the well-planned flower border, created with bees in mind, there will be perennials such as comfrey, polemonium, campanula, delphinium, nepeta and hesperis; a large patch of blue cranesbill, *Geranium pratense*, would be very popular.

There are several hardy biennials which you must also include in the border. Wallflowers and forget-me-nots are an essential feature of the scented garden in spring and the furry-leafed mulliens, or verbascums, are another feature and an equally good bee plant. The quality of the leaves varies considerably so you must take care to keep only the best seedlings with the most felted leaves; there will always be plenty to select from.

Among the best hardy annuals for bee-forage are limnanthes, clarkia, eschscholzia, linum, nigella, poppy and nasturtium. They can all be sown directly into their flowering positions, or you can grow some of them as hardy biennials, particularly nigella. Another favourite, *Echium* 'Blue Bedder', is a hairy plant with intense blue flowers which has a long flowering period. *Salvia patens* is probably one of the best blue plants. Grow this as an annual, or else hope that the small tubers which it grows from will survive hard winter frosts and reappear in the spring.

Nearly all the herbs are loved by bees: rosemary, which flowers in late spring, borage, balm, sage and, of course, the different thymes. Many midsummer and autumn herbaceous plants are important for honey: Michaelmas

daisies, globe thistles, monarda, mignonette, meadowsweet and heleniums.

An important characteristic of many butterflies and moths is that they themselves are scented, since scent plays a direct part in their sexual attraction. Flowers which are fertilized by them usually have a heavy, sweet scent, like that of honeysuckle, jasmine, lilac, wallflowers and narcissi. The scent of these flowers, resembling that of the insect, serves to attract ardent suitors, who end up fertilizing a flower instead of another insect; such is the craftiness of nature!

It is believed that flowers have evolved in relation to the insects which visit them. So the conclusion could well be that, were it not for the scent of butterflies, some flowers might never have developed a fragrance; in which case we are deeply indebted to the butterfly kingdom. Butterflies are most active on fine sunny days, in gardens with a warm, sheltered aspect, as they will neither breed nor feed in cold, windswept gardens. They like flowers which are mauve, blue, deep pink, crimson and saffron yellow. In fact some of these proud creatures prefer flowers which are the same colours as their own wings.

As it does in the evening, scent in a shady woodland has the advantage over colour. Many woodland flowers such as lily of the valley and daphne are pale in colour but heavily scented, which makes them more noticeable in the twilight and easier for night-feeding moths to find.

Man soon discovered the sweetness of honey, and for centuries he has captured swarms of wild bees and made hives for them to live and store their honey in. He then steals some of the honey for his own use, so it is natural and just for him to plant those flowers which will supply food for the bees.

One essential factor in having butterflies in the garden is to make sure that you have the right place and plants for them to overwinter and breed on. The Tortoiseshells love to spend the winter in a warm blanket of ivy, grown up a wall or kept low as ground cover. There is no need to choose ordinary dull-green ivy; there are many with beautifully marked and variegated leaves: *Hedera helix* 'Goldheart' will keep its glorious golden tints even in the shade, and during the summer *H. colchica* 'Dentata Variegata' makes a wonderful complementary backdrop to a golden-toned herbaceous border.

You must arrange to keep a patch of nettles in an unfrequented corner of the garden, or else grow them in large pots to stand in sunny corners, as this is where Red Admirals, Tortoiseshells and Peacock butterflies like to lay their eggs. Painted Ladies choose thistle leaves and their caterpillars feed on anchusa and nettles. You should have *Viola canina* for the Fritillaries and *Cardamine pratense* for the Orange Tips. In late summer when most butterflies are about, you must have several purple buddleias, the powder blue *Ceratostigma willmottianum*, hardy fuchsias and hyssop.

Sedums are an essential part of the butterfly garden. When in flower *Sedum spectabile*, with chalky, mauve-pink flowers, is covered with Peacocks and Tortoiseshells hovering and landing. The cultivars 'Meteor' and 'Brilliant' are darker in colour, and the pink 'Autumn Joy' is a fitting companion for the blue ceratostigma; its muted colour also blends well with grey-leafed plants. Two late-flowering herbaceous plants which must be included are asters and ligularias. In my garden, the orange-yellow flowers of *Ligularia przewalskii* are alive with Peacocks flitting about on sunny days in August. There is a wide selection of suitable asters, and my advice is to experiment and find out which grows best in your garden. My firm favourite is *Aster novae-angliae* 'Elma Potschke', a ravishing cerise that needs some cooler colour to calm it down; grey is a good foil and so is a pale blue, but I have yet to find its perfect mate.

'The bee is little among such things as fly, but her fruit is the chief of sweet things.'
Bees and butterflies animate the garden, assisting in pollination and cross-fertilization. By encouraging them in your scented garden you will help the plants to produce their flowers and fruits.

Say it with flowers

The use of emblems to signify special things and the assignation of hidden meanings to commonplace items was an accepted practice long before the language of flowers was introduced from Persia during the 18th century. This preconditioning no doubt assisted in the avid acceptance of the floral code by European and American ladies.

'Happiness is to hold flowers in both hands', say the Japanese. Certainly every woman, whatever her age and status, loves to be 'bunched' with a bouquet of flowers. Some long to be given the most expensive, exotic orchids, while others find more to appreciate in a humble posy from the meadow or garden. But until the 1920s – when the fashion died out, no doubt because of more relaxed communication between the sexes – there would have been the added fascination of a secret message conveyed by the flowers themselves.

In popular tradition each bloom had its own meaning, often several meanings, as there were many advisers on the subject of 'flower emblems', and not all agreed. The flax flower might mean 'domestic industry' according to one authority, but 'I feel your kindness' to another, while a white poppy could signify either 'my bane' or 'my antidote' – a confusion which might have serious consequences if misunderstood.

From early times, emblem books were an indispensable tool of artists, craftsmen and writers. Typically, an emblem book would contain illustrations of plants and flowers, accompanied by an exposition of each flower's allegorical significance. This might take the form of a story, drawn from the Bible, folklore, or classical literature, telling how the flower gained its attribute. For instance, under an engraving of the red rose you might read how the rose was white, until Venus, running wildly through the woods mourning her dead lover Adonis, cut her foot on a brier and stained the roses red with her blood, and so the red rose came to symbolize 'love'.

So important was a knowledge of flower meanings considered to be that even practical books on gardening included them. Henry Phillips in his *Flora Historica* of 1829 describes flowers for the formally patterned parterre. Each description starts with the emblematic meaning of the flower: the yellow day lily, 'this fragile beauty is made the emblem of coquetry, because its flower seldom lasts a second day'; 'The Peony is given as a representative of bashful shame' and 'The sunflower is made the emblem of false riches because gold of itself cannot render a person truly rich.'

The 19th-century woman – and her lover – made a cult of the Language of Flowers. But how did the symbolism of flowers, so well understood in the Middle Ages and Renaissance, become this 'florigraphy' in which one could send all but the most finely detailed of messages?

In 1718, Lady Mary Wortley Montague sent a letter from Constantinople to a friend at home in England, describing the secret messages that Turkish women sent to their lovers. These love letters were not sent in words but in flowers and tokens. Each flower, thread of silk or gem had a saying attached to its name which the Turkish girls had learned by heart so that they could decipher these subtle missives. When Lady Mary's letters were published in 1763, it was the language of flowers which attracted her readers, as it suited so well their current passion for gardening.

But the real popularity of flower-language began around 1818 with *Le Langage des Fleurs* by the pseudonymous 'Mme Charlotte de la Tour'. This volume was translated into several languages. Richly illustrated versions appeared, their fine engravings and hand-tinted drawings set to satisfy the 19th century's great appetite for all things botanical. Many books were written on the subject, often by women, and it provided the means for them to exercise

What the Flowers Say
Other scented plants with a message

Achillea millefolium	War
African marigold	Vulgar minds
Almond flower	Hope
Alyssum	Worth beyond beauty
Amaryllis	Splendid beauty
Apple blossom	Preference
Balm	Pleasantry
Basil	Hatred
Bluebell	Constancy
Borage	Bluntness
Cactus	Warmth
Carnation, striped	Refusal
– yellow	Disdain
Clematis	Mental beauty
Coriander	Hidden worth
Crown imperial	Majesty
Heather	Solitude
Heliotrope	Devotion
Hop	Injustice
Hoya	Sculpture
Hyacinth	Sport, play
Jasmine, white	Amiability
– yellow	Grace and elegance
Lantana camara	Sharpness
Laurel	Glory
– flower	Perfidy
Lily, white	Purity
– yellow	Falsehood
Lily of the valley	Return of happiness
Meadowsweet	Uselessness
Mignonette	Your qualities surpass your charms
Mock orange	Counterfeit
Narcissus	Egotism
Oenothera	Inconstancy
Orange blossom	Bridal festivity
Pelargonium, dark	Melancholy
– lemon	Unexpected meeting
– rose scented	Preference
– scarlet	Folly
Rose, eglantine	I wound to heal
– single	Simplicity
– white bud	Heart innocent of love
– yellow	Jealousy
Rosa chinensis	Beauty always fresh
– moschata	Capricious beauty
– Mundi	Variety
– muscosa	Voluptuousness
Rosemary	Remembrance
Rue	Disdain
Selenicereus	Transient beauty
Snowdrop	Consolation
Southernwood	A jest
Stephanotis	You can boast too much
Sweet william	Gallantry
Tulip, yellow	Hopeless love
Vervain	Enchantment
Violet, blue	Faithfulness
– sweet	Modesty
Wisteria	I cling to thee
Witch hazel	A spell

With the pull of a string, this paper posy reveals the hidden meaning of the flowers. This pretty floral language appealed especially to Victorian sensibilities and provided ladies and gentlemen with a polite and proper means of expressing their innermost feelings.

Say it with flowers 2

the sentimental demeanour so popular at the time. The well-brought-up young lady could add to her practical yet genteel accomplishments an understanding of the language of flowers. In Victorian England women, stifled by an overbearing sense of propriety, had to be models of wifely and maidenly virtue. But they had romantic impulses and found a means to express ardent messages through the otherwise innocent gift of flowers.

And how delightful it must then have been for a young girl to discover that she could express her feelings to her undeclared lover without giving away their secrets to others: a fern ('I am fascinated by you'), an iris ('I have a message for you') or love-lies-bleeding ('It is hopeless, but I am not heartless').

A swarm of floral dictionaries followed

'Mme de la Tour's' work; many were plagiarized from earlier books, but others had their own variations on the theme. In the 1870s, Captain Frederick Marryat wrote *The Floral Telegraph*, in which he instructed his fair readers how, by means of an ingenious system of ribbons and knots, to send such messages as 'Mama always goes to sleep before dinner'.

The most romantic writers, however, believed that old is best. I have Mrs. Wirt's *Flora's Dictionary*, an intriguing book, given to me by a good friend in Philadelphia, who inherited it from her grandfather. Perhaps he wooed my friend's grandmother with a spray of ivy, symbol of matrimony.

Flower language is out of fashion today, but we still acknowledge it when we say, 'Say it with flowers'. Why not revive some of these traditions? When you have friends to dinner, decorate the table with honeysuckle ('generous affection'), acacia ('friendship') and nutmeg-scented pelargonium ('an expected meeting'). You can include sprigs of parsley for 'festivity' – this is bound to elicit questions, and the explanation will charm your guests.

When you are going away for a few days, leave a posy of sweet peas ('departure') and white clover ('think of me') to hold the fort till you get back. If your son or daughter is facing an important examination, encourage them with angelica ('inspiration'), red clover ('industry') and pink cherry blossom ('education').

Flowers are the traditional gift for people who are unwell, but a bundle of herbs – chamomile ('energy in adversity'), fennel ('strength'), allspice ('compassion') and if you have it, of course, Balm of Gilead for 'cure', make an original and clean-scented bouquet. Better to leave out the useful evergreen bay, though, as to the initiated it means 'I change but in death'.

But the language of flowers is quintessentially romantic. A florist's selection arriving at the door the morning after a promising first introduction speaks volumes.

Assuming the best, celebrate the wedding with a lot of red roses and myrtle for 'love' and Cape jasmine for 'joy'. Include sage ('esteem'), peppermint ('warmth') and the oak-leaved pelargonium ('true friendship') if you like herbs. If you add marjoram for 'fertility', remember to plant white lilac ('innocent youth'), primrose ('early youth') and sweet sultan ('happiness') in time for the expected christening.

A tussie mussie or tuzzy muzzy, is a small nosegay made entirely of scented flowers and leaves. Like the pomanders carried by Renaissance courtiers, tussie mussies were believed to afford protection from plague. In colonial America, these fragrant posies were carried by women to sustain them during the long Sunday prayer meetings. Later, tussie mussies were a popular way of conveying messages in the language of flowers.

The arrangement of the flowers is quite formal, consisting of rings of leaves and sprigs of herbs and scented flowers encircling a central bud, usually a rose. Flowers for a tussie mussie should be cut with long stems. Florist's wire wrapped around the stems of the outer flowers will help you to bend them outward without snapping them. When the bunch is completed, tie a pretty ribbon around the top of the stems to bind the bouquet together.

Basics of flower arranging

Flowers should always be picked either before the sun has reached them or else late in the evening. Fill a bucket with cold water and stand it in a shady place in the garden so that you can plunge the flowers neck-deep into the water as soon as they are picked, to prevent immediate wilting. A golden rule is to put all cut flowers in deep water until you need them – for twelve hours if possible.

Before you actually arrange the flowers, some will need special attention and treatment. Plants which will retain their freshness much longer if you hold the ends of their stems in boiling water for a minute are broom, mimosa, buddleia and mignonette. Try to prevent the steam getting on to the flowers or the petals may suffer. There are others, such as heliotrope, hellebore and nicotiana, that should have their stems held for a moment in a candle flame. With all shrubs with hard wood, it is as well to strip off all leaves below the water line, and then lightly crush the bottom 3cm/1½in of the stem. Lilac, roses, lonicera and philadelphus are examples of shrubs to be treated like this.

Flowers such as water-lilies, which naturally close at night, can be kept open by dropping a blob of candlewax between the petals.

When trimming hollow-stemmed plants be sure to cut away the solid stem to open the hollow end. With flowers such as tulips and daffodils, the stem-ends should be held in boiling water for several seconds, or under running water, to clear away the mucus they emit.

As well as treating particular flowers in special ways to make them last longer, there are a few simple tips which apply to all flower arrangements. First of all, never stand bowls of flowers near central heating vents or radiators, and do not leave them in full sun – they will wilt within the hour. Keep the water fresh and clear by putting a piece of charcoal or a copper coin in the bottom of the container, and do remember to top up the water regularly so that the flowers have something to drink.

Many winter-flowering plants will not release their scent in the coolness of the garden, but indoors the warmth will bring it out. I love to make small, restrained winter posies to stand on a fireside table. I use sprigs of either winter honeysuckle or wintersweet as a base, add sprays of honey-scented *Virburnum farreri* or *V. bodnantense*, and then spiky sprigs of rosemary or branches of sage. Few people make use of herbs in floral decoration, which is a pity as the leaf shapes and colours of herbs are most attractive. A few well-marked leaves of ivy or scented-leaf geranium and a flowerhead or two of a greenhouse-raised pelargonium, added for colour, will complete your arrangement.

Iris unguicularis is one of the earliest and most beautiful of the winter flowers. Pick them just before the buds open and you will be able to watch them unfurl indoors.

In the spring all the daffodils and 'Pheasant's Eye' narcissi will be out, as will the variously coloured wallflowers.

But the greatest scope for flower arranging is provided by the summer-flowering annuals and herbaceous plants. Peonies, lupins, bergamot and sweet peas are but a few of the scented flowers that can be used to make riotous, extravagant arrangements to celebrate the beauty of the scented garden in summer.

Out of doors you must bury your nose in many flowers before you fully appreciate their fragrance – the shrubby *Paeonia delavayi* is one of these – but a few of the blooms, picked and put in a vase, have a strong and surprising scent. Herbs such as rosemary, sage, hyssop, lavender and mint will also be in flower and can be used to fill out a bouquet.

There are few fragrant flowers which are not suitable for cutting and arranging. A group of small vases such as those shown *below*, filled with freshly picked flowers including branches of *Eucalyptus gunnii*, the Cider gum, and clove-scented carnations, makes an eye-catching display and brings the pleasure of the scented garden into the house.

Bulbs, corms and tubers

Beautifully illustrated bulb catalogues arrive through the post each autumn, enticing us to spend our money on bulbs of every sort. How grateful I am to have them, for they tell when and how to plant the bulbs, how tall they will grow and exactly what conditions they like, making it all so simple.

How different it must have been three or four hundred years ago: no catalogues, and only William Turner's or John Gerard's herbals, if you were lucky. But maybe it was more exciting to receive an unfamiliar, dormant bulb, not knowing what would emerge from it.

All bulbs once grew in the wild; many of them have now been brought into our gardens for their qualities of colour and scent or for their decorative value. But what of the past? We know that colchicum and scilla were cultivated for medicinal purposes as early as 1800 BC, and that the Egyptians grew anemones, lilies and narcissi, for these flowers were among the funeral tributes discovered in the tombs of the ancient Egyptian Pharoahs. The Assyrians grew the Madonna lily, *Lilium candidum*, and so did the Minoans in Crete, if we may believe surviving wall paintings.

The Greek Theophrastus, in his *Enquiry into Plants* written about 340 BC, describes narcissi, saffron crocuses, lilies, ranunculus and gladioli among other plants. Mithridates, King of Pontius, famous for his antidotes for poison, used the juice of the Madonna lily bulb against snake bite. Dioscorides in the 1st century AD wrote extensively about bulbs. Each succeeding writer increased the repertoire of known plants, cultivated in gardens chiefly for their medicinal properties rather than for their beauty; although the lily, the rose and the violet were grown primarily for their elegance.

Returning Crusaders brought bulbs from the eastern Mediterranean countries and Asia Minor to France and Britain. In the Middle Ages the general trend was to grow plants for use rather than beauty, but by the 16th century, particularly in France, Italy, England and Holland, garden design was assuming a new importance. Bulbous plants performed a major role in knot gardens during spring. You have only to turn the pages of the early herbals, or *Hortus Floridus*, written in 1614 by Crispin van de Passe, to find alliums, lilies, hepaticas, crocuses, narcissi, muscari, hyacinths and the inevitable tulips, with petals of purple, white, saffron-yellow, crimson and scarlet with 'glistening white flames, a wonderful marvel of nature'. Tulips seemed to come in every colour except blue. How fortunate we are that the introduction of new bulbs was thus recorded.

We must not forget the importance of the colonization of South Africa by the Dutch, for that country provided freesias, oxalis and gladioli. And, as mentioned earlier, in the 1730s John Bartram of Philadelphia, more than anyone else at the time, was responsible for introducing new seeds and bulbs to England.

The introduction of tulips to Europe dates from much earlier. In 1554 Busbecq, ambassador from the German Emperor Ferdinand I to the Ottoman Empire, observed near Constantinople 'an abundance of flowers everywhere – narcissi, hyacinths and those which the Turks call Tulipam – much to our astonishment, because it was almost mid-winter . . . Greece abounds in narcissus and hyacinths remarkable for their fragrance . . . the tulipam, however, have little or no smell, but are admired for their beauty and variety of their colours.' This, I believe, is the first reference to tulips in western writing.

Busbecq took tulip seeds, and probably bulbs, to Vienna, and the fame of the flowers quickly spread. From this small beginning a great industry sprang, for in 1562 a merchant in Antwerp received a consignment of bulbs from Constantinople, and tulips were soon

Of all the sweetly scented plants in the garden, only the rose is as highly prized as the lily. Both are among the oldest flowers in cultivation and a display of the ivory-white Madonna lily, *Lilium candidum*, *left*, would be a credit to any garden.

Iris florentina, *right*, which has the delicate scent of violets, is cultivated in Tuscany for the production of orris root powder.

being grown in Holland, England and France. In all probability these were not a species of wild tulip, but the self-coloured cultivated tulips which have the habit of breaking into striped and feathered variegated forms. They became the cause of 'Tulipomania', the wild financial gambling in tulip bulbs which consumed Holland for three years between 1634 and 1637. If the owner of a self-coloured tulip found that it had 'broken' and was unlike any other known tulip, he could sell it for a huge sum of money so, not surprisingly, anyone in Holland who had a spare square yard grew tulips, hoping for a fortune. The crash came when the Dutch government ordered a halt to tulip speculation.

However, the foundations of the Dutch bulb industry had been laid by 1600, and since that time the Dutch have done more than any other nation in raising new varieties and hybrids. This is also the case with narcissi and hyacinths, as well as many genera of bulbous and tuberous plants such as crocuses, irises, muscari and leucojums. Today there can be no haphazard pollination on the off-chance of getting a unique flower. Details of exactly what characteristics are wanted in a new bloom are decided upon, and the parent flowers are then selected with the utmost care. Even then, only one seedling in a thousand may produce a new variety worth growing commercially. When you next smell the sweet scent of your hyacinths, think of all the time and thought that has been involved in producing this marvellous flower.

So many people are under the impression that bulbs are spring flowers only and for the rest of the year have little to offer in the garden. How utterly wrong they are. Some of the sweetest perfumes to be found in autumn and winter emanate from tiny crocuses, cyclamen and snowdrops.

The earliest flowering crocus is 'Gold Bunch' or *C. ancyrensis*: usually this will be in bloom in time to greet the New Year. It is generous in flowering, so each corm will provide you with several blooms, yellow outside and tangerine inside. The plant is small and delicate and looks lovely pushing between paving stones, or brightening the rockery in

The hyacinth is probably the most familiar fragrant bulb for indoor growing; its perfume will easily fill a room. This still life, by the early 19th-century French artist Philipe Rousseau, shows pot-grown crocuses and a hyacinth rooting in water.

midwinter. It is not expensive or rare; it has a sweet scent, seeds freely and will sow itself if left undisturbed. But perhaps one of its most useful assets is the rough, netted jacket which surrounds the corm and, in an astonishing way, prevents mice from regarding it as a part of their rightful diet. I hate to think how many other types of crocus are consumed by the mice who live in my garden walls!

C. sieberi and *C. susiana* also have this protective jacket. *C. sieberi* comes from Greece and Crete and appears in profusion in early spring. It is an indispensable crocus, coloured a delicate lilac-blue with scarlet stigmas, which, unfortunately, does not set seed readily. The species *C. chrysanthus* provides 'Blue Giant' and 'Blue Pearl', two of the best blues, and also the lovely 'Lady Killer', with outer petals dark purple, and the inner ones a shiny white.

You can have a succession of delicately scented snowdrops all through the winter. They look beautiful in drifts and, by dividing them as they finish flowering, you can create generous clumps under deciduous trees or anywhere else they can be left undisturbed. They come from the eastern Mediterranean and, surprisingly, did not appear in the west until the 19th century. *Galanthus elwesii*, named after Henry Elwes (renowned for his classic book, written with Augustine Henry, *The Trees of Great Britain and Ireland*), are sure to be the first to flower. You will recognize them by the large green markings at the tip and base of the inner segments. *G. nivalis* is the common snowdrop – if any flower can be common so early in the year – with narrow, strap-shaped leaves and pure white flowers with a touch of green. They will multiply quickly, as will the double form, 'Flore Pleno'; and all have a refreshing spring-like scent.

The rewarding tiny *Iris reticulata* never fails. It has the same netted or reticulated corms as *Crocus sieberi*, hence the name. The plants appreciate a warm corner and, in my garden, corner is the precise word, for I have planted them at the corners of the borders, so that I know exactly where to search for them early each spring, as they push their way through the soil. I often think that were these irises to flower at the height of summer, I might not get such intense pleasure from their wonderful colours as I do at the end of winter. Their strong violet scent is amazing too; I like to get timid garden visitors on to their knees in order to hear what they think of the scent! *Iris histrioides* blooms a

week or two later, with clear gentian-blue flowers and a scent of primroses.

Early spring holds the excitement of the appearance of the first narcissi. Of the Cyclamineus narcissi, 'February Gold' and 'Peeping Tom' are both about 30cm/12in high with clear yellow flowers and a honey-like scent; group these with *Scilla mischtschenkoana tubergeniana*, each of whose soft blue petals has a darker streak. When spring is firmly established, the rich scent of jonquils and the Tazetta narcissi is carried sweetly on the air.

In most gardens it is difficult to find the appropriate place to plant hyacinth bulbs. Perhaps because they have become so firmly identified as house plants, the pale blues and pinks do not look right among the yellows of crocuses and daffodils. So I have reached the firm conclusion that the best thing is to let them bloom indoors, and then to plant them out in the garden as soon as the flowers fade. This year I have put them in the rose beds hoping that when next spring comes they will not look out

Dutch flower pieces of the 17th and 18th centuries, such as this one by Van Dael, did much to increase the popularity of flowers they portrayed, and were as much a celebration of nature's marvels as a display of the artist's skills. In this painting, a Centifolia rose is surrounded by fragrant 'Pheasant's Eye' narcissi.

of place. One thing is certain, their sweet strong scent will be greatly appreciated.

Late spring sees the flowering of the deliciously scented *Narcissus triandrus* 'Silver Chimes', whose petals are pure white and the trumpet a creamy yellow. It grows to 30cm/12in and should be planted at the front of the border.

The summer months are enriched by the lily, the flower that shares with the rose the most praise in literature, and is one of the most frequently painted flowers in the history of art. The monks in the Middle Ages planted the Madonna lily in their herb gardens; it has always grown well in cottage gardens and certainly it has one of the best scents of all.

To get the most from the lilies planted in your garden, there are a few special points to remember. Lily bulbs are composed of scales with no outer covering and must never be allowed to dry out, so never leave them unplanted. If you do not have time to plant them for a day or two, then cover the bulbs with damp peat or moss. In the garden they love a good, rich soil, but must have sharp drainage; a cushion of sand underneath each bulb is wise. They like their roots in the shade and their heads in the sun, and a suitable place for them is under shrubs – they look lovely growing through grey *Senecio* 'Sunshine'.

In late summer the acidantheras and outdoor freesias should be flowering and, frost permitting, should continue to scatter their scent about the garden until the end of autumn. Freesia bulbs will probably not survive any frost, so you must either dig them up and store them for the winter, or else be prepared to buy a few fresh bulbs every spring.

By now we have come almost a full circle of the seasons, for the earliest snowdrop, the autumn-flowering *Galanthus nivalis reginae-olgae*, will be blooming before its leaves appear. I never wish to pick any, since I know that if I do, I will be reducing the opportunity for self-seeded plants to increase my stock.

Finally, every garden should have a few bulbs of the lovely winter-flowering *Crocus laevigatus* in a sheltered sunny spot. It is worth putting a protective cloche over the flowers to prevent the rain splashing mud on to their attractive petals, which are white to lilac, heavily lined and feathered on the outside. In Greece, where these crocuses grow wild, they are found in stony places where the winter rains cannot dirty them.

The plants to grow

Any bulbs and corms that you can plant in the garden, then forget about until they make their appearance, often year after year, are a wonderful bonus, especially if they tend to increase as well. Most of the bulbs mentioned here fall into this category, but corms of *Acidanthera* (a native of the Ethiopian highlands where it revels in a frost-free, well-drained soil with plenty of sunshine to ripen the corms) are vulnerable to winter frosts so should be planted in spring. Then they will flower in late summer, after which the leaves will die down sufficiently for you to dig up the corms when tidying up your borders for winter. The narrow strap-shaped leaves are about 60cm/24in long, and from these grow taller spikes with six to eight star-like flowers. *A. bicolor* is white with a maroon blotch and the variety *A. bicolor murielae* has longer, more graceful and arching sprays. There is a pure white species *A. candida*, and also *A. gunnisii*, which is white tinged with pink.

They are all worth growing as house-plants or for use as cut flowers, for the highly fragrant blooms carry their scent well indoors.

Theophrastus used the name *Akoros* for a plant with an aromatic rhizome. *Acorus calamus*, sweet flag, is probably the plant he was referring to, as all parts of the plant are fragrant: the creeping rhizome, the iris-like leaves and the unimpressive greenish-yellow flowers all carry a comforting spicy aroma. Cardinal Wolsey, who fell foul of Henry VIII, was, apparently, very fond of the leaves as a strewing herb and was, among other things, accused of being too lavish with this costly commodity. When it is crushed it produces a cinnamon scent which I have even noticed when planting it. I bought this from the wonderful nursery of Beth Chatto who specializes in growing a wide selection of unusual plants. She also has a variegated form *A. calamus* 'Variegatus', described thus: 'Handsome sword-like leaves boldly variegated cream and green with rose-pink bases in spring. Deliciously scented.'

Its place in the scented garden is in moist ground for, being a semi-aquatic herbaceous perennial, this is another pool-side plant. It rarely flowers in gardens, but the strong, spiky leaves make a bold contrast to rounded shapes.

Amaryllis belladonna, a large, bulbous plant from South Africa, is sometimes known as the belladonna lily, and could well be called the prima donna lily for unless you live in a warm, moderate climate, you must be sure to give it

the right treatment if you hope to have any success. Plant the bulbs at least 15cm/6in deep in summer on a dry sunny bank or at the foot of a south-facing wall, in well-drained soil and sheltered from wind. They are undoubtedly temperamental about flowering, and hate any disturbance once they have settled into a flowering rhythm. As soon as the flower stems appear through the soil they grow at a great rate and it is a daily excitement to watch their progress. The drooping, funnel-shaped flowers are usually rose-red, but can vary from dark

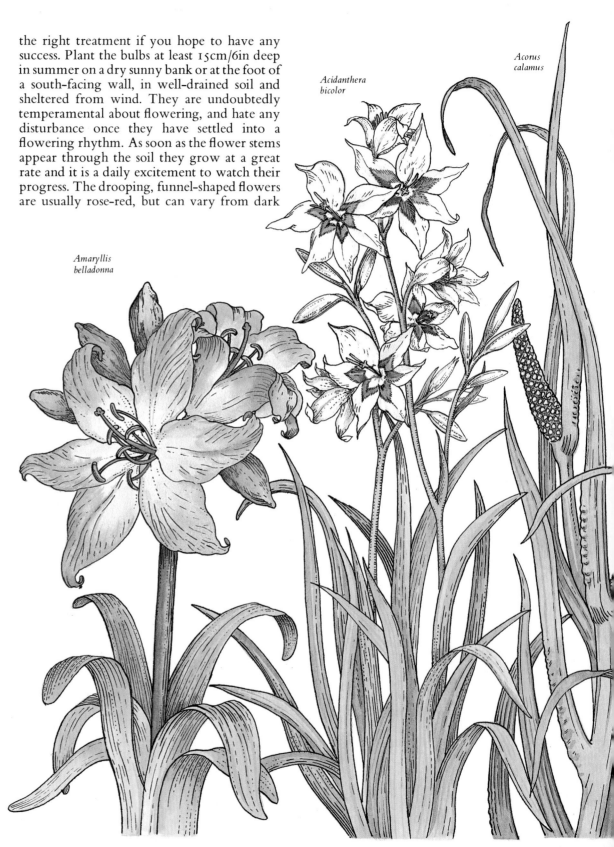

Acorus
calamus

Acidanthera
bicolor

Amaryllis
belladonna

pink to white. The leaves come through in winter or early spring after the flower stems have died down.

The St. Bernard lily, *Anthericum liliago*, is a beautiful hardy member of the lily family, native to the European Alps. The flowers are pure white, tipped with green and richly scented, especially if you can grow them in a group. They will appreciate a mulch or light covering of bracken in winter, particularly if this season is harsh in your area.

Convallaria majalis is a plant that has a permanent place in almost every gardener's heart. Commonly known as lily of the valley, this sweetly scented flower should have a special patch in the garden reserved for it. It loves a shady corner where it can increase undisturbed each year by means of creeping root stocks. Do not neglect the plants in the autumn, when the flowers have all been picked, and they have died back. Give them a generous dressing of well-rotted manure, leaf mould or compost; you will then reap your reward next spring when, with every leaf, a flower stalk will pierce through, bearing 'white flowers like little bells with turned up edges,' as Culpeper so accurately described them.

Pink and red varieties have been grown – if we are to believe all that the old writers tell us. And I am inclined to believe faithfully all Philip Miller wrote in his *Gardener's Dictionary* over 200 years ago, in which he described a double variety 'beautifully variegated with purple and white'. For those who love variegated leaves *C. majalis* 'Variegata' has effective longitudinal golden stripes. They retain their colour best in a sunny position so it is a useful plant to liven up the foliage at the front of the border.

Solomon's seal, *Polygonatum multiflorum* or *P. × hybridum* is an ideal garden partner for lilies of the valley as it likes the same growing conditions. Sweet-scented violets and primroses are good companions too.

For those who like to achieve the exotic, crinums with their giant-sized bulbs are a challenge. Given the right conditions they will be a source of tremendous pleasure, especially for their intense evening fragrance.

They are natives of the warmer parts of the world so naturally require a warm spot. The most hardy sort is the hybrid *Crinum × powellii*, with a fountain of bright green strap-shaped leaves reaching up to 90cm/36in long. Its umbels of reddish flowers are carried on 60cm/24in stems and are honey scented. Give the plant a rich soil in a sheltered south-facing border with good drainage, and plant the large bulbs by midsummer so that they will have time to settle before the winter. The necks of the bulbs should be just above ground level and will profit from protection from hard frosts. *C. moorei*, a parent of *C. × powellii*, and a native of Natal, is nearly hardy in regions with mild winters and will succeed in a well-protected spot. The flowers are buff-pink and have a pungent fragrance.

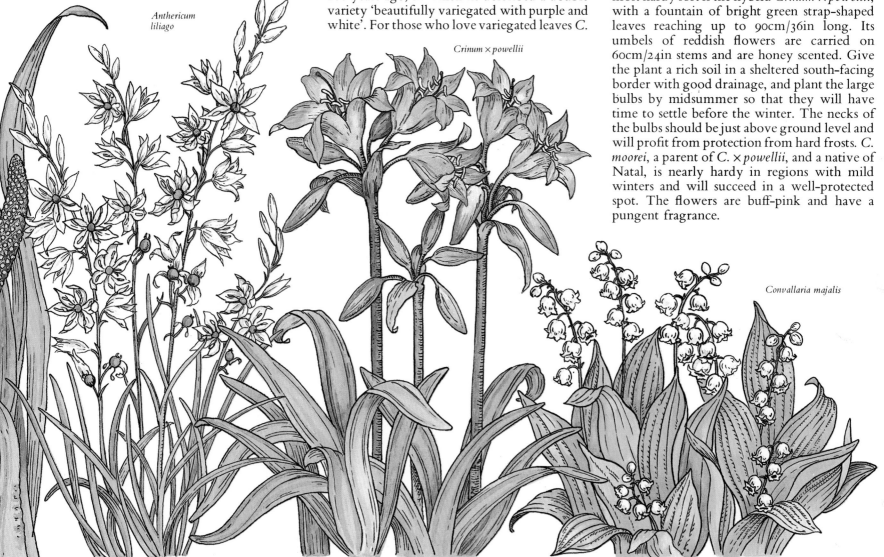

Anthericum liliago

Crinum × powellii

Convallaria majalis

If I were creating a new garden one of the first plantings I would make would be of carefully selected crocuses. You can have these in bloom from late autumn until spring and many of them have a sweet scent. The very first to flower, even before the leaves appear, is *Crocus speciosus*, which always causes me a moment of amazement when I see groups of its great blue goblets growing under deciduous trees in early autumn. This crocus has a faint but lovely scent and once the first seedlings are three years old you will have an annual increase in flowers. But be careful not to cut down the leaves before they fade, even though they do look untidy in early summer.

C. longiflorus blooms next, deliciously scented (probably the most heavily in the group), with delicate, soft lilac flowers and outstanding, brilliant scarlet stigmas. This species is superb in window boxes and makes wonderful potted plants, the better to enjoy the scent.

The saffron crocus *C. sativus*, flowers in autumn and is, according to John Parkinson writing in 1629, 'the true saffron that is used in meates and medicines . . . the flowers are of a murrey or reddish-purple colour, having a shew of blue in them.' The stigmas, he says, are a 'fierie red colour, the true blades of Saffron which are used physically . . . All these blades

being pickt . . . are laid and pressed together into cakes and afterwards dryed very warily.' Today this species does not increase as well as many others.

C. laevigatus fontenayi is without question one of the most desirable, for it flowers in winter – a time when our gardens are at their least interesting. The soft lilac and white flowers have a pronounced and sweet scent. Make sure that you get the true *fontenayi* variety with attractive buff or biscuit colouring on the backs of each outer sepal.

C. tomasinianus is among the easiest to naturalize and in midwinter can make a marvellous fragrant carpet of pale lavender flowers. *C. susianus*, the Cloth of Gold crocus, flowers somewhat later, and is followed by the *C. chrysanthus* cultivars with their glorious colour range of yellows, mauves, blues and whites, some with a tawny streak and others with stripes and feathering, and all fragrant.

Most of us are familiar with the florist's forms of the Persian cyclamen. Flowers of the hardy species growing in the wild are miniature versions of these, but far more delicate and herein lies their charm.

Cyclamen balearicum, *C. creticum*, *C. purpurascens* (syn. *C. europaeum*), and *C. persicum*, have the well-known fragrance of lily of the valley. *C. persicum* is native to the eastern Mediterranean and the flowers, which appear in spring, are usually pale lilac or white with a dark purple blotch on each petal. Unfortunately this

Galtonia candicans

Cyclamen persicum

Galanthus nivalis

Crocus chrysanthus

Crocus laevigatus fontenayi

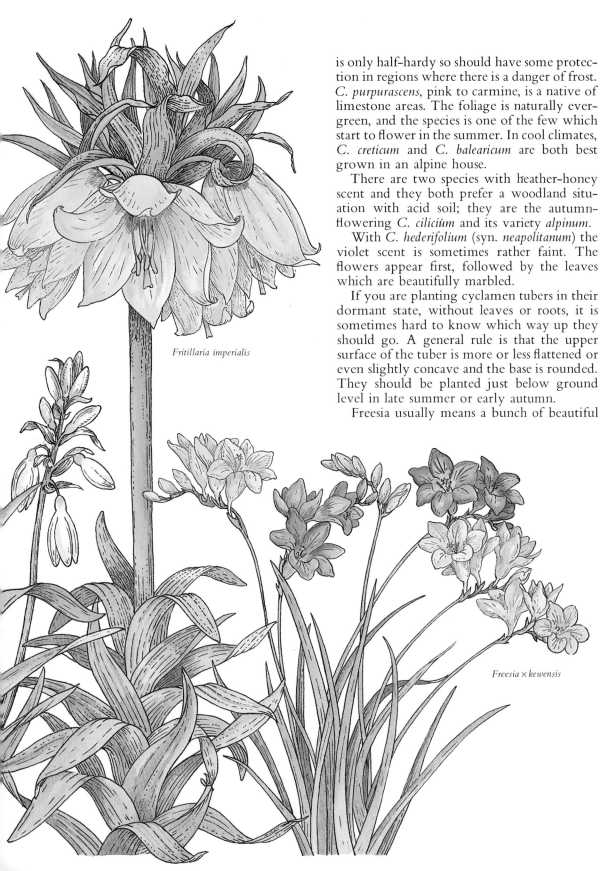

Fritillaria imperialis

Freesia × kewensis

is only half-hardy so should have some protection in regions where there is a danger of frost. *C. purpurascens*, pink to carmine, is a native of limestone areas. The foliage is naturally evergreen, and the species is one of the few which start to flower in the summer. In cool climates, *C. creticum* and *C. balearicum* are both best grown in an alpine house.

There are two species with heather-honey scent and they both prefer a woodland situation with acid soil; they are the autumn-flowering *C. cilicium* and its variety *alpinum*.

With *C. hederifolium* (syn. *neapolitanum*) the violet scent is sometimes rather faint. The flowers appear first, followed by the leaves which are beautifully marbled.

If you are planting cyclamen tubers in their dormant state, without leaves or roots, it is sometimes hard to know which way up they should go. A general rule is that the upper surface of the tuber is more or less flattened or even slightly concave and the base is rounded. They should be planted just below ground level in late summer or early autumn.

Freesia usually means a bunch of beautiful scented florist's flowers presented by a grateful guest. One day, several years ago, on a visit to Syon House in southwest London, I was amazed to see and smell a group of freesias growing in a sheltered bed outdoors in mid-summer. I had always associated them with winter and spring and definitely with green-house cultivation. I then discovered that the Dutch now provide prepared corms for planting outdoors from mid-April to flower in late summer. I am, of course, referring to Britain but in warmer, frost-free countries, the corms I grow in my greenhouse would flower outside.

Challenges in the garden are stimulating, and luckily a failure one year does not dampen the enthusiastic gardener's ardour. Crown imperial, *Fritillaria imperialis*, is a typical example in my life. I have seen and coveted it growing on a bank along a village street, with its majestic flowerheads peering over a low wall – so arresting I could not but stop to look up into the pendant bells to see the drops of nectar on the base of each petal. In a spring garden its blatant, aristocratic character puts it in a different world from other spring flowers such as the gentle wood anemones and primroses. But the moment you handle the bulbs a foxy smell overwhelms you. Nothing daunted, I plant them 7–10cm/3–4in deep, slightly tilted, on a comfortable bed of sand for drainage, then wait hopefully until next spring. One year, maybe, all my bulbs will bloom, but I am still grateful if only a few do so.

I am not a snob about snowdrops. I love them in great sweeps in the winter garden, coming up fresh and smelling delightfully of spring and honey and moss, with their delicate nodding heads waiting for admiration. *Galanthus elwesii*, one of the best known with its inner segments marked heavily with green at the base, has spread wonderfully in my garden. So has *G. nivalis*, the common snowdrop of European origin. I love the double form especially for arranging indoors, surrounded with ivy leaves. These must all be planted in great masses; but I am utterly content with my handful of *G. nivalis reginae-olgae*, which flowers in the autumn before the leaves push through, and each year causes surprise and delight.

The pure white bells of the hyacinth *Galtonia candicans* are very sweetly scented. Left undisturbed this pretty plant will increase steadily, sending up tall (60cm/24in) flower stalks faithfully each year.

Lilium henryi

Lilium auratum

Lilium candidum

The delicate *Gladiolus tristis* was first mentioned in English by Philip Miller who grew it at the Chelsea Physic Garden in 1745. Surprisingly, he does not allude to its scent, but the cream or soft yellow flowers do give off a strong clove scent in the evening. In fact, the presence of three or four flower stems indoors will make a strong impact, while outside they also seem to scatter their scent generously. Other scented gladiolus species, also from South Africa, are *G. alatus*, smelling of sweet brier, and *G. carinatus* and *G. gracilis*, both of which have a violet scent. All these are modest in size compared with the giant gladioli commonly grown today, and should be grown under glass in all but the warmest climates.

Iris germanica, the old common flag which has been cultivated in gardens for hundreds of years, and flowers in spring, has a rich fruity scent. *I. florentina* which provides the scented orris root is even older. The Greeks sprinkled powdered orris root over clean linen to perfume it, and it may be the white iris described by William Turner in the third part of his herbal of 1568. The true strength of the scent, which is pronouncedly that of violets, does not become apparent until the root is dry.

I. pallida dalmatica, said by Gerard to 'smell exceedingly sweet, much like the orenge flower', has pale blue flowers appearing in early summer and is distinguished from *I. germanica* by its pale glaucus leaves. The two cultivars *I. pallida* 'Argentea variegata' and *I. pallida* 'Aurea variegata' both have vanilla-scented

Iris stylosa
(syn. *I. unguicularis*)

Iris reticulata

flowers, and the added attraction of handsome variegated leaves that create a real patch of interest even in winter.

I. graminea, a beardless spring-flowering species, is essential for its 'plum tart' scent. The purplish flowers with blue falls are hidden among the arching leaves. The great gardener E.A. Bowles in *My Garden in Spring* wrote, 'I have a strong conviction that the first real breath of spring that I inhale in the garden comes from *I. unguicularis*.' The scent, he says, is indistinguishable from *Crocus longiflorus*. These popular winter-flowering irises, better known as *I. stylosa*, if given exactly the right conditions, will provide a succession of lavender-lilac flowers all through the winter. The buds hide themselves among the dense grassy leaves. Pick these for indoors and they

Iris florentina

will open in the warmth, giving off such a delicious scent that one is almost glad it is still winter. The ideal site is against a warm sunny wall with poor, but well-drained soil. Always refrain from disturbing them.

My other top favourites are the *I. reticulata* cultivars. They hold themselves so proudly, defying the elements, and are as happy in pots indoors as they are in the garden. They come in colours of sky blue, deep blue, purple and almost white, usually with bold yellow or orange splashes on their falls. Their scent is of sweet violets, very much like the orris root. These little bulbous irises will increase year after year and so will the lovely *I. histrioides*. This amazingly beautiful iris, blue with black and gold markings, is almost stemless.

I am always surprised that leucojums are unknown to so many gardeners. They are akin to snowdrops, but each segment of the perianth is equal, unlike snowdrops which have three large and three smaller petals. The lovely Loddon lily *Leucojum aestivum*, 45cm/18in tall, is scentless but the spring snowflake *L. vernum*, only 15cm/6in tall, with solitary flowers slightly larger than snowdrops, has a deliciously pronounced fragrance. Gerard called them bulbous violets and said, 'they are cherished in gardens for the beautie and rareness of the floures, and sweetnesse of their smell.'

My selection of three lilies for illustration here is specially chosen, one for an acid soil, the next for an alkaline or limy soil and the third because it is so beautiful it should be in every garden. Having made my choice, I was delighted to find all three are among the list of 'Easiest and Easy' lilies in that classic book, *Lilies of the World*, which was written by Judge Woodcock, a respected lily grower, and J. Coutts – a past curator at Kew Gardens.

Lilium auratum, variously known as the lily of Japan and the queen of lilies, bears more flower heads on one stem than any other lily. The name *auratum* means 'ornamented with gold' and, indeed, it is: each waxy-white flower has a golden ray down the centre of each crimson-spotted petal and, for good measure, the six stamens are covered with red pollen. In fact, the warmth of colouring complements the flower's spicy aroma. The plants flower in late summer and are very hardy and easy to grow on an acid soil in a sheltered place.

L. candidum, the Madonna lily of dazzling whiteness, is the oldest of cultivated lilies with a place on each page of garden history. It was

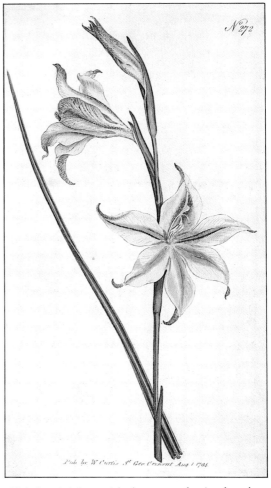

Gladiolus tristis has a rich clove scent that is released only in the evening.

grown in ancient Crete and Egypt and in monastic gardens; it is seen in Renaissance paintings and is beloved in English cottage gardens. Some people find the heavy honey-like fragrance a bit overwhelming, but the plant is breath-taking. It is totally hardy, likes to remain undisturbed for years, with its roots shaded but its head in full sun and does well on limy soil. If you allow the stem and leaves to die down naturally so that no goodness is robbed from the bulb, you will find new leaves appearing immediately; in fact, this lily has only a very brief resting period.

The sweet-smelling, orange-flowered *L. henryi*, discovered in 1888 in the Yangtse region of China, loves a limy soil and is extremely hardy. The black stems appearing through a group of mauve or purple phlox are a lovely sight in the autumn border.

Muscari, the grape hyacinths, are among the most free-flowering spring bulbs, tough yet beautiful, suitable for the rock garden, the front of the border or for naturalizing in grass.

Muscari armeniacum, the most commonly seen species, has 23cm/9in stems with dense clusters of bright cobalt blue flowers, shaped like small bells with a thin but distinct white rim. The bulbs increase year after year, flowering at the same time as primroses and polyanthuses, pushing their way between these or through aubrieta and other low edging and rock plants. The cultivar 'Blue Spike' is the double form and less spreading.

M. botryoides, in its blue as well as its white form, is only 15cm/6in tall and is an ideal rock plant. *Muscarimia moschatum* (syn. *Muscari moschatum*), the most sweetly scented grape hyacinth, now becoming rare in cultivation, turns a dull yellowish-olive as the flowers age. If you can find a few bulbs, plant them near the house or in pots ready to bring indoors. John Gerard grew them in his London garden and described them in his *Herball* of 1597, saying 'they are kept and maintained in gardens for the pleasant smell of their floures, but not for their beautie'. He also knew and grew the 'Ashe-coloured muscari'. I wonder if this is still in cultivation? All these species have a mellow honey fragrance, the perfume of the last two being tinged with musk and easily imparted to passing breezes.

Looking through the specialists' catalogues one becomes dazed by the innumerable cultivars of daffodils and narcissi. They all have an earthy scent of freshness and growth, but many also have a rich, sweet scent, usually more pronounced in the medium- and small-cupped types. The shallow cup is an adaptation that makes it easier for moths and butterflies to pollinate the flowers, the strong perfume not only guiding but attracting the insects.

The Jonquilla narcissi have a distinctive fragrance, sometimes so strong that it is almost overpowering. Usually they are not more than 38cm/15in tall with several flower heads on each stem. In my garden I grow *Narcissus* 'Trevithian' and *N.* 'Baby Moon'. The first is a soft lemon yellow with a shallow cup and very fragrant. The buttercup-yellow *N.* 'Baby Moon' is smaller in every way, and flowers rather late, so it tends to be overlooked in the outburst of spring excitement.

In the Poeticus narcissi group, *N.* 'Actaea' is the largest, with snow-white perianth and a very striking cup, yellow margined with deep red. This and the 'Pheasant's Eye' narcissus *N. poeticus recurvus*, take over the scene in spring. Plant them in groups under trees where they can be left undisturbed and they will give years of pleasure.

The old Tazetta narcissi which grow wild in Spain and France, and right across the Near East to China and Japan, have a wonderful scent and are equally good in the garden or the house. I have had *N.* 'Cheerfulness' and its form, 'Yellow Cheerfulness', growing between herbaceous plants for years. They need no attention and their strong stems carry the double flowers with ease.

Then there are the miniatures that have a strong perfume. *N. canaliculatus*, good for pot cultivation, and the Lent lily *N. pseudonarcissus*, only 15cm/6in high and suitable for naturalizing; both have a cool woodland perfume.

To the discerning nose *Puschkinia libanotica* has a faint but sweet scent. Since it is only 10cm/4in high and of a retiring nature, it is not always possible to appreciate this plant fully. The flowers are almost white with a blue streak. Plant drifts of these between the dark blue *Scilla sibirica* and the very early *S. mischtschenkoana* 'Tubergeniana' from northern Persia. There is no point in planting these bulbs in an unfrequented part of the garden; they must be in a place where you walk every day in the winter, otherwise they will bloom unseen and unappreciated for their scent. They all have a drifting fragrance and if you have the patience to pick and arrange these small blooms for a living room posy you will be richly rewarded.

A question I am often asked is, 'How does one buy bluebells?' and I fully understand the dilemma as for some reason the plant has

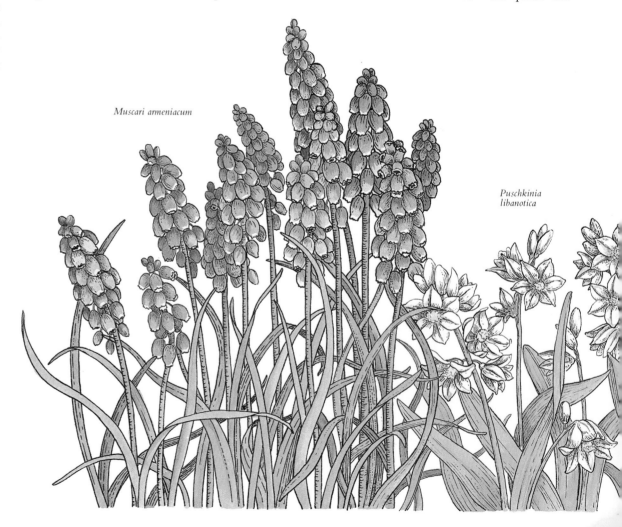

Muscari armeniacum

Puschkinia libanotica

two names. Sometimes it is listed as *Scilla nutans*, otherwise as *Endymion non-scriptus*. It needs a moist and shaded situation.

I do not think of tulips as scented flowers, in fact, a fragrance only emerges in certain species such as *Tulipa celsiana* (syn. *T. persica*) and *T. gesneriana*. Both are old species, and from the latter our garden tulips have been developed.

T. gesneriana was the first tulip to be sent from Turkey to Europe in 1554 by the ambassador Busbecq. It is short stemmed, bowl-shaped and varies in colour, being sometimes red, sometimes yellow. *T. celsiana* was a later introduction from the Atlas mountains of north Africa. The star-shaped flowers are yellow inside and tinged with red outside. But for me, the tulip with the best scent is *Tulipa sylvestris* which has been grown in British gardens since the 16th century. Each 45cm/18in stem has two or three yellow-tinted flowers, with green on the outer sides of the petals. It is of a more graceful habit than the stiff garden cultivars, and its pronounced perfume makes it worthy of a place in every spring garden. It increases by underground stolons and a few bulbs will soon create a fragrant patch.

Tulipa sylvestris

Narcissus 'Actaea'

Narcissus 'Trevithian'

Scilla sibirica

Forcing a winter bouquet

One of my favourite garden jobs is 'doing the tubs'. Each year the containers have more or less the same theme, but the plantings vary. One thing I am certain about is that to make spectacularly successful tubs you must always use far more plants than you would in the equivalent space in the open border.

The summer tubs always have standard *Lippia citriodora* as a centrepiece. My standard lippias are lifted with a good ball of soil in the autumn and put into containers which must be kept dry and free of frost all the winter. They are pruned in late spring, as you would prune prime standard fuchsias, and are brought back into growth, ready for their summer tubs.

One rule I try to keep is to make a note in my garden diary as to where in the garden more bulbs would be welcome, then when the bulbs come out of the tubs they can be put straight into their chosen permanent homes, not left lying about, deteriorating.

We must never take too much for granted in the garden, without making our own contribution. Bulbs need to build up a reserve of food in order to produce a good display of flowers the following year, so do not forget to feed them. There are two ways of doing this; you can either give them a dose of general fertilizer each spring, or else, and this is what I favour, spray the leaves with foliar feed. This must be done when the leaves are still growing strongly and able to take in any goodness that is offered.

If you have no garden, only a patio, porch or roof garden, you still have plenty of scope and can enjoy planting scented bulbs in containers. Always keep your eyes open for containers, so when the moment comes in the autumn, you will have these to hand. They may be made of fibreglass which is light to handle, crockery or cast-cement; they may be urns, stone troughs or wooden boxes. This is where your imagination will help in choosing the bulb to suit the container or vice-versa. Drainage is vital, so it is an advantage if the containers have drainage holes in the bottom.

Having collected the containers, these are the basic rules for planting the bulbs. If the container has drainage holes, put a layer of broken flower pot crocks at the bottom; this will prevent waterlogging. Add about 2.5cm/ 1in of moss or leaf mould, then a mixture of good garden soil and peat in a ratio of 2 to 1 and a handful of bonemeal. This is all you will need. Plant the bulbs at the same depth that you would in the garden. A rough guide is to cover the neck of the bulb with soil equal in depth to the length of the bulb, except for hyacinths and narcissi which are best left with their necks above soil level. I finish off my planting with a covering of moss to make the final result more attractive.

If the container has no drainage holes then you should fill it with bulb fibre, available from florists' shops or garden centres. Be sure to purchase enough for the job; nothing is more annoying than to arrive home and find you need more. If it is left dry, any surplus will keep until the following year.

It is most important that the fibre be evenly moist, so what I like to do is to soak it in a basin or bucket of water for several hours, then squeeze out any surplus. Put a layer of fibre in the container, judging the height so the necks of the bulbs will stand free. Never, under any circumstances, press the bulb down into the fibre. If you do this it will compress the fibre and, as the roots grow, the bulb will be pushed upward by the roots' attempt to penetrate downwards. So put the bulbs lightly on the fibre and then fill in between them, this time being firm with your fingers.

Having planted the bulbs, the choice is either to stand the containers outside, preferably under a north wall, and cover them with straw or peat; or else to leave them in a dark place indoors where the temperature will not rise above 12°C (54°F); the garage is a good place.

Success in forcing bulbs such as hyacinths and narcissi depends on allowing enough time for a good root system to develop; ten weeks is preferable before you bring the bulbs into the light. To have flowers at Christmas time, make sure you order specially prepared bulbs in August, plant them in September, and bring them into the light and a slightly warmer temperature by the first week of December. By then the flower buds should be just standing out of the neck of the bulb. Bring the bowls indoors, stake the plants if necessary and gradually provide a warmer temperature. Do not immediately put them into a warm room.

Hyacinths and narcissi are the ideal flowers for scenting your rooms at Christmas time. The bulb catalogues will always tell you which are the best narcissi available for forcing, and it is as well to take their advice. In the Poeticus group I believe it is hard to beat the old-fashioned *N. poeticus recurvus* 'Pheasant's Eye'.

You can plant narcissus bulbs in just pebbles and water, and the chief difficulty you will experience may well be keeping the blooms upright; you must somehow anchor them before they become too vigorous.

Crocuses, *Iris reticulata*, chionodoxas and scillas are all lovely growing in pots indoors, bringing their fragrance and delicate beauty with them. I like to plant them in shallow containers in ordinary garden soil, leave them outside to grow-on naturally, and then bring them indoors as the flower buds break.

Temperamentally we are all different; so are bulbs. When the bulb catalogues arrive at the end of summer, Christmas seems far away, but we should discipline ourselves to make our bulb orders early, so as not to miss the right time for planting.

Use this chart as a rough guide to planting depths for container-grown bulbs.

cm
in

Cyclamen persicum

Puschkinia

Lilium candidum

Scilla sibirica

Acidanthera bicolor

Galanthus nivalis

Narcissus 'Trevithian'

Iris reticulata

Muscari

Lilium auratum

Fritillaria imperialis

A choice of containers and an abundance of bulbs imaginatively used will provide you with a lovely indoor show of scented flowers in winter.

The scents of spring

Not many people will have had the good fortune to experience an amazing sight such as that seen by Ernest Wilson in the Hupeh province of China in 1908. He was a plant hunter from Gloucestershire and we can easily imagine the intense pleasure he felt when he came upon great drifts of *Lilium regale* scenting the air. Two autumns later he returned and arranged for 7000 bulbs to be dug up and shipped to North America, for by then he was working for the Arnold Arboretum at Jamaica Plain, Massachusetts. It is thought that, from this one consignment of bulbs, all the regal lilies grown in gardens are derived. Although it is not possible for us to naturalize these lilies in our gardens, most of us have, at some time, been amazed at the wondrous sight of a blanket of cyclamen, or a whole carpet of daffodils, growing with abandonment along woodland banks or under trees.

Happily, quite small patches of bulbs and corms can naturalize themselves; anyone who has an odd unplanted corner, a place under boundary hedges or round the boles of large trees should try to establish a few cyclamen. Patience will be needed, but I am always surprised how quickly long-term plans materialize. For the scented garden, perhaps the member of the species which spreads most easily is *Cyclamen hederifolium* (syn. *C. neapolitanum*). The flowers appear in late summer, followed by attractive ivy-like leaves that are mottled or marbled in an amazing variety of patterns. The foliage persists from the end of summer through the winter until spring, serving as excellent ground cover. When the foliage has died down, give the corms a mulching of leaf mould or rich compost to encourage next year's growth.

If your garden soil is limy, then a good choice is the late-flowering *C. purpurascens* (syn. *C. europaeum*) with almost evergreen leaves. One of my favourites is *C. balearicum*, whose spring flowers have a lovely fragrance, but this species needs a relatively frost-free home. I believe that these cyclamen, with their lovely foliage and scented flowers, give as much value throughout the year as any garden plant. Watching the seed heads develop is extremely interesting. They form at the end of the flower stalk which retracts into a tight coil. As the seeds ripen, usually in late summer, the coil slackens and the seed capsule, carried close to the corm, begins to split; this is the moment that you must watch for if you wish to collect the seeds. Sow them in pans of compost at once, while the seeds still have a covering of mucilage. Alternatively, you can allow them to sow themselves and collect the seedlings, keeping them safely in pots for a year until they are large enough to put out in the garden. During that year do not let the soil in the pots dry out.

I have created a lovely strip of cyclamen under a yew hedge in just this way. The soil under the hedge is dry and the situation shady, so nothing else, except weeds, would grow there. Now the area is colonized and I will start elsewhere with the next batch of seedlings. Sound advice when buying cyclamen is to purchase them when they are 'in the green' with their leaves out. Then they will suffer no setback. Dormant corms can sulk for a year or two before deciding to produce any leaves.

There are two gardens I know well where *Crocus tomasinianus* has naturalized freely, and when the flowers open up the bees arrive in their hundreds; it is one of the great joys of sunny days in early spring. The flowers have a deliciously fresh scent and the owners of these gardens tell me that the plants have spread without any help. The grass through which the crocuses grow is cut in the autumn and then left until the crocus leaves have faded.

Other scented bulbs for naturalizing in grass or under deciduous trees and shrubs are chionodoxa, scilla and snowdrops. *Scilla sibirica*, with prussian-blue bells and grey-blue anthers, has increased steadily in my garden over the years, and in spring has a commanding position under the lime trees along the drive. The blue chionodoxas I planted four years ago have also spread; a few of the pink form, *C. luciliae* 'Pink Giant', were also planted, with ground cover of bronze-coloured ajuga.

A rewarding springtime task is dividing the snowdrops. They will seed themselves, but the quickest way to increase your stock is to dig up a few clumps as the flowers fade, separate the bulbs, and give each individual bulb its own home. It may be an afternoon's work, but in two years every bulb will, in turn, have become a small clump!

No bulbs naturalize more effectively than daffodils. To most gardeners they are the heralds of spring. When April comes five happy months of gardening will follow – the

'Fair daffodils, we weep to see
    You haste away so soon . . .'
A patch of naturalized daffodils and narcissi, like the sweetly scented 'Pheasant's Eye' shown here, are the heralds of spring, and a spot in the garden should be set aside for their cultivation, in a place where the bulbs can be left undisturbed, year after year.

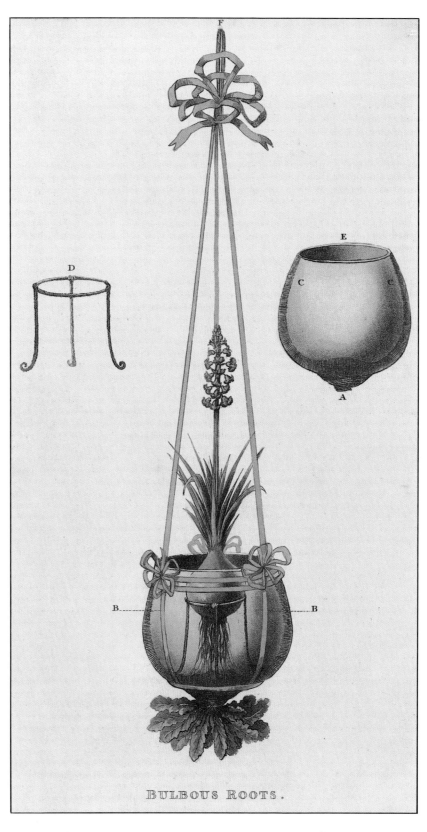

BULBOUS ROOTS.

Rooting hyacinths in water rather than soil is not a new idea, as this early 19th-century engraving demonstrates. Although the apparatus looks fairly complex, a similar arrangement could be made using an earthenware bowl and a wire frame modelled on the one shown in the print.

The plug is ingenious; another plant is grown upside-down through the drainage hole, sealing it with the roots.

sunshine maybe is unreliable, but the flowers are not. You can never have too many daffodils. Plant them anywhere they can remain undisturbed: under deciduous trees or shrubs such as philadelphus, whose emerging leaves will hide the daffodils' dying foliage; in the orchard; in light woodland; around the edge of a swimming pool or patio. I feel strongly that it is a virtue to plant drifts of only one species. Growing in this way, in well-defined groups rather than in mixed varieties, they give so much more pleasure.

Choose the scented varieties carefully. The pink *Narcissus* 'Louise de Coligny' has a white perianth and a pink crown; *N.* 'Cheerfulness' and 'Yellow Cheerfulness' both have double flowers with up to five heads on each 40cm/16in long stem. *N. plenus moschatus* loves growing undisturbed in the grass. The Cyclamineus narcissus has only a faint scent, but it is early flowering – a welcome quality – and is ideal for naturalizing. Pride of place must be given to the Jonquilla narcissi; break the rule here and plant a mixture and then try to make the difficult decision as to which has the best scent.

Herbs

One of the oldest manuscripts to survive is the *Enquiry into Plants* of Theophrastus, the ninth book of which contains the remains of a Greek herbal as well as information about the rhizotomists, as the herb-gathers and herbalists were first called.

Herbals were intended to instruct the reader on the healing properties and practical uses of plants gathered in the wild or cultivated in the garden. For instance, Theophrastus writes that the juice of the herb lysimachia stops bleeding.

One of the first illustrated herbals is by Krateuas, physician and rhizotomist to King Mithridates, who drew all the herbs he included, giving a brief description of their medical uses. His work was passed down to us through other herbals, such as the *Juliana Anicia Codex*, written c. AD 516.

The herbal of Dioscorides, physician to the Roman army in Asia in AD 50, is immensely important to the history of herbal remedies. It was translated into Latin in the 6th century and widely used during the Middle Ages under the title *De Materia Medica*. In 1655 John Goodyear translated it into English; the book was edited and republished as recently as 1933.

Another Greek herbal which has survived through transcription is the so-called *Pseudo-Apuleus* by Apuleus. During the 9th century this was copied into Latin by the monks at Monte Cassino and a beautiful Anglo-Saxon version exists in a codex transcribed c. 1120 at the Abbey of Bury St Edmunds, Suffolk. This is now in the Bodleian Library, Oxford.

This brief outline of herbals should serve to demonstrate the importance of herbs throughout man's history, and to discover their place in the garden we must again turn to the written word.

A great monastery was built at St Gall in Switzerland during the 9th century. All that remains of this establishment are the plans, but these include a layout of the three gardens. One of these was the 'physic' or herb garden, made up of sixteen beds, each for a different herb. The other two are designated a vegetable and a fruit garden, which was also the monks' burial ground.

Near by at the Abbey of Reichenau, the monk Walafrid Strabo was also making a garden. He described the plantings and uses of this garden in the poem *Hortulus*, which was translated into English in 1966 by Ralph Payne and published by the Hunt Botanical Library, Pittsburgh. It serves as an inspiration to myself

and to many other gardeners. The monastery gardens were responsible for preserving many horticultural practices and keeping plants in cultivation that might have disappeared.

The Renaissance brought a revival in the applied sciences, and discoveries in the fields of medicine and botany were closely allied. In 1530, as Leonardo da Vinci was studying anatomy and drawing from 'life' (actually, corpses), Brunfels published the first herbal illustrated with 'living portraits of plants'. The plants were drawn from nature by Hans Weiditz, and the *Herbal* included many plants not represented in the ancient works.

The clergyman and naturalist William Turner wrote the first two books relating to plants native to Britain. As a student he had been inconvenienced by not being able to find the names of certain herbs in Greek, Latin or English, 'such was the ignorance in simples at that tyme'. Therefore, he annotated his books in Greek, Latin, English, Dutch and French.

One of the most jovial gardening authors of the 16th century was Thomas Tusser who wrote *Five Hundred Points of Good Husbandry*. In this extremely useful and entertaining book, Tusser categorizes the many herbs popular at the time: 'Necessary Herbs to Grow in the Garden for Physic', 'Herbs, Branches and Flowers for Windows and Pots', 'Strewing Herbs of All Sorts' are just a few of the headings given to the categories.

But the most renowned author is John Gerard whose *Herball* was published in 1597. Gerard was clearly a lover of plants, but his work does not add much to our knowledge of Tudor garden design and the place of herbs in the scheme of things horticultural. For this we must turn to Gervase Markham, John Parkinson, and Thomas Hyll.

Just as flowers were banished during the 18th century landscape movement, so herbs disappeared from the garden scene, and what had once been the most common part of a garden became an oddity. This sad situation persisted until the mid-19th century when the planting

'A good housewife may, and will, gather store of herbs for the pot, about Lammas, and dry them and pound them and in winter they will do good service.' Thus wrote the 16th-century herbalist John Gerard, and in the painting *Spring* (1595), by Lucas van Valkenbosch, the mistress of the fine garden in the background can be seen tutoring her maid on the values and uses of the botanical wealth so carefully nurtured in Renaissance herb gardens.

of a small herb garden was regarded as a pleasant novelty. But eventually good sense prevailed, and under the patronage of Victoria Sackville West and Gertrude Jekyll, herbs returned to their rightful place in the garden.

Our food is basically of two kinds: that which is mild-tasting, like cereals, meat and certain vegetables, and forms the basis of our diet, and the strongly flavoured which must be mixed or diluted, usually by blending with the mild flavours. The art of seasoning has developed through the centuries, each country creating its distinctive seasonings according to which herbs grow best in that region, resulting in the spicy curries of the east, the sweet fruit flavourings of the Middle East and the milder herb seasonings of European dishes. In the United States, the varied climate nurtured the raw ingredients necessary to flavour the varied cuisines that arrived from the four corners of the world as the nation developed.

When eating we enjoy both taste and smell, and these two senses combined provide our gastronomic pleasures. Food is mainly sweet or sour, and this is what determines how we season it. Many people use little seasoning; just salt and sugar. We have a misconception that in medieval Europe food had to be highly spiced in order to hide any odour or taste of decay. This I do not believe, primarily because spices were very expensive and far beyond the means of ordinary people. But herbs were growing in gardens and so the natural thing for people to do would be to use the leaves to flavour food. I think it is far more likely that medieval cooks used spices to perk up the relatively uninteresting foods which were allowed on the days of abstinence appointed by the Church.

Today we have saucepans and can cook foodstuffs separately, but in earlier days, with only an open fire to cook over, the most natural thing to do would be to throw all the food into one cooking pot. The result would have been a potful of mixed sweet and sour food, and because ginger and cinnamon combine well with both, these spices were widely used. For example, mince meat pies were made of chopped meat and dried fruit seasoned with ginger and cinnamon. On days of abstinence when meat was not allowed, the pies contained only the dried fruit and spices, which is how the pies are made today.

As we know, the use of herbs is not restricted to the kitchen; they are also an invaluable beauty aid. The Egyptians used many spices

and scented resins in their religious rites, for burials and for personal hygiene. They used scented oils in the bath and to massage their bodies. The flower perfumes of ancient Egypt were produced by soaking or macerating quantities of scented petals and leaves in olive oil and from the excavations of early Egyptian tombs we have learned which herbs and flowers were used. Olive and willow leaves, blue lotus petals, cornflowers, wild celery and mandrake were found in the tomb of Tutankhamun; in another grave, pomegranate, flax, clover, vine, currants, peach blossom, henna, walnut, myrtle, woody nightshade, sweet marjoram, bay, laurel and narcissus were discovered – quite a collection.

At the zenith of Rome's importance the women used herbs in their cosmetics, making face packs of egg white, honey and wine mixed into barley meal with the juice of narcissus bulbs. The rose was grown for garlands and decorations and became so essential to everyday life that Roman gardens were full of them. Dried flowers and petals were used to fill cushions and to scent toilet waters and baths to comfort tired limbs. Pliny knew that 'A crown of mint exhilarates the mind,' and Ovid lamen-

ted, 'Alas there are no herbs to cure love.'

In the days when the Roman soldiers made very long marches each was given a ration of salt, and this is where our expression 'A man worth his salt' comes from. The Romans brought herbs and horticultural knowledge to all parts of their empire, and though some plants were neglected during the Dark Ages, many were preserved in monastic gardens, where they were cared for and used by the monks, who no doubt exchanged plants as they travelled between religious houses and foreign countries – much as gardeners do today.

Much that is written about the use of herbs in the past is based on supposition but there are facts which stand out as authentic, enabling us to study the place of herbs in history.

Walafrid Strabo wrote that he grew culinary and medicinal herbs, melons, roses and lilies.

There is an extant plan of the monastery garden at Canterbury, Kent created in 1165, and here the herb garden occupied a space between the Dormitory and the Infirmary. There was a *gardinarius* who cared for the flowers which were used in the church and who also tended the orchard and vineyard. At great functions the priests were crowned with

flowers, and walked in processions wearing garlands that often were made of red roses.

During the reign of King Henry VIII, with the dissolution of the monasteries, the art of gardening in England must have come more and more into the province of the landed gentry and their gardeners. The first books on practical gardening were written at this time, and Thomas Hyll tells us exactly which vegetables and herbs were being grown in the 1560s. They were largely the same as those grown by Strabo in the 9th century and are, in fact, representative of what we grow today. Hyll prefaces his instructions to gardeners by describing the various plants and pot herbs, which included vegetables and sweet smelling herbs, 'as well for use of physick as for pleasure, to carry in the hand and to serve the pot'.

Richard Gardiner of Shrewsbury, who in 1599 wrote the first book entirely devoted to vegetables, clearly thought that too much money was wasted importing vegetables. 'It is not unknown . . . what great abundance of carrots are brought by foreign nations to this land, whereby they have received yearly great sums of money . . . and all by carelessness of the people of this realm of England.'

By the late 17th century salads, or sallets, were of importance. The diarist John Evelyn wrote a *Discourse on Sallets*. He was greatly influenced by the gardeners Le Nôtre and La Quintinie who worked for Louis XIV at Versailles. Louis insisted on having a daily supply of fresh fruit and vegetables at his table and, no doubt, John Evelyn wished for the same for his monarch.

In 1683 John Worlidge recommended that lettuce, purslane, corn salad, spinach (to be eaten raw or boiled), endive, chervil and so on be grown in the herb garden. Of 'sweet herbs' – this new expression came into use during the 17th century when sweet and sour foods became distinct – 'they are very necessary for compounding many excellent Condiments, to add a relish to the best pottage. These are mints, sage, marjoram, thyme, savory, hyssop.' Really our herbs have changed but little.

Herbs are nature's priceless gift to the gardener: the plants are an attractive addition to the flower garden, the fragrant leaves flavour our food and relieve our ailments, and the flowers provide nectar for the bees and petals for pot pourri and other perfumed comforts. A thoughtfully planted herb garden can be as eye-catching as a field of lavender in flower.

The plants to grow

In the herb garden the four most useful species of allium to grow are garlic, chives, tree onions and Welsh onions. All are perennials with hollow stems, characteristic of the genus.

The tree onion, *Allium cepa proliferum*, forms crowns of small bulbils at the tops of tubular stems 60cm/24in tall. These tiny onions are useful for imparting a mild onion flavour to stews and salads. If left on the plant the bulbils eventually drop to the ground and quickly root, so increasing the plant, or you can take offsets from the main bulb in autumn.

A. sativum is garlic, and is grown from the offsets or cloves which comprise the bulb. The cloves should be planted either in autumn or spring, 15cm/6in apart and 2.5cm/1in deep. By summer each clove will have formed offsets. When harvesting the mature bulbs, reserve a few for next season's planting.

A. schoenoprasum is the impressive botanical name for the simple chive. Growing in deep green, spiky clumps, they make a decorative edging for the herb or vegetable garden. Chives grow about 30cm/12in tall and enjoy a site in full sun. To keep a succession of young growth available, gather a few stalks from each plant regularly throughout the summer, cutting near to the ground to encourage new growth. A few plants covered with large jars in winter will enable you to cut chives in early spring.

A. fistulosum, Welsh onions, are very like chives, but are larger and evergreen and for this reason are useful in the winter garden.

Angelica
archangelica

Artemesia
dracunculus

Artemesia abrotanum

Anethum
graveolens
(syn. *Peucedanum
graveolens*)

Althaea officinalis, better known as marsh mallow, grows best – as the name implies – on marshy ground near the sea. The powdered root mixed with sugar and water was used to make the original marshmallow candy.

Although many herbs are shrubs or perennials, when you plant a herb garden it is important to allow space for annuals. Two of the most useful in the kitchen today were, in the past, most often found in the home medicine chest: *Anethum graveolens* (syn. *Peucedanum graveolens*) and *Anthriscus cerefolium*, better known to us as dill and chervil. Both should be sown *in situ* in the spring; afterwards, successive sowings should be made to ensure plenty of fresh leaves as the summer advances. I find that chervil grown in dappled shade will self-sow, but dill, being only half-hardy, is better if freshly sown each year. Dill likes a place out of the wind for, if you thin the seedlings to 23cm/9in apart, they grow easily to 120cm/48in on single strong stems. The soft feathery leaves are useful for flavouring many foods and should always be added at the last minute so that their flavour is not destroyed. Dill seeds are sharply aromatic and can be used to flavour wine vinegar, root vegetables, and to add a piquancy to fruit cake. Dill water, made by steeping seeds in water, has long been a remedy for hiccoughs and stomach-ache; a teaspoon for the baby and a tablespoon for you is what the 17th-century apothecary would have prescribed.

Chervil is sweeter than dill and is a good mixer; in fact, it helps to bring out the flavour of other herbs. The French are very fond of chervil and have given it a place in *fines herbes*. Sow the seeds at random and at short intervals for a good crop of this useful herb. As they appear, cut down the flowers to encourage more leaf growth, but allow a few plants to run to seed for next year's crop.

Once there is *Angelica archangelica* in your garden you will always have it, yet I would not call it an invasive plant, for unwanted seedlings are easy to remove. It is a statuesque perennial, flowering in its second year on strong 2m/6ft stems arising from the centre of a rosette of bright green leaves. The best way to start the plant in your garden is to buy a container-grown seedling. Take care to transplant it without disturbing the tap root; alternatively, gather and scatter the seeds the moment they ripen for they quickly lose their viability.

The most useful artemisias for the herb garden are southernwood and tarragon. *Artemisia abrotanum*, southernwood, has been a popular garden plant since the 16th century. The scent is quite pungent, but refreshing, and lingers on your fingers when the plant is touched. It has feathery grey-green leaves and a tough, woody stem which, left unpruned, will grow to a height of 120cm/48in. In this form the whole plant has an air of untidiness. Pruned hard to within 7–10cm/3–4in of the ground every spring, it will make a sturdy low hedge, admirable for edging rose beds or for making

divisions in the herb garden. It can be clipped again in summer.

Never grow tarragon, *A. dracunculus*, from seed; if you do you will be certain to have the coarse, vigorous Russian variety. French tarragon is an altogether superior plant, but not so strong-growing, so you must nurture it. To get the best crop, plant it in a well-drained soil in full sun. Before the worst of the winter sets in, give it a protective covering of peat or dried bracken. It responds to careful root division, preferably in spring. French tarragon grows to about 60cm/24in and has smooth, pointed, narrow leaves, whereas the leaves of Russian tarragon are divided at the tip. The flavour is sharp, but subtle, and chewing a leaf will make your tongue tingle.

A. camphorata is very like southernwood, but the foliage is greener and narrower and has a distinct camphor fragrance. Its leaves and those of southernwood were used long ago as strewing herbs and to keep moths out of linen cupboards. *A. absinthium*, wormwood, is one of the bitter herbs of the Bible, and was used to flavour the addictive liqueur absinthe.

Anthemis nobilis (syn. *Chamaemelum nobile*), chamomile, is an aromatic perennial with finely cut leaves. The stems lie flat, rooting as they go along, forming a dense mat, so making a delightful scented lawn. The daisy-like flowers, borne on 30cm/12in stems, should be clipped off to keep the plants compact, and can be dried to make chamomile tea. The cultivar 'Plena' has double flowers, but the non-flowering 'Treneague' is best for lawns.

To establish a lawn, plant seedlings in spring 20cm/8in apart in carefully prepared soil. The lawn will take a year to establish and must be watered in dry weather and regularly weeded. For its first winter, cover young plants with dried bracken to protect them from frost damage. The next summer you may walk on it or roll it to encourage the new stems to root.

Asperula odorata (syn. *Galium odoratum*), known for generations as sweet woodruff, has the delightful scent of new-mown hay. It is a low-growing, slow-spreading perennial with minute white flowers set off by leaves that grow in whorls, like tiny ruffs, up the stem. The scent of the dried leaves is most pronounced and they are a useful addition to pot pourri. In the past, bunches of this herb were hung from ceiling beams to cool and perfume the air – an interesting alternative to air-conditioning.

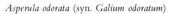

Asperula odorata (syn. Galium odoratum)

Anthemis nobilis

In 1597 John Gerard wrote of the herb borage: 'Those of our time do use the flowers in salads to exhilerate and make the mind glad.' I believe that when you read words like that, or 'maketh merry' it is in reference to the fragrance of this or any other herb dispelling the side effects of unpleasant odours or humours.

Borago officinalis is a hardy annual with large grey-green leaves, that are somewhat coarse and bristly, and bright blue flowers with jet-black anthers. Borage grows up to 50cm/20in tall, and in the garden makes an attractive foil for red bergamot.

Seeds sown in the spring are quick to germinate and should, if possible, be sown where they are to bloom, for they do not appreciate transplanting unless they are quite small. They will self-sow, so look out for seedlings.

The Romans brought borage to Britain and we know that the Pilgrim fathers carried the herb to New England in 1631. I first saw borage in a nearby cottage garden where it grew luxuriantly. I gathered seeds and scattered them in my herb garden and the resultant plants have thrived and seeded ever since.

With me, the plants are at their best in late summer, and the cucumber fragrance and taste of both leaves and flowers make borage a pleasant addition to cool drinks.

Calamintha is an old-fashioned herb also mentioned by Gerard, yet now it is seldom seen in cultivation. If you bring *Calamintha grandiflora* from its wild state into the garden it will increase in stature and provide yet another mint flavour for herbal teas. Grow it in the rock garden or in the front of your herb bed.

'You shall see mine orchard, where in an arbour we will eat a last year's pippin of my own grafting with a dish of caraways.' How enticing it sounds, as Shakespeare puts it in *Henry IV*, but I do wonder exactly how Falstaff ate his dish of caraways. Were the apples stewed with caraway seeds, put in a dish and carried to the arbour? *Carum carvi* or caraway, is a biennial or short-lived perennial grown for its aromatic seeds. It will grow in ordinary conditions, preferring an acid soil, but resents a damp winter bed. Sow the seed in spring for an autumn harvest, and at the end of summer for use the following year. It is a tall plant, up to 90cm/36in in height. The thread-like leaves have a faint fragrance and make evergreen mounds, attractive all through the winter, which are hardy enough not to succumb to

Coriandrum sativum

Carum carvi

Chrysanthemum balsamita (syn. Balsamita major)

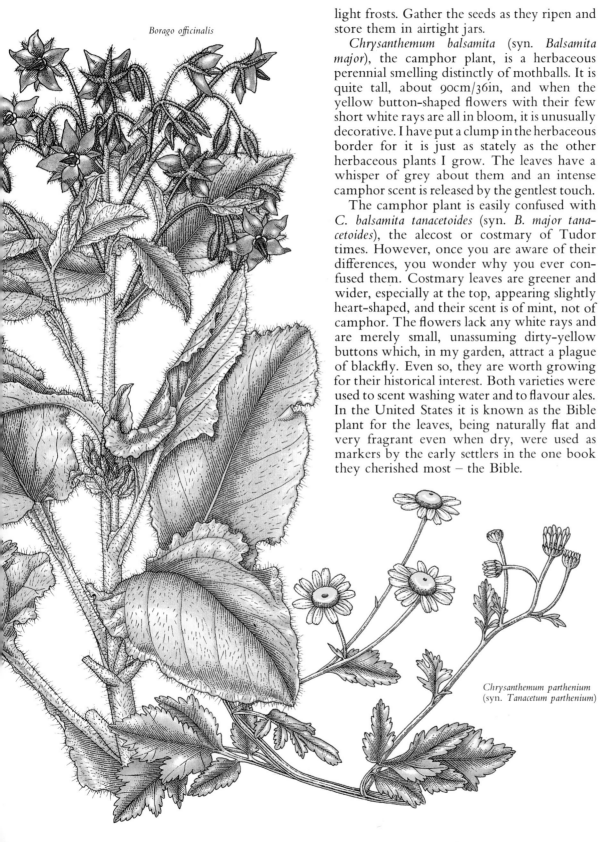

Borago officinalis

Chrysanthemum parthenium
(syn. *Tanacetum parthenium*)

light frosts. Gather the seeds as they ripen and store them in airtight jars.

Chrysanthemum balsamita (syn. *Balsamita major*), the camphor plant, is a herbaceous perennial smelling distinctly of mothballs. It is quite tall, about 90cm/36in, and when the yellow button-shaped flowers with their few short white rays are all in bloom, it is unusually decorative. I have put a clump in the herbaceous border for it is just as stately as the other herbaceous plants I grow. The leaves have a whisper of grey about them and an intense camphor scent is released by the gentlest touch.

The camphor plant is easily confused with *C. balsamita tanacetoides* (syn. *B. major tana-cetoides*), the alecost or costmary of Tudor times. However, once you are aware of their differences, you wonder why you ever confused them. Costmary leaves are greener and wider, especially at the top, appearing slightly heart-shaped, and their scent is of mint, not of camphor. The flowers lack any white rays and are merely small, unassuming dirty-yellow buttons which, in my garden, attract a plague of blackfly. Even so, they are worth growing for their historical interest. Both varieties were used to scent washing water and to flavour ales. In the United States it is known as the Bible plant for the leaves, being naturally flat and very fragrant even when dry, were used as markers by the early settlers in the one book they cherished most – the Bible.

C. parthenium, or *Tanacetum parthenium*, the name under which it now sometimes appears in floras, has an interesting history. Plutarch records that it was used to save the life of a man who fell from the Parthenon, hence its specific name. Commonly called feverfew, Gerard suggests that it should be bound to the wrists 'as a most singular experiment against the ague'. With its strong aromatic scent, it is said to purify the air and keep diseases at bay and so should be planted near the house.

Feverfew is a perennial which seeds itself very freely in the garden. It is about 50cm/20in high, with ferny leaves that last through the winter. The small, daisy-like flowers have yellow centres and grow in panicles. The golden-leaf feverfew makes a striking plant when grown in bold groups under dark evergreens such as holly or yew, or as filler plants in paving. The common name implies that it was once used as a medicine to drive away fevers, and recently the idea has come about that a daily dose of feverfew leaves will cure migraine. How much truth there is to this I cannot vouch. The leaves produce an essential oil with an aroma similar to chamomile and when dried they retain the strong antiseptic smell.

Coriandrum sativum, coriander, is an annual belonging, as do so many of the herbs with pungently scented seeds, to the Umbelliferae family. Although the leaves and flowers are quite attractive, the seeds are of more value. A native of the eastern Mediterranean, coriander seeds are used as one of the main flavourings for highly spiced Indian curries.

For a succession of ripe seeds make the first sowing *in situ* in early spring, with several successive sowings. In Middle Eastern countries the fresh leaves are used for garnish and flavouring as we use parsley.

The common fennel, *Foeniculum vulgare*, is another Umbelliferae. It is a hardy perennial, growing as tall as 1.5m/5ft, with feathery green or bronze leaves and large flat umbels of tiny yellow flowers. It is of great value in the garden as the leaves make such a handsome contrast to solid foliage and its presence lightens the overall effect. If you cut the stems right down during the summer, new young leaves appear at once; in this way it is possible to use fennel in the front of the border, but do remember to put one where it can freely seed itself as fennel plants, especially the cultivar with bronze leaves, are lovely to give to fellow gardeners, and the seeds can be used to flavour gin.

Hyssopus officinalis, another herb in the labiate family, is a native of the Mediterranean countries; it thrives in sunshine and on a well-drained soil and its narrow leaves have a strongly aromatic, almost medicinal, scent. The flowers are usually blue and, less frequently, white or pink. It will grow to 60cm/24in but you can keep it compact by hard pruning in the spring; this pruning is essential if you use it as an edging in the herb garden. There is a dwarf form, *H. officinalis aristata*, or rock hyssop. Plant this in crevices and walls and for a low dividing hedge between other small herbs.

In Psalm 51, King David, lamenting his sins, cries 'Purge me with hyssop and I shall be clean: wash me, and I shall be whiter than snow.' It was for its cleansing qualities that hyssop became renowned in ancient times. The distilled oil from the leaves is antiseptic and branches were used as strewing herbs to ward off vermin and the noxious odours of everyday medieval life.

Hyssop is not especially noteworthy except when it is in full flower, for then it is a paradise for bees and butterflies.

Laurus nobilis, the sweet bay, is an aromatic shrub or small tree, honoured by the ancient Greeks and Romans who regarded it as a symbol of valour. Distinguished poets were crowned with bay leaves, or *Bacca Laureus*, from which comes the terms *baccalauréat* and Bachelor of Arts.

Bay plays an important part in the herb garden and in the kitchen. During the first few years of its life it is slightly tender, but when thoroughly established it is usually only the new, young growth which gets cut back by severe frost. I planted a bay hedge in my Cotswold garden in 1977 and that winter it was cut to the ground by icy winds and frost, but the next spring, lovely new growth with especially robust leaves appeared from ground level. Bay trees may be grown in tubs and trimmed as standards or pyramids to make decorative features to stand either side of a doorway. Used in the herb garden it can be allowed either to branch out as it wishes, or clipped and trained as described above.

Lavender is far too well known to require a detailed description. You can never have too much of it in your garden, especially when it is in flower and the bees are about. However, sometimes there is confusion over the naming of the species. *Lavandula angustifolia (L. spica or L. officinalis)*, Old English lavender, grows wild in the Mediterranean region. When it was first cultivated as a crop in Britain, it was discovered that the climate there produced the best quality oil. Hot sun brings out the essential oil content in most plants, but in the case of lavender, gentle summers similar to those of the British Isles are best.

After four or five years, an Old English lavender plant will become 90cm/36in tall with an equal spread. It makes an ideal hedge on top of a low retaining wall where the soil is sure to be well drained.

Two good smaller cultivars are *L.* 'Hidcote' with dark mauve flowers and strongly aromatic leaves and *L.* 'Dwarf Munstead' whose flowers are paler and very fragrant. Both are suitable for low hedges anywhere in the garden. I have them at the entrance to my vegetable garden and often as I rush out to pick vegetables for a meal the fragrance slows me down, causing me to pause and enjoy the present instead of feeling rushed. The attractive pink *L.* 'Nana Rosea' is fractionally smaller. I am surprised it is not more often grown; everyone who comes to my garden admires it, yet seems unfamiliar with it.

Harvest lavender flowers just before they fully open and dry them in a dark, ventilated cupboard. Later you can use them to make those winter contentments – lavender bags and pot pourri. It is essential for the well-being of the bushes to clip off the flower stems after flowering, but any major pruning must be left until the spring when you can see where new growth is starting. Never cut below this or you may end up with dead stumps.

The French lavender, *L. stoechas*, is less hardy and needs winter protection in cool climates where there is danger of frost. It makes a small bush only 30cm/12in high, from which squarish spikes of mauve flower heads reach out. The spikes have a topknot of pale bracts. It is a plant worth cosseting, and so is the even more tender, lacy-leafed *L. dentata* or fringed lavender.

Levisticum officinale, lovage, is a hardy perennial that grows taller each summer as its roots develop until, after four or five years, a plant could reach 1.5m/5ft. Therefore, it pays to think well ahead and plant it in the right place unless, of course, you want it only for the

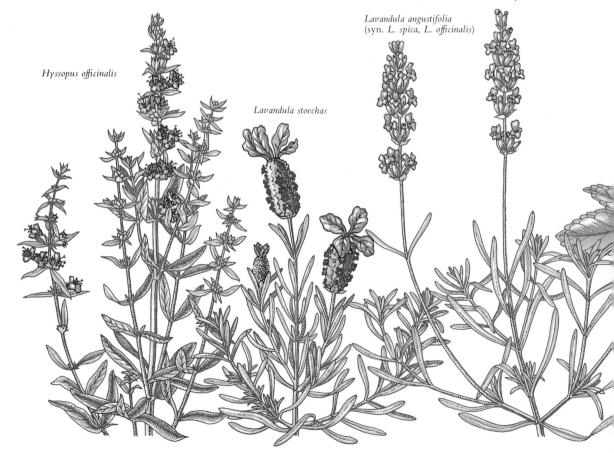

Hyssopus officinalis

Lavandula stoechas

Lavandula angustifolia
(syn. *L. spica, L. officinalis*)

flavour of the leaves and do not want seeds. The leaves have a distinct taste of celery, but never use too many for they are extremely strong.

The very name lemon balm has a relaxing effect on me and evidently the citrus tang of its fragrant leaves does the same for bees. *Melissa officinalis* has been used by generations of bee-keepers to entice swarms into their new homes, and once there to remain quietly – knowing how touchy bees can be, the scent must have a soothing quality.

Balm is a hardy, perennial herb, growing to 90cm/36in, with crinkly leaves and insignificant white flowers on one side of the square stems. Unless you have an aversion to variegated leaves, grow *M. officinalis* 'Aurea'. Clumps of this will brighten a dull corner for it is one of the plants which do not lose their variegation in shade; but it is even better in full sun. Seedlings from this form will invariably be green, so directly the bees have had their feast of nectar, cut the flower stems right down to avoid any seed being set. There is also *M. officinalis* 'Allgold' which, as the name implies, has golden leaves.

Levisticum officinale

Laurus nobilis

Melissa officinalis

There are many species of mint worthy of a place in the herb or scented garden and all have certain characteristics in common. They are aromatic perennial herbs with opposite leaves that are usually toothed, and the flowers appear in whorls up the square stems. Mint spreads by means of underground rhizomes, and should be controlled. The aromatic leaves have a variety of uses.

The most common species *Mentha spicata*, spearmint, has bright green, smooth leaves about 5cm/2in long, sharply pointed and unevenly toothed. To keep a ready supply of fresh leaves for the kitchen it is wise to cut the stems to ground level at least once in the season. Cut a quarter of the mint bed each week in midsummer and new stems will quickly spring up.

Twenty years ago I had a present from an old gardening friend whom I would describe as so identified with her plants that when she was working among them it was hard to discern her. My present was several roots of *M. × villosa alopecuroides* or Bowles apple mint. The broadly oval leaves, rather hairy and wrinkled, sprout from stout square stems and give me a great sense of satisfaction. The plant grows to 110cm/45in, spreads unashamedly and makes

much better mint sauce than its *spicata* relation.

Both of these mints must be kept in check. I have them planted in a narrow bed contained between a wall and a path. Precisely because the plants are so vigorous, do not neglect them; lift them every other year, dividing and replanting their roots as you go. Each autumn, put a few roots in a box in the greenhouse or cold frame and you will have welcome sprigs of fresh mint early in the year.

M. suaveolens (rotundifolia) has a less robust relative with variegated leaves splashed with

pure white and pale cream. The smell is distinctly of fresh apples and I am always grateful for its surprising resilience when it reappears each spring. Try growing species tulips, such as *Tulipa greigii* or *T. sylvestris* among it for a pleasing effect in the border.

Two outrageously invasive mints are *M. × piperita citrata* and *M. × gentilis*, neither of which do I regret having introduced to my garden – not that I have much choice, both are there to stay, being hard to exterminate. I mention this so that, should you choose to give

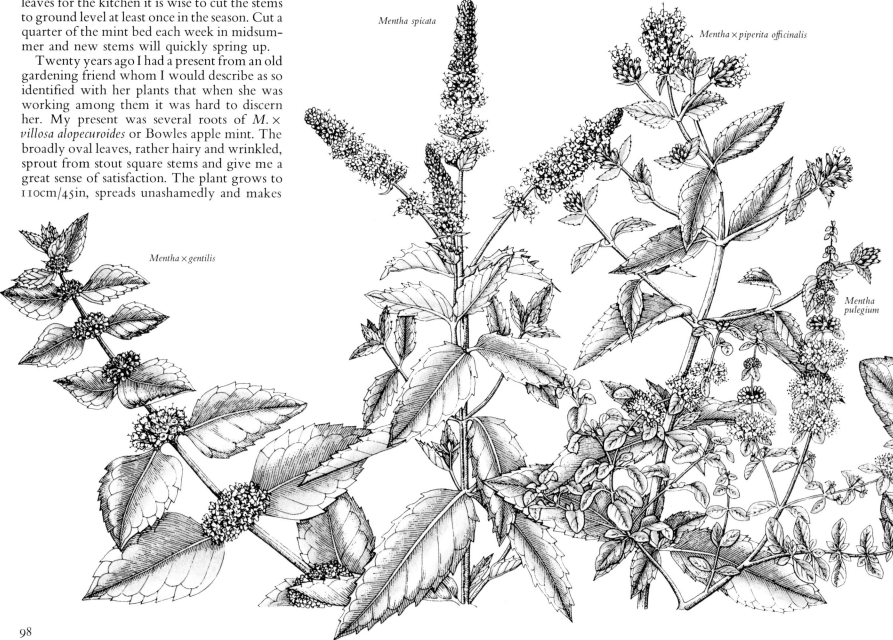

Mentha spicata

Mentha × piperita officinalis

Mentha × gentilis

Mentha pulegium

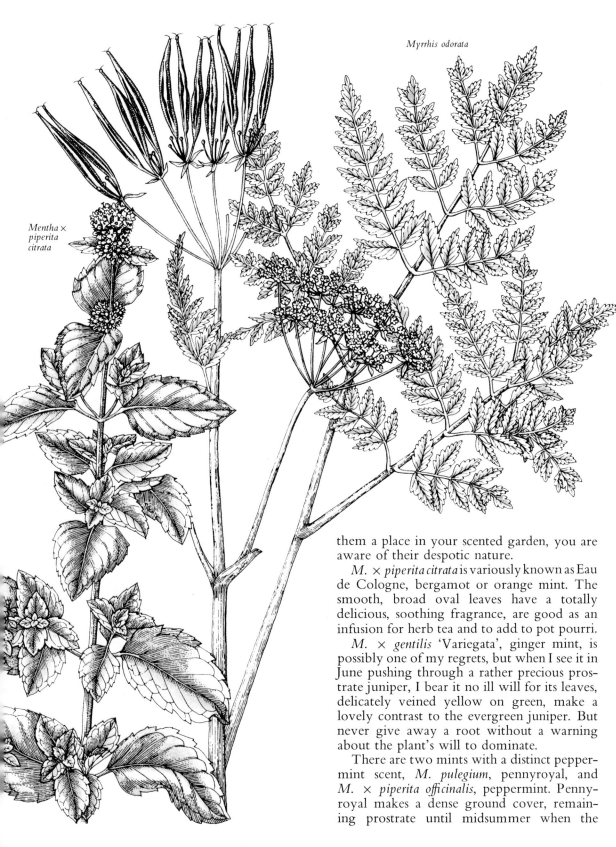

Myrrhis odorata

Mentha × piperita citrata

flower spikes push up and demand your attention. Planted beside a path it will gently encroach, just enough so that you tread on it and release its pungent, peppermint aroma.

The 9th-century monk Walafrid Strabo explains why he grew pennyroyal in his monastic herb garden:

They say that Eastern doctors
Will pay as much for it as we pay here
For a load of Indian pepper . . .
Believe me, my friend, if you cook some
  pennyroyal
And use it as a potion or a poultice, it
  will cure
A heavy stomach . . .
When the sun is blazing down on you in
  the open,
To prevent the heat from harming your
  head, put a sprig
Of pennyroyal behind your ear.

The stem of *M. × piperita officinalis*, white peppermint, has a purple tinge as do the leaves, and the whole plant has a distinct peppermint flavour. Invasive, yes, desirable too, so beware where you plant it; not in the middle of a herb bed, but contained between paving stones or, if you are truly practical, with the roots confined in a bottomless bucket.

Smallest of the mints is *M. requienii*, only 2.5cm/1in tall, a real carpeting plant, with tiny round, pungently peppermint leaves. Put it in cracks in the paving, right at the edge of a bed or use it as a green carpet in a trough of scented plants. But remember that it appreciates moisture and partial shade.

Myrrhis odorata, sweet cicely, is a beautiful member of the Umbelliferae family. The leaves are thrice pinnate, apple green on top and whitish underneath. As they age the whole leaf and stem become cream coloured. It is hardy, perennial and utterly graceful. The aromatic leaves taste like sweet liquorice and so do the shiny black seeds as they ripen. Chop the leaves into a salad and use a few to flavour stewed rhubarb. They also make a lovely addition to a picture made of pressed flowers.

Once established in the garden, preferably in semi-shade, the root will thicken and each year the plant will reappear and grow to 75cm/30in. The seeds take a long time to germinate – sown in a cold frame in autumn, they will sprout the following spring. I find that the easiest way is to allow the seeds to self-sow around the parent and then move the seedlings on when they are still quite young.

them a place in your scented garden, you are aware of their despotic nature.

M. × piperita citrata is variously known as Eau de Cologne, bergamot or orange mint. The smooth, broad oval leaves have a totally delicious, soothing fragrance, are good as an infusion for herb tea and to add to pot pourri.

M. × gentilis 'Variegata', ginger mint, is possibly one of my regrets, but when I see it in June pushing through a rather precious prostrate juniper, I bear it no ill will for its leaves, delicately veined yellow on green, make a lovely contrast to the evergreen juniper. But never give away a root without a warning about the plant's will to dominate.

There are two mints with a distinct peppermint scent, *M. pulegium*, pennyroyal, and *M. × piperita officinalis*, peppermint. Pennyroyal makes a dense ground cover, remaining prostrate until midsummer when the

The two most reliable species of basil to grow in gardens in countries where the climate is moderate to cool are *Ocimum basilicum*, sweet basil and *O. minimum*, bush basil. They are half-hardy annuals so have a relatively short outdoor life. Make an early sowing indoors with gentle heat, for a characteristic of basil seed is that it will not germinate in cold ground. However, in warm soil under glass or outside in the summer, germination takes a few days.

Both sweet and bush basil have bright green shiny leaves and these have a remarkably pungent, rather clove-like aroma. Bush basil leaves are much smaller and slightly less aromatic, though Gerard says, 'The whole plant is of a most pleasing sweete smell'.

Given a good start followed by plenty of sunshine and grown in a well-drained soil, it should give an abundance of leaves – try a handful chopped and sprinkled on sliced fresh tomatoes; basil also mixes well with french beans. Encourage the plants to become bushy by nipping back any long growths to three or four buds. Basil is also a splendid pot herb. I have often seen it flourishing better on a sun-filled kitchen windowsill than in my garden – on warm days the scent will reach you in fleeting spicy breaths. This is especially true of the variety 'Dark Opal'.

Basil is indigenous to India and southwest Asia, and no doubt Alexander the Great was entranced by its taste and took seeds home to Greece, where it was quickly appreciated as a herb of special quality. Bush basil, however, is a native of Chile and did not reach Europe until 1573, the age of seafaring adventurers who criss-crossed the Atlantic.

Basil belongs to the Labiatae family and so does marjoram. *Origanum vulgare*, common or wild marjoram, grows particularly well on chalk and limestone soils. Both the leaves and the spikes of pale purple flowers are fragrant and rather spicy; if you add them to a salad they will provide a sharp, tangy taste.

Every early writer on herbs, from William Turner and Nicolas Culpeper onward, mentions marjoram with approval. This herb had a variety of interesting uses, as John Parkinson explains:'The sweete marjeromes are not only much used to please the outward senses in nosegays, sweet bags and washing waters, but are also of much use in Physicke.'

The golden form of marjoram, *O. vulgare* 'Aureum', should be in every herb garden. Grown in full sun it makes a wonderful sunny splash, and as it is quite low growing, makes a weed-proof ground cover as well.

As with most of these fragrant herbs, if you cut the plant hard back once during the summer, before it becomes straggly, new shoots will appear fresh and strong. It is easy to propagate by division or by cuttings of young growth, 5–7cm/2–3in long.

I use the leaves of parsley and aromatic seeds almost every day in my cooking, but have never tasted parsley seed. Leaves of parsley, *Petroselinum crispum*, are used as a garnish for their two outstanding qualities: their appetizing attractiveness and the fact that they remain fresh looking for so long. Traditionally, parsley seed is difficult and slow to germinate, an idea which has arisen because the seed is hard and must have enough moisture (as well as gentle warmth) before it will shoot. If you moisten the sowing compost well before planting and provide a warm but not hot temperature, the seed will usually germinate within ten days. Outside you must always water the seedbed well before sowing.

Parsley comes in various shapes and sizes. *P.* *sativum* is the Hamburg or turnip-rooted parsley, and its leaves are not as curly as those of *P. crispum*. But I find that the form with the most curly leaves has the best flavour and makes the prettiest plants for edging. I allow a few of my best plants to flower, and the seeds which ripen provide me with plenty for next year's crop.

Rosmarinus officinalis, rosemary, has been loved and cultivated for centuries. In 1370 Queen Philippa, wife of the English monarch Edward III, received a piece of motherly advice from the Countess of Hainault. She wrote to her daughter, 'The leves layde under the heade whanne a man slepes, it doth away evell spirites.' In view of the fact that Edward III provoked the Hundred Years' War, I doubt

Origanum vulgare

Ocimum basilicum

Ocimum minimum

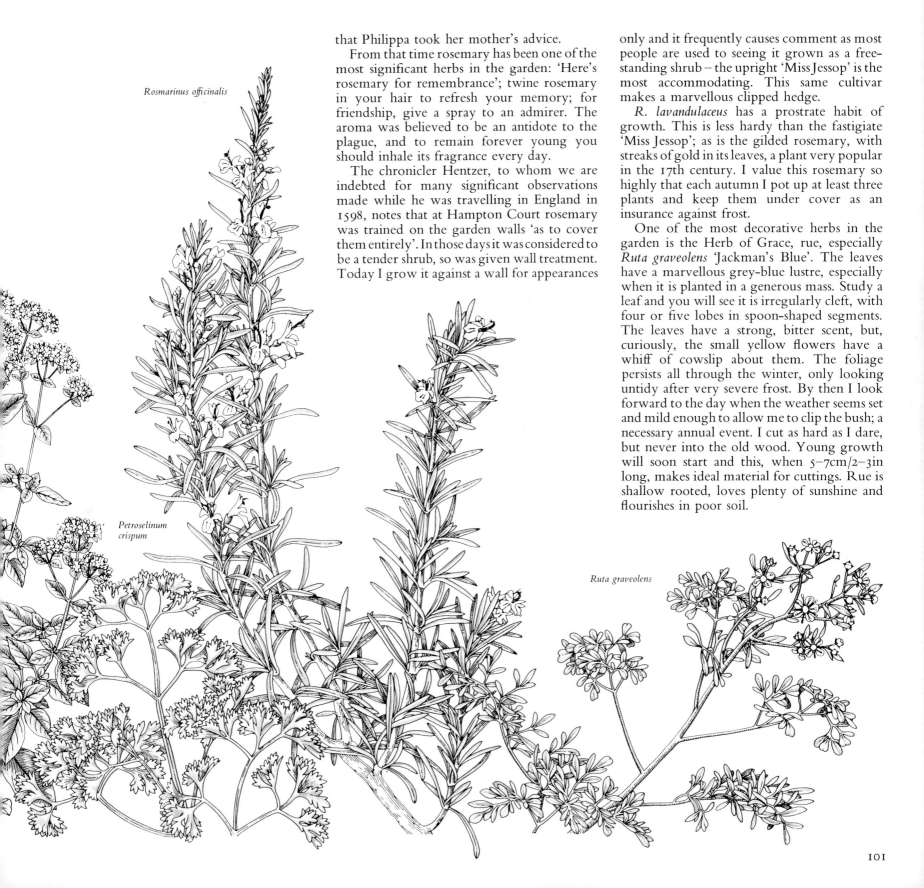

Rosmarinus officinalis

Petroselinum crispum

Ruta graveolens

that Philippa took her mother's advice.

From that time rosemary has been one of the most significant herbs in the garden: 'Here's rosemary for remembrance'; twine rosemary in your hair to refresh your memory; for friendship, give a spray to an admirer. The aroma was believed to be an antidote to the plague, and to remain forever young you should inhale its fragrance every day.

The chronicler Hentzer, to whom we are indebted for many significant observations made while he was travelling in England in 1598, notes that at Hampton Court rosemary was trained on the garden walls 'as to cover them entirely'. In those days it was considered to be a tender shrub, so was given wall treatment. Today I grow it against a wall for appearances only and it frequently causes comment as most people are used to seeing it grown as a free-standing shrub – the upright 'Miss Jessop' is the most accommodating. This same cultivar makes a marvellous clipped hedge.

R. lavandulaceus has a prostrate habit of growth. This is less hardy than the fastigiate 'Miss Jessop'; as is the gilded rosemary, with streaks of gold in its leaves, a plant very popular in the 17th century. I value this rosemary so highly that each autumn I pot up at least three plants and keep them under cover as an insurance against frost.

One of the most decorative herbs in the garden is the Herb of Grace, rue, especially *Ruta graveolens* 'Jackman's Blue'. The leaves have a marvellous grey-blue lustre, especially when it is planted in a generous mass. Study a leaf and you will see it is irregularly cleft, with four or five lobes in spoon-shaped segments. The leaves have a strong, bitter scent, but, curiously, the small yellow flowers have a whiff of cowslip about them. The foliage persists all through the winter, only looking untidy after very severe frost. By then I look forward to the day when the weather seems set and mild enough to allow me to clip the bush; a necessary annual event. I cut as hard as I dare, but never into the old wood. Young growth will soon start and this, when 5–7cm/2–3in long, makes ideal material for cuttings. Rue is shallow rooted, loves plenty of sunshine and flourishes in poor soil.

Salvia officinalis, the culinary sage, is a small shrub with persistent leaves which are invaluable in the kitchen, and I regard it as an indispensable plant in the garden. I like to grow it and the purple-leafed 'Purpurascens', in groups of at least five plants spaced 30cm/12in apart to make a bold effect. There is a narrow-leafed variety which has grey, slightly wavy leaves of a good texture.

S. officinalis 'Tricolor' has attractive leaves of a mixture of purple, cream and green. It is not so vigorous as the other forms, and must be given pride of place against a wall if you want it to succeed. *S. officinalis* 'Icterina' has leaves splashed with gold, but I do not find it as decorative a plant as the others; perhaps I have failed to get the best from it.

It is wise to treat these sages as you do other woody herbs; in fact, begin as you mean to go on and clip them every spring and then, as the summer goes on, give them another more gentle trimming. Walafrid Strabo knew this too, for in his poem telling about his garden he observes:

> Unless the new growth is cut away, it turns
> Savagely on its parent and chokes to death
> The older stems in bitter jealousy.

The name salvia is derived from the Latin *salvus*, safe or well, an allusion to the powerful healing properties attributed to the genus since ancient times. But, as has often happened in the history of herbs, the healing virtues have been forgotten as sage has become used more as a kitchen herb. Always remember though, 'He that would live for aye, Must eat sage in May'.

Spring is also a good time to take soft-wood cuttings; these will root in two to three weeks in a propagator with bottom heat. Another sure way to increase your plants is from hard-wood cuttings put in a frame in winter.

One herb that always exceeds my expectations is *Sanguisorba minor* (syn. *Poterium sanguisorba*), salad burnet. Its unpromising appearance in the seed box changes dramatically after it is planted out in the herb garden, for sunshine brings out the leaves with their unusual formation, and the curious greenish-grey hue takes on a lick of pink. The foliage is delicate and, to me, has a nutty flavour, although some say it tastes of cucumber. Grow it and decide for yourself, enjoying it for its flavour and appearance. The leaves persist in

Satureia montana

Saponaria officinalis

Thymus vulgaris

Sanguisorba minor
(syn. *Poterium sanguisorba*)

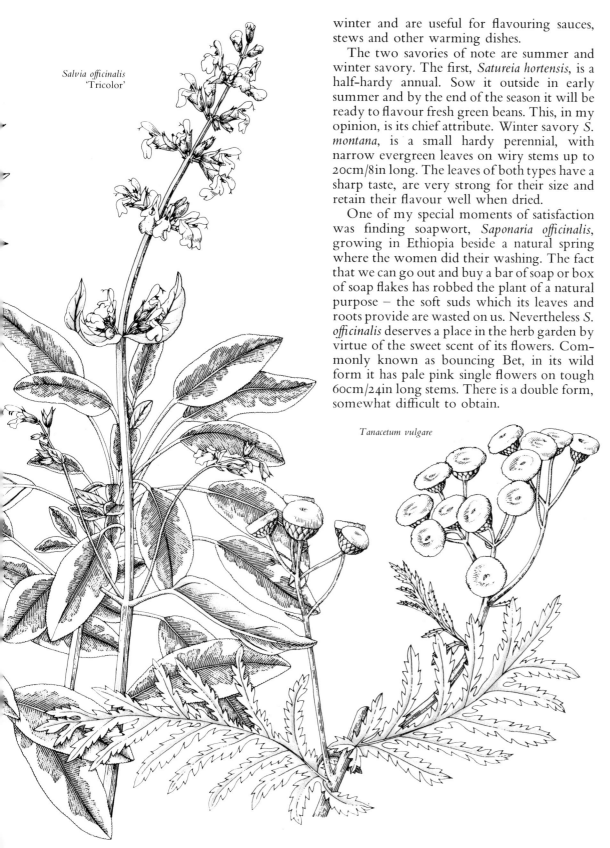

Salvia officinalis
'Tricolor'

Tanacetum vulgare

winter and are useful for flavouring sauces, stews and other warming dishes.

The two savories of note are summer and winter savory. The first, *Satureia hortensis*, is a half-hardy annual. Sow it outside in early summer and by the end of the season it will be ready to flavour fresh green beans. This, in my opinion, is its chief attribute. Winter savory *S. montana*, is a small hardy perennial, with narrow evergreen leaves on wiry stems up to 20cm/8in long. The leaves of both types have a sharp taste, are very strong for their size and retain their flavour well when dried.

One of my special moments of satisfaction was finding soapwort, *Saponaria officinalis*, growing in Ethiopia beside a natural spring where the women did their washing. The fact that we can go out and buy a bar of soap or box of soap flakes has robbed the plant of a natural purpose – the soft suds which its leaves and roots provide are wasted on us. Nevertheless *S. officinalis* deserves a place in the herb garden by virtue of the sweet scent of its flowers. Commonly known as bouncing Bet, in its wild form it has pale pink single flowers on tough 60cm/24in long stems. There is a double form, somewhat difficult to obtain.

It is my belief that we gardeners should take heed of what the ancient writers said; the Greeks associated tansy, *Tanacetum vulgare*, with immortality. Whether it was because of its persistent roots or the 'everlasting' quality of its flowers I do not know, but experience has taught me that once planted in a border it is virtually impossible to eradicate and, if allowed, will spread irrepressibly. It is tempting, however, for its dark green ferny leaves are much divided and very beautiful; when crushed they release a pleasant camphor scent.

Thyme is a dwarf shrub or sub-shrub, sometimes prostrate. The leaves are usually narrow and their strong aromatic scent makes them one of the most useful and often used herbs in the kitchen for flavouring savoury dishes. There are many varieties, all of which can be easily propagated from cuttings taken in spring and summer, or by layering. *Thymus serpyllum* makes a perfect tiny lawn, the scented leaves giving off a strong perfume when they are walked on. The flowers are either pink, crimson, mauve or white and when in full bloom are visited by hundreds of honey-bees. Its creeping habit and lax growth make it ideal for planting in cracks in a garden wall.

You can grow *T. vulgaris*, the common culinary thyme, from seeds. From a single sowing you will get quite a range of flower shades, from pale to deep mauves.

The intensely aromatic grey-leafed thyme which I found growing wild on the hillsides in the south of France is one of my favourite herbs in the garden, for its scent has an incense-like quality. The thin stems are very wiry and tough and the flowers quite pale.

Lemon thyme, *T. × citriodorus*, has rich green leaves and grows to about 30cm/12in and, as its name implies, has a pronounced and clean lemon scent and taste. The form 'Aureus' is distinct for its variegated golden leaves, which are at their best in winter and early spring. 'Silver Queen' is a highly desirable cultivar with lemon-scented leaves splashed with cream and silver; again this is at its best in winter, a time when we are grateful for a bit of colour.

These are my first choice for the herb garden, but a collection of thymes should include *T.* 'Albus Compactus', only 15cm/6in tall; *T. herbabarona* the caraway thyme, a strong carpeter with an equally strong flavour, used in bygone days to season a baron of beef, and finally, *T. serpyllum* 'Minus', the most prostrate growing of all, has tiny pale mauve flowers.

Puzzles and patterns

L'Ambrogiana, shown here in a painting by Van Utens, was the hunting lodge of the Grand Duke Ferdinando I. It was built in 1587 at Montelupo, west of Florence.

The garden design is based on four 'proportions' as advised in *La Maison Rustique*, which was published in 1583 and later translated by Gervase Markham.

The knotte garden serveth for pleasure:
The potte garden for profitte.
Horti serviunt voluptati:
Hortus holitorius utilitati.

This exercise appeared in a Latin grammar written for Eton and Winchester scholars in the year 1519 and contains one of the earliest known references to knot gardens. In 1520 the Duke of Buckingham gave his gardener John Wynde a reward of three shillings and fourpence 'for diligence working and making knotts in the duke's garden.' The duke's brother-in-law, Henry Percy, Earl of Northumberland, also paid a labourer to 'attend hourly for setting of erbis and clipping of knottes, and sweeping the said garden cleaner hourly.' From these references we can surmise that knots were coming into fashion in the early years of Henry VIII's reign. While Buck-

ingham was busy at Thornbury, Cardinal Wolsey, King Henry's minister, was building his palace at Hampton Court, and there making a new garden where, according to his contemporary George Cavendish, he had 'knottes so enknotted it cannot be expressed'. These elaborately knotted beds adjoined his private rooms and from the windows of these apartments he could look down upon the knots to enjoy their pattern fully.

Although knot designs were quite a familiar motif during the Middle Ages, used in mosaic floors, on painted walls and patterned ceilings, by the 15th century the word knot had come to mean a decorative wooden carving placed at the intersection of ceiling beams. The later designs for knot gardens bear a striking similarity to these wooden motifs, which may, in fact, have served as early patterns for garden

plantings. During the 16th century the first practical books on gardening appeared: *The Proffitable Art of Gardening* and *The Gardener's Labyrinth*. Both were written by Thomas Hyll and each contains patterns for knot gardens (though some of his schemes are so intricate, they would be better suited to needlework than spadework!).

Mr. Hyll's readers were members of the newest layer of the social strata – the middle class. These solid merchants had built for themselves some of history's finest manor houses and I like to think that it was the ladies, always keen to keep in step with the latest fashions, who influenced their husbands' instructions to the gardeners. As Hyll proclaims, 'mazes and knotts aptly made do much set forth the garden.' I can just imagine the ladies discussing the new vogue for knot gardens and considering how best to use one in the grounds of their fine houses. To top it all, there were countless exciting flowering plants arriving from the New World. This was the age of discovery, innovation and, most importantly, of peace, which came with the defeat of the Spanish Armada: what climate could be more conducive to that gentlest of pastimes – gardening? 'If delight may provoke men's labor, what greater delight is there than to behold the earth apparelled with plants, as with a robe of embroidered workes, set with orient pearles and garnished with diversitie of rare and costly jewels.' So wrote John Gerard, herbalist and gardener to Lord Burghley, in the preface to his great *Herball* in 1597.

In 1583 *La Maison Rustique* appeared with sixteen different knot patterns. Gervase Markham translated this into English and thus we are indebted to him for giving the clearest instructions on how to make a knot garden. The threads of the knot had to be continuous, without beginning or end. If the threads were interlaced it was a closed knot and could not be walked within. The interlacing threads should be made of different herbs, to emphasize the overs and unders of the pattern. If the threads did not interlace then the knot was open and could be walked in.

Markham said that the most suitable herbs for making the threads were pennyroyal, lavender, hyssop, rosemary, sage, chamomile and thyme. Later writers, after experience of knot gardening, advised the use of box as the most useful herb for the threads as it retains a more even shape and can be kept tidier.

If there was sufficient space in the garden then four knots or 'proportions' should be made and, if possible, these sections should have a border of interlacing threads set with taller and thicker herbs than those used in the centre.

The peace of 17th-century England was marred by civil war and the collapse of the monarchy, and as a consequence ornamental gardening went into decline. But following the Restoration in 1660 two writers, Leonard Meager and Stephen Blake, began publishing designs for knot gardens. This was a hundred years after Thomas Hyll and ideas for small gardens had not radically altered, although the grand gardens were being much influenced by the elaborate parterres being laid out by Le Nôtre for the Sun King, Louis XIV, at Versailles.

Leonard Meager's designs were for open

a Scale of 32:Foote

'Here I have made the true lover's knot, To tie it in marriage was never my lot.' This is the rhyme Stephen Blake put with his pattern for the lover's knot shown here. To emphasize the interlacing pattern of a closed knot, the threads should be planted with herbs of varying colour. In Elizabethan days, low-growing herbs such as dwarf hyssop and box, marjoram and thyme would have been used, but today, taller herbs such as purple sage, dwarf lavender, teucrium and southernwood may be used to form quickly grown threads. But whichever herbs you do select, they must all grow to the same height to avoid a totally unacceptable up-and-down appearance.

knots. He says box is the 'most durable, and cheapest to keep to sette knottes . . . Hyssop is handsom, thrift is well liked . . . some use Gilded Marjoram . . . violets will thicken and be handsom if oft cut.' He also recommends 'lavender-cotton, rosemary if oft cut, lavender and sage.' His remarks are possibly rather ambiguous and details are left to the imagination of the reader. I believe that the taller herbs were for edging and the lower ones for infilling.

Stephen Blake, in 1664, kept to the idea of interlacing closed knots, captioning his designs with rhyming couplets such as:

Here I have made the true lover's knot,
To tie it in marriage was never my lot.
This use of emblems was a familiar mode of expression to Elizabethan and Stuart intelligentsia.

Another interesting knot innovator was Samuel Gilbert who, in his *Florist's Vademecum* of 1682, gives designs for both a square and an oblong garden. He edges his quarters with narrow railed beds to be filled with good

earth for flowers. Gilbert was a leading grower of Florists' flowers, mainly carnations, dianthus, auriculas, primroses and hyacinths – all sweet smelling. One feature of this style was to use flowers of one colour to infill between the rails, then they looked, as John Parkinson observed, 'as divers coloured ribbons'. I often think how pretty a little knot garden could be using an interlacing pattern and infilling between parallel threads of box with spring flowers all of one colour, such as grape hyacinths, scillas, anemones or wallflowers.

When looking for inspiration for a knot garden pattern, take a look at a book about 16th-or 17th-century architecture that has examples of decorated ceilings. Also, heraldic badges were fashionable at the same time as knot gardens – the Duke of Buckingham's badge was a knot and Henry Percy's a manacle – and could have served as patterns for the laying out of knot gardens. The curved moulding of a ceiling motif could be translated into the threads of herbs and the elaborate pendant bosses by standard hollies, rosemary, juniper or

Puzzles and patterns 2

lollipop honeysuckles. (Henry VIII had carved wooden heraldic beasts on poles at the corners of his gardens.)

Having decided the pattern, draw the knot design on paper using a pair of compasses or a set of French curves to help in drawing clean curves. Next draw a square grid over the pattern. As it is this grid which will enable you to transfer the knot to the garden site, it must be in proportion to the dimensions of the plot.

To appreciate the full beauty of a knot garden you should be able to look down on it, so try to place it directly under an upstairs window; perhaps one in a hallway or in a bedroom.

As Gervase Markham says, 'you must keep your level to a haire, if you fail in this you fail in your whole work.' Prepare the ground carefully, removing large stones, breaking up the soil to a fine tilth. Make every effort to level the ground, either stamping it well underfoot or, preferably, rolling it with a lawn roller.

Using small wooden stakes, divide the sides of the plot into the measurements of the grid. Hammer the stakes firmly into the ground at each point. To mark the grid lines tie a length of string between each opposite pair of stakes. Using the knot pattern as a guide, draw the threads on the ground. I have discovered the best and simplest way to do this is to fill a bottle with dry sand and then carefully pour the sand along the design lines. Be sure to use only the driest sand or it will not pour at all easily.

Finally, the threads should be planted with slips or rooted herbs in spring. Markham stresses that the whole plan must be most carefully laid out and executed so that it is pleasing to the eye while the threads establish themselves.

In a closed knot garden the spaces between the interlacing threads should be filled with coloured earths. This is where the influence of heraldic badges is again apparent, for the coloured earths recommended are all heraldic colours. For yellow, clay or sand should be used; for white, coarsest chalk or lime; for black, best and purest soil; for red, broken useless bricks; for blue, chalk and coal dust mixed. Spread these all in their chosen quarters and beat them with a flat beetle and the 'lustre will be beautiful.'

Although the threads of an open knot do not interlace, the pattern is still symmetrical and geometric. The narrow paths created by the thread in turn create small enclosures which should be filled with flowers suitable for nosegays and garlands. Traditionally, these were auriculas, cornflowers, cowslips, poppies and primroses. This type of knot garden is especially captivating in the spring when most of these flowers bloom.

The knot garden, being evergreen, makes a contribution even in winter. The plants that I have found to be most satisfactory for the threads are box, in variety; *Teucrium chamaedrys*, or wall germander as it was called in Elizabethan times, and cotton lavender. These all respond well to clipping and grow evenly. Phillyrea is good for clipping and is admirable for a mound at the centre of the knot and at the corners. I have used an upright form of rosemary as a low hedge to surround the knot garden, but it has to be clipped twice a year to keep it looking well tutored. For height at each corner I have put variegated holly, *Ilex* 'Golden King'. Honeysuckle grown up a stake and then clipped into a lollipop top is effective and, most importantly, sweetly scented. The best plants for this are the early and late Dutch varieties.

The design of the garden, *above*, which was created for Expo '58 at Brussels, Belgium, could be adapted to form the pattern for a knot garden.

The plans, *left* and *right*, from *The English Gardener* by the 17th-century garden designer Leonard Meager, could also be used to make a knot in the average garden. Instead of having lawns and flower borders, grass paths could form the threads and the beds created between them could be filled with scented flowers. The beds could be edged with neatly clipped dwarf box or germander. Depending on the size of the garden, the whole area or just a small part of it could be made into a knot.

The essential difference between a knot garden and a herb garden has always been its purpose – remember 'The knotte garden serveth for pleasure, The potte garden for profitte'. The so-called 'potte garden' provided the vegetables and herbs for the kitchen pot; carrots, onions, leeks, cabbage, parsley, sage and other herbs were all called 'pot herbs' by the early gardening writers.

That kindly Yorkshireman, William Lawson, wrote *The Countrie Huswife's Garden* in 1618. This was the first book for lady gardeners and in it he declared that he had been gardening for forty-eight years before putting pen to paper. His advice to country women was that 'we should have two gardens; a garden for flowers and a kitchen garden . . . because your Garden flowers shall suffer some disgrace, if among them you intermingle Onions, Parsnips, &c.' Yet he told the ladies that they should grow roses and lavender with their vegetables as these 'Yield much profit and comfort to the senses'. A pleasantly relaxing idea: to enjoy the smell of lavender when stooping to pick the peas!

Until quite recently I had the firm conviction that it was better to grow herbs all round the garden. Then when I was feeling hot and bothered trying to produce a good luncheon for Sunday guests, I could slip into the garden and cool off by walking through my borders collecting handfuls of herbs – parsley for garnish, mint for sauce to accompany lamb, sage to chop into a salad with chervil and chives, and borage flowers to float in the cool

drinks. I like to hold the herbs in my hand as I gather them, rather than use a basket, for their refreshing aroma stays on my fingers like a lingering perfume.

Then one day I came to the decision, as must many a busy housewife before, that a herb garden near the kitchen door was essential – some days are just too cold or rainy for restorative jaunts out to gather herbs. So I prepared a bed in a convenient place and began gathering in the herb plants and assigning them new homes.

Just as a knot garden must have a firm geometric pattern, so the herb garden must have a balanced plan and the best site – one which has well-drained soil and receives the maximum sun and warmth to help bring out the plants' best scents. The surest way to discover a plant's requirements is to consider its natural habitat. Many of the strongly aromatic herbs like lavender and rosemary, thyme and

This design for a herb garden is based on my own. At first glance it appears similar to a knot garden, yet in the best traditions of herb garden design, the purpose is first, practical and second, pleasurable, because the areas delineated by the decorative clipped box borders are filled with culinary and medicinal herbs. The taller growing and shrubby herbs, such as sage lovage and rosemary, are planted in the central diamonds and low-growing and creeping herbs, such as chives and pennyroyal, are grown in triangles around the edges of the plot. These spaces are also ideal sites for planting annual herbs like basil and chervil. Herbs enjoy full sun and should be planted in well-drained soil; if possible, the garden should be sited near the kitchen door.

sage are native to Mediterranean countries, where they grow on sunny hillsides. Others such as mint, fennel, lovage and myrrh prefer a richer soil and will tolerate shade.

Having chosen the site, sit down and draw out a plan of the proposed beds. If the garden is to be square or circular you will need a central feature: a sundial or bay tree, or a beautiful pot which you can keep filled with floral treasures. Place the herb beds symmetrically around this. These small beds should not be too broad, 120–150cm/48–60in is quite enough, then you will not tread on the soil when you are working and weeding. This is a good opportunity to make decorative paths of bricks, blocks or pebbles set in cement which will add another texture to the overall effect. Do not miss the chance to include a different level, steps down into a sunken area in the centre or raised beds for herbs that are especially particular about well-drained soil.

Decide if you wish to use an edging or a pattern of box. If so, the plants will have to be prepared. Box cuttings root best if taken in the spring or autumn and may be put directly into their final home. Root several spare cuttings for infilling in case of sudden loss in the border. The scent of box is very strong and pleasant to some people, but heavy and overpowering to others. Queen Anne had all the box pulled up from the garden at Hampton Court, as she found it so unpleasant. Personally I do not notice the scent where box is used as a dwarf edging, but on damp spring days the scent hangs very heavily about the old box bushes

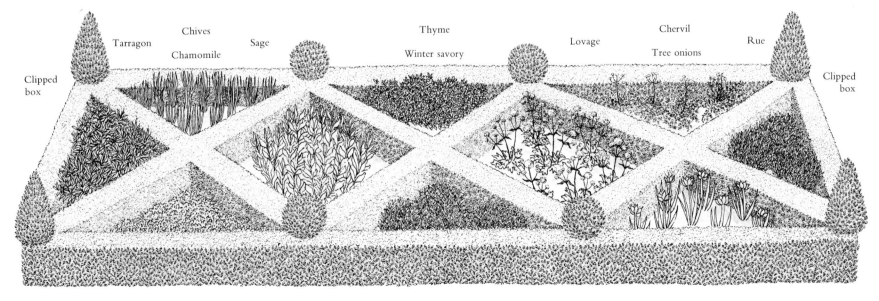

Chives
Tarragon
Chamomile
Sage
Thyme
Winter savory
Lovage
Chervil
Tree onions
Rue
Clipped box
Clipped box

Puzzles and patterns 3

growing round our house. Perhaps in this case it is sheer quantity that adds weight to the perfume. A good substitute for box is evergreen wall germander. As mentioned before, it is a very hardy plant which stands clipping and roots most easily from cuttings.

Make a list of herbs you want to grow. Begin with the evergreens and greys, as these will make the framework of the garden and be most apparent in the winter. These plants include rosemary, bay, lavender, sage, rue, hyssop and southernwood. Next list the very tall perennial herbs which die down in the winter to use as special features, such as fennel, angelica and lovage. Slightly less statuesque are myrrh, balm, borage, tanacetum and saponaria. Finally, add the low-growing and carpeting herbs such as thyme, chives, sweet woodruff, dwarf hyssop, marjoram, basil and the indispensable parsley. Look at your plan and begin filling in the planting area with herbs of the appropriate heights.

In a large garden you can include old-fashioned roses: the almost thornless 'Ispahan', 'Marie Louise', or 'Quatre Saisons'; mingle them with honeysuckles, and different cultivars of lavender, for example, the dark-flowered 'Hidcote' and the pale 'Dwarf Munstead'. These, interspersed with pink-flowered lavender, make a lovely contrast and provide wonderful nectar for the bees. *Lavandula angustifolia*, the Old English lavender, forms a taller and more spreading bush that is very suitable for planting next to garden steps.

If you have only a narrow strip for the herb bed, perhaps along the side of the house, then choose the herbs you love best, those you know you will use most often in your cooking. My choice would be a bay tree with rosemary and sage to form the framework. Between these I would plant a group each of chives, marjoram and winter savory, and allow enough space for sowing annuals: parsley, chervil and basil. I would endeavour to create enough space for one lovage plant and a tall fennel. Two or three thymes could be tucked in as ground cover at the base of the rosemary bushes and bay tree. With a selection similar to this you would have enough herbs for most occasions and some to dry for winter use. Mint and balm must go elsewhere, perhaps in a pot nearby as they are both too invasive for a small herb garden.

My own herb garden is a long narrow strip edged on each side with old black bricks rescued from the blacksmith's shop when he

moved elsewhere. The basis of the design is five diamond shapes running down the centre, outlined in box. Inside these diamonds there are rue, dwarf hyssop, grey sage, meadowsweet, lovage and tarragon. The edging triangles formed by these shapes and the path are filled with chives, chamomile, thymes of all sorts, golden marjoram, winter savory, strawberries with variegated leaves, tree onions, chervil, dill and anything new that comes my way. The angles of the diamonds are all marked by box bushes clipped into balls, with pyramids 45cm/18in tall at each corner.

Form in the herb garden is as important as it is in the flower garden, indeed even more so, for most herbs lack colour even when they are in flower. But their dazzling spectrum of aromas, tastes and textures fully compensates for this shortcoming. Once you have cooked with fresh herbs you will never willingly do without them as food will seem flat and unappetizing.

Dried herbs are a second best. I dry mint, basil and tarragon for titivating our winter food, but they have the unmistakable character of a substitute and remind me that I am waiting for the spring.

All through the centuries herbs have been profoundly appreciated, and one of my favourite writers, John Worlidge, clearly had the right idea. In 1677 he wrote: 'Endeavour to make the principle Entrance into your garden, out of the best Room in your House, your Walks being places of divertisement after a sedentary repast. The Aromatick Odours they yield, pleasant refreshments after a gross diet, and such innocent Exercises the best digestive to weak Stomacks. And let your principle Walk extend itself as far as you can . . . adorned with the choicest Plants for Beauty and Scent, and that there may be a succession of them through the year, not without Flower pots, which grace the best of Gardens.' Scent can still relax our nervous tensions, and what better way to achieve this than with the help of the herb garden?

When planning your herb garden it is a good idea first to draw the scheme on a piece of graph paper and note the plants in position, bearing in mind their height and habit of growth. When deciding which plants to grow together, one idea is to establish a theme, planting together the herbs used for tisanes, herbs for leaf and seed, or any of the other combinations suggested by the plans shown here.

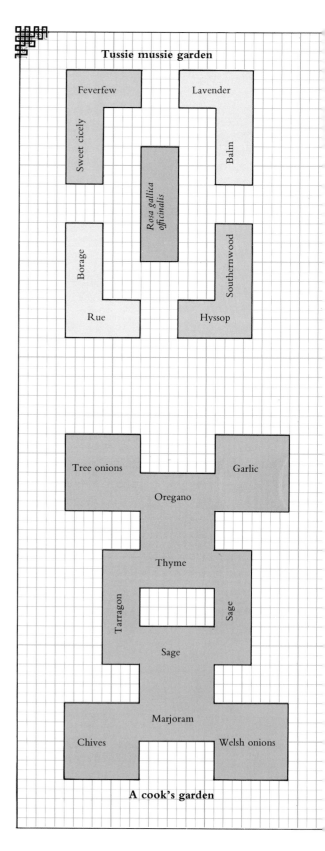

Tussie mussie garden

Feverfew — Lavender

Sweet cicely — *Rosa gallica officinalis* — Balm

Borage — Southernwood

Rue — Hyssop

Tree onions — Garlic

Oregano

Tarragon — Thyme — Sage

Sage

Chives — Marjoram — Welsh onions

A cook's garden

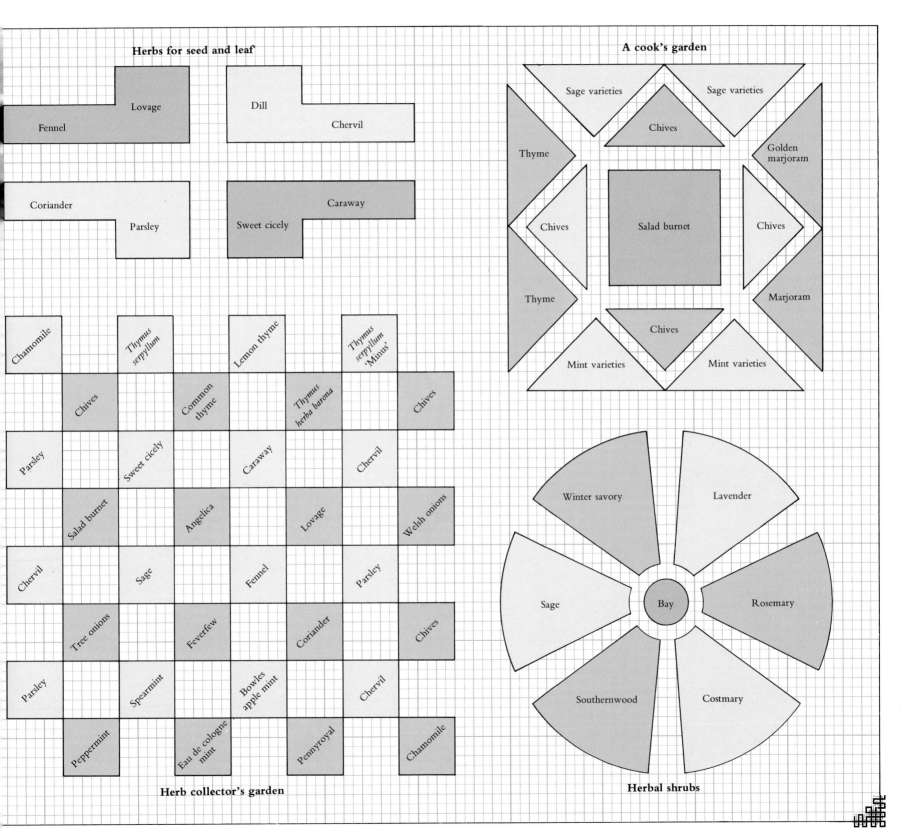

Herbs for seed and leaf

Lovage
Dill
Fennel
Chervil
Coriander
Caraway
Parsley
Sweet cicely

A cook's garden

Sage varieties
Sage varieties
Thyme
Chives
Golden marjoram
Chives
Salad burnet
Chives
Thyme
Marjoram
Chives
Mint varieties
Mint varieties

Chamomile
Thymus serpyllum
Lemon thyme
Thymus serpyllum 'Minus'
Chives
Common thyme
Thymus herba barona
Chives
Parsley
Sweet cicely
Caraway
Chervil
Salad burnet
Angelica
Lovage
Welsh onions
Chervil
Sage
Fennel
Parsley
Tree onions
Feverfew
Coriander
Chives
Parsley
Spearmint
Bowles apple mint
Chervil
Peppermint
Eau de cologne mint
Pennyroyal
Chamomile

Herb collector's garden

Winter savory
Lavender
Sage
Bay
Rosemary
Southernwood
Costmary

Herbal shrubs

109

A movable feast

There are two types of indoor herb growers: those who are obliged to do so throughout the year simply because they have no place outdoors to cultivate herbs, and those who bring a few herb plants indoors in the winter time so as to have fresh leaves for cooking. But the same rules apply for them both!

Most herbs like direct sunlight, so have your pots or hanging basket in or near a south-facing window. In the summer the night temperature should drop to at least 15°C/62°F to simulate an outdoor environment. High humidity is important, so a bathroom or kitchen is an ideal place. Plant the herbs in a good compost and see that drainage is provided and that the plants are regularly watered. In most cases a little and often is better than an occasional drowning.

Buy a peat-based compost mixture from a garden centre, but remember that the fact that it is peat-based means that fertilizer has been added which will, in time, get used up. You must, therefore, add some more fertilizer yourself. Foliar feeds are excellent since plants are able to take up food more quickly through leaves than through roots.

Hanging baskets may be used indoors or out, but in either case make certain that the basket is hanging above head level and not in a place where you will constantly have to dodge it. Choose a place which is accessible for easy watering and tending of the plants. Remember, when you are watering you will have to lift the watering can up to the basket, so allow yourself plenty of elbow room.

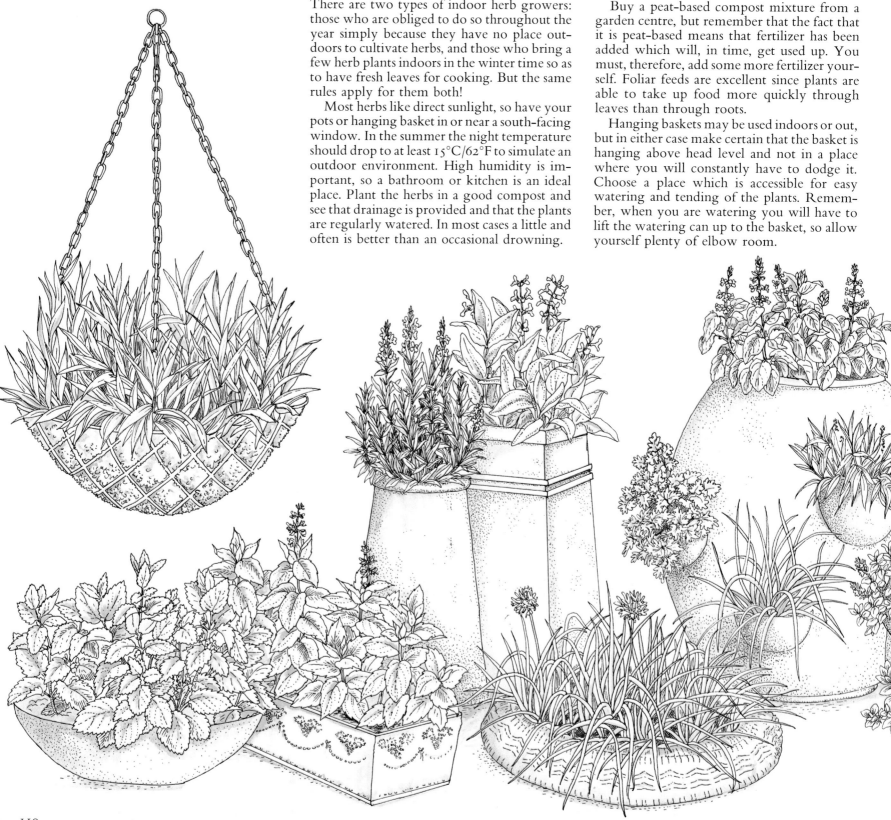

Make sure the basket is securely hung, because by the time it is full of soil and has been watered, its weight will be considerable. Your hanging basket may be made of plastic or metal, whichever is available. First line this with spaghnum or any moss you can find, but put it in so that the 'mossy' side is facing. If moss is not obtainable then a lining of well-perforated polythene is essential to keep the soil from disappearing through the mesh of the basket. Fill the basket with your chosen compost, almost, but not quite, to the top.

How often we hear people say: 'I only have to look at a potted plant and it dies.' If you obey certain golden rules your scented plants and herbs in pots and hanging baskets will flourish.

Most plants grow smaller indoors or in pots than they do in the garden, but none the less, avoid giants like fennel, angelica and lovage and forget about horseradish and marshmallow. Second, buy well-rooted plants that have had a good start. When you buy plants always choose them very carefully, selecting bushy specimens

Fish	Poultry	Pork & Veal	Beef & Lamb	Game	Salads	Vegetables
Bay	Parsley	Caraway	Bay	Bay	Chives	Caraway
Chervil	Rosemary	Marjoram	Marjoram	Fennel	Fennel	Chives
Dill	Tarragon	Rosemary	Mint	Marjoram	Oregano	Fennel
Fennel	Thyme	Sage	Oregano	Sage	Parsley	Lovage
Lovage			Rosemary	Savory		Parsley
Parsley			Savory			
			Thyme			

Thyme Basil Chervil Marjoram Parsley Chives Dill

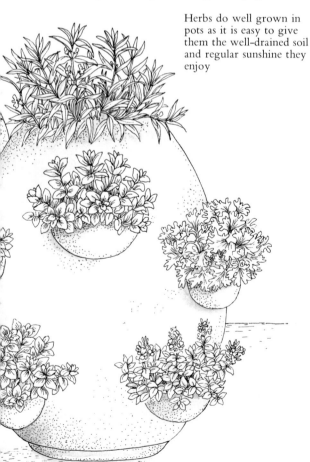

Herbs do well grown in pots as it is easy to give them the well-drained soil and regular sunshine they enjoy

with plenty of new growth springing from the base. Then turn the leaves over and make sure there is no greenfly lurking there. If when you get them home you find any insect pest, isolate the plants for a few days while you deal with it. For immediate action, you can pick up the pot, covering the soil with your fingers, turn it up-side-down and swish the leaves about in soapy water. Then use a spray. Nothing is more annoying than to introduce a pest to a greenhouse or windowsill garden.

When planting a hanging basket, begin at the centre, choosing herbs that grow upright: chives, parsley, basil and sage. Around the edge plant prostrate herbs such as thymes, nasturtium, and prostrate rosemary. Marjoram keeps low if you clip it constantly and so does dwarf hyssop.

I would never mix mint with other herbs in a hanging basket, for a well-justified fear that it would take over. However, mint does well indoors, so plant it in a sizeable pot and keep it on the windowsill, cutting the stems often.

If you have a long windowsill facing south you can provide yourself with all the herbs you need for cooking. Grow pots of parsley, chives, hyssop, thyme, rosemary, basil and sage. You can use either clay or plastic pots, (the latter retain moisture longer), but make sure the pots have good drainage by covering the bottom with broken crocks.

If you have a patio where you can stand your pots, there is plenty of scope. Start by collecting attractive and original containers. Do try to use containers with drainage holes, but if you have an attractive one without them, you must put a deep layer of pebbles or crocks, since it is disastrous to let the herb roots sit in water.

Fill the pot with good loam to within 2.5cm/1in of the rim. Put a tall plant, such as rosemary or sage, in the middle and circle it round with prostrate thyme.

Large parsley pots with lipped holes all around the sides are ideal for herbs. You can have great fun filling them, choosing a different herb for each hole. Begin by filling with compost as high as the first set of holes, then plant these up with, possibly, a selection of thymes. Put them in firmly. Continue in the same way, using marjoram, chives, balm, parsley, winter and summer savory, and some french tarragon. The top should be most carefully planted and would look pretty with a scented pelargonium, or an ivy leaf variety, for colour. I have a half-barrel filled with purple sage interplanted with a collection of *Iris reticulata*. The irises come through each spring just at the moment it is time to clip the sage.

You can experiment with many combinations of colourful annuals planted among your herbs and your patio herb garden will give endless pleasure and use.

Herbal receipts and conceits

Picking herbs when they are at their most fragrant, carefully putting them to dry and then blending and storing them away for later use is a most satisfying occupation. But for the occupation to be profitable, it is of the utmost importance that the harvesting be done properly so that the herbs will dry correctly, retaining their flavour and colour. All parts of a herb may be dried: the root, the leaf, the flower and the seed; but there is a special method for the harvesting and preparation of each part.

The roots should be gathered in the autumn when they are fully mature. Dirt should be carefully removed by gently scrubbing the roots under running water, taking care not to bruise them or to scratch the skin, as this may cause rot to set in while they are drying. Place the clean roots on sheets of newspaper spread over wire racks, and put them to dry in a cool, dark cupboard that is absolutely free from moisture. It may take several months for the roots to dry thoroughly.

In the engraving, *left*, *Habit de parfumier* by Nicolas de Larmessin, a man who trades in perfume wears the various soaps, pastilles, and scented waters that he sells. His rather alarming headgear is a smoking incense brazier.

The floral clock, *near right*, from *Le Livre des Parfums* purports to tell the time of day when each of the flowers represented is at its most fragrant. Among the flowers are the rose, water-lily, violet, pink, and heliotrope.

The roots of angelica, lovage and fennel can be treated in this manner and then used for flavouring by grating them into soups and stews. Orris root powder is made from the dried roots of *Iris florentina* and smells of violets; it is an essential ingredient in pot pourri and was once used to scent washing water.

The general principle of harvesting herb leaves is to do it before the plants produce flowers. Gather the leaves early in the day when the morning dew has been evaporated by the sun, but the leaves have not been warmed. Never pick more than you have time to deal with immediately; this applies especially to mint. Do not be tempted to gather great armfuls when you realize that the plants will soon be forming flowers; pick only a few bunches a day.

Harvest lavender flowers when they first open, always cutting a full length of stem; this will keep your bushes tidy. When you are harvesting seeds, wait until they are fully ripe and ready to drop, then cut the stems and turn the seedheads into a paper bag. Peg the bag to the drying line described below, and before long the seeds will have fallen into it and be ready for storing.

Before you start to pick, decide where you will hang the herbs to dry. The place must be warm and completely dry and free from dust, which probably indicates a closet or cupboard. Arrange lengths of string like clothes lines, and gather up some clothes pegs. Tie the herbs with long stems in small bunches and hang them upside-down. Shorter-stemmed herbs, such as basil and thyme, I put into paper bags, with a few holes in the bag to allow air circulation. Use the clothes pegs to attach the bags to the line and leave them for a few days. Touch the leaves gently from time to time, and directly you feel that they are brittle and dry, carefully take down one bunch at a time. Put it on a sheet of paper, strip off the leaves and rub them between your palms to break them up. If you want a finer texture, rub the leaves through a kitchen sieve.

Put the herbs into glass jars with airtight lids. Take the time to label the jars; otherwise you will be amazed later at how easy it is to be puzzled by the contents, since one crumbled herb looks very much like another. Store the jars in a dark place: daylight causes the flavour to fade.

Some herbs, such as parsley, chervil, tarragon, thyme and lovage, freeze well. Wash the leaves after gathering, chop them as desired, then put them into plastic bags or pots and place these in the freezer. An alternative and enjoyable way of storing herbs in the freezer is to use the ice-cube trays from your refrigerator. Put anything from borage flowers to chopped herbs, rose petals or whole raspberries into the trays and then fill them with water. When frozen, put the ice-cubes into plastic

containers and store them in the freezer. Bring out the cubes when the appropriate moment arises: put raspberries mixed with blue borage flowers into summer drinks, and the chopped herbs into a cold consummé.

Fresh herbs growing outside the kitchen door, just waiting to be picked, are a joy. Use them for cooking, for your home-made cosmetics, herbal baths, sleep-inducing pillows or simply for sweet-smelling posies.

There are certain expressions used in cookery books which should be explained. *Fines herbes* means herbs, cut up very finely, which are added to an omelette, stew or fish dish. The traditional combination is chives, parsley, chervil and tarragon, but I like to create a balance, using no more than three ingredients and choosing between chives or spring onions, parsley, chervil, marjoram, thyme or winter savory, and mint or balm.

A *bouquet garni* is, quite simply, a few sprigs of herbs tied into a bunch and then dropped into stew or soup as it simmers on the stove; bay leaf, parsley and thyme are the classic combination. The volatile oils in the herbs which give them their flavour can be boiled

away, so do not add the *bouquet garni* too soon – 10 minutes before serving is quite long enough.

A good idea for a special luncheon party on a summer's day, when you wish to offer your guests that extra something, is herb butter – nothing more than finely chopped herbs blended into softened butter. A *ravigote* is a mixture of chopped herbs such as tarragon, chives or burnet to sprinkle on fresh salad. In the United States individual small bowls of *ravigote* are provided for dinner guests – a custom that other countries should certainly adopt.

Angelica

Cut young angelica stalks into pieces 5cm/2in long. Put them in a bowl and cover with boiling water to which you have added a tablespoon of salt; leave to soak for 24 hours. Then peel the stems and boil them for 20 minutes in a syrup made from 700g/3 cups sugar and 500ml/2 cups water. Remove from the syrup and leave to drain. The next day, boil the pieces again in the same syrup. By now the stems should be quite transparent and still green. Drain again and dry, then roll in fine white sugar and store in an airtight jar.

Basil

'The smell of basil is good for the heart and for the head,' wrote John Gerard. Basil is one of the most desirable culinary herbs as it has a strong and very distinctive taste. Use fresh basil on sliced tomatoes, french and runner (string) beans and in vegetable soups; it lends an exotic flavour to herb butter.

Pesto is the classic Genoese basil sauce that can be used on all types of pasta and, when added at the last minute, gives a distinctive taste to soups and stews. It is based on the recipe given by Elizabeth David in *Italian Food*. She suggests using it on baked potatoes and remarks that an equally good sauce can be made with fresh parsley. Using a pestle and mortar, pound a large bunch of basil leaves with one or two cloves of garlic. Add a pinch of salt and 1oz pine nuts or walnuts. Add 1oz grated Parmesan cheese. Pound this mixture to a smooth paste. Then gradually incorporate 4–5 tablespoons of finest olive oil. Mix well.

Borage

Make a punch of fresh fruit juice, with or without wine. Float borage flowers in the jug at least one hour before serving to allow the cucumber flavour of the flowers to infuse.

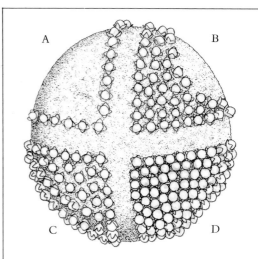

One of the earliest references to a pomander, and the expression from which the word we use today is derived, appears in the medieval poem *Roman de la Rose*, where it is called a *pomme d'embre* or apple of amber. The first pomanders were nuggets of rare scented resins, which were carried in small boxes, such as those shown *below*, suspended from chains. They were, according to Bulleyn's *Bulwark* (1562), 'to be worne against foule stinkyng aire'.

Cardinal Wolsey carried a pomander of an orange stuck with cloves, and a less expensive alternative was an apple stuck with cloves; these were called 'comfort apples'.

To make an orange pomander, select a medium-size, thin-skinned orange.

Beginning at the stalk-end, quarter the orange with a line of cloves forming a channel to take a ribbon if desired **A**. Push them firmly into the skin spacing them one clove-head width apart **B** and **C** because as the orange dries out it shrinks considerably **D**.

When the orange is completely covered in cloves roll it in a mixture of 1 teaspoonful each of orris root powder and cinnamon. Wrap the orange in greaseproof or waxed paper and store in a dark cupboard for several weeks to mature. Tie ribbon around the orange, making a large-looped bow at the top from which to hang it.

Herbal receipts and conceits 2

Before the 17th century, herbalists were recognized as medical authorities and early herbals are a rich source of plant lore and illustration. As botanical science advanced, the traditional medicinal qualities of plants were obscured by the horticultural. But the herbalists' knowledge did not die out, and many of today's synthetic drugs owe their origin to natural remedies obtained from plants.

Chamomile

Dried flowerheads of chamomile make a delicious herb tea that is an effective aid to digestion. Simply steep the flowerheads in boiling water for 5–10 minutes. Sweeten with honey if desired.

Coriander

Coriander seed mixed into a fruit cake batter, pumpkin pie filling or any other dessert flavoured with cinnamon and cloves, adds a fresh, spicy taste to familiar flavours.

Dill

Therewith her Vervain and her Dill,
That hindereth Witches of their Will.
During the Middle Ages this herb was thought to repel the spells of witches, although warlocks used it to work their magic. In colonial America small children were given handfuls of dill seed to chew to keep them quiet during long Sunday sermons. Thus the seeds became known as 'meeting seeds'.

The leaves of dill are best used fresh to add a piquant flavour to fish, meat such as pork, salad dressings with a sour cream base and white sauces.

The seeds are extremely useful and are chiefly used to flavour cucumber pickles and to make dill water, a teaspoonful of which is a traditional cure for flatulence and hiccoughs. It is very easy to make: boil a teaspoon of the seeds in 600ml/$2\frac{1}{2}$ cups water for 30 minutes and then strain the water into a clean bottle.

Fennel

Fennel sauce should be in every cook's repertoire. Mix 2 tablespoons chopped fennel leaves in 500ml/2 cups béchamel sauce, and use the sauce with fish and egg dishes.

Fennel plants set masses of seed that should be used to make a refreshing decoction. Put a handful of seeds in a bowl and pour over 500ml/2 cups boiling water. Bend over the steaming bowl and put a towel over your head. Let the steam flow across your eyes, first closed and then open. You will find this most relaxing as it cleanses and freshens the eyes after a day in a polluted town atmosphere.

Garlic

Of all the herbs, I think garlic has the most incredible properties attributed to it: from the horror story fiction of a necklace of garlic cloves protecting the wearer from werewolves and vampires, to its use during World War I as a wound-dressing. During epidemics of plague in Europe, it was said that those who ate garlic regularly were completely protected.

The purifying properties of garlic are legion; it cleanses and stimulates the blood, is recommended for lowering high blood pressure, aids the digestion by keeping the stomach lining in good condition and an intensive course of garlic is reputed to clear blemished skin. For those who feel it would not be kind to friends or family to pursue these remedies, odourless garlic pills are available from health food stores.

Parsley

Parsley is probably the most important culinary herb. It is rich in vitamins C and A, as well as available iron, and it is the one herb which can be dried in heat without its flavour being destroyed. Lay the leaves in a hot oven (200°C/400°F) for not more than 5 minutes, turning them once. They will become crisp but stay green. Store in airtight jars and use in the same way as fresh parsley: for garnishes, chopped over cooked vegetables and in soup. In fact there is no savoury dish which is not improved by the addition of parsley. It may be used instead of basil to make pesto sauce.

Rosemary

The Romans regarded rosemary as a sacred herb, which would give happiness to the living and peace to the dead. But whatever its more aesthetic qualities may be, it is certainly one of the most useful culinary and cosmetic herbs.

As a herb for cooking it is pungent, especially when used fresh. Dried rosemary may be left on the stem; that way you can crumble as many leaves as you need into the pot.

I always use fresh leaves in preference to dried, and to me a sprig of rosemary laid over the breast of a roasting chicken, or chopped into bread crumbs and used as a stuffing, is infintely preferable to any other herb. Yorkshire pudding (popovers) served with roast beef has a far more interesting flavour if you add a teaspoonful of chopped rosemary to the batter.

Tea made from an infusion of the leaves is reputedly a cure for headache, and it certainly helps relieve congestion when you have a bad cold.

Sage

Sage is a great help to the digestion. After a large meal an infusion of two sage leaves in a cup of boiling water is much better for you than a cup of coffee. Also try chewing a leaf or two before a big meal or before eating food which you normally find hard to digest: pork is often flavoured with sage leaves for this very reason. A delicious herb bread can be made by adding crushed dried sage leaves and finely chopped fried bacon to your favourite bread recipe. Add 2 teaspoons of sage per pound of flour when sifting it; then add 200g/1 cup of chopped bacon when kneading the dough.

Summer savory

This is another of my favourite herbs, with its delicate aroma and taste. Use the leaves fresh or dried in salads, soups and stews or with fish and chicken, but it is at its best with french beans and new peas. An infusion of the leaves is good for digestion and the herb is a friend to weight-watchers: Gerard says, 'It maketh thin'. I have no proof of this, but he also recommends it for use with peas and beans and 'other windie pulses', so there we can agree.

Lavender is a great favourite for its distinctive fragrance, and is widely used to make sachets or sweet bags for scenting linen. While mixtures of lavender flowers and herbs enclosed in fine cotton and lace-trimmed pouches are extremely pretty, the following method for making lavender sticks is a quick way to achieve the same sweet-smelling results.

Gather the lavender just before the flowers open, cutting it with long stalks. Make bunches of 12 to 18 stalks and tie each bunch securely under the flowerheads as shown in **A**. Do not make the knot too tight as you might break the stalks.

Carefully bend the stalks back over the flowerheads as shown in **B**. Space the stalks evenly around the flowers.

Finally, tie the stalks together just by the flowerheads as shown in **C**, using a pretty ribbon.

Put the completed stick to dry in a moisture-free, dark cupboard for several days.

There are so many ways in which you can use your garden herbs other than in cooking that I often wonder how people without a herb garden can possibly manage.

The two most effective herbs for keeping flies away from food in the kitchen are rue and southernwood hung in small bunches by the kitchen doors and windows. Lay sprigs of artemisia in the linen cupboard and you will never be troubled by moths.

If you are stung by insects rub parsley leaves on your skin; the pain of a bee sting can be alleviated by onion juice, or the juice of crushed savory leaves.

Herbs for the bath

There is no need to buy expensive bath oils as many of the best scented oils may be found in the herb garden. The quickest way to scent your bath is to pick a large spray of rosemary and hold it under the hot water as the bath fills, but it is more effective to make a decoction of rosemary leaves and add this to the bath water.

In high summer, when the roses are in full bloom, go into the garden in the early morning and gather a bowlful of rose petals to float in your bath – the heat of the water will bring out the essential oil in the petals and it will float on the surface of the water.

Make yourself a muslin or cotton bag about 15cm × 10cm/6in × 4in with a drawstring opening. Fill it with your favourite blend of herbs, either fresh or dried. Depending on your mood you can use lemon verbena, rosemary, lavender or rose petals for fragrance; balm, chamomile, elder flowers or lime, hyssop or meadowsweet to help you relax; pennyroyal, marigold, borage, sage or tansy to enliven you; comfrey and mint mixed to soothe tired limbs.

If you have time you can make a decoction of the herbs by boiling them for 15 minutes; then use just a small quantity of this mixture to scent your bath.

Elderflower face cream

Warm a clear oil, such as almond oil, with lanolin in the proportion of 4 to 1. Put freshly picked elderflowers into this and keep warm, for 30 minutes. Strain into small jars.

Cosmetic herbs

This is the moment to explain the difference between an infusion, a decoction, a maceration, a distillation, an extraction and an *enfleurage*.

An *infusion*, or *tisane*, is made from herb leaves and flowers by pouring boiling water over them in a china teapot, then leaving the mixture to infuse for at least 5 minutes. The timing is critical since if the herbs steep for too long, the taste could be bitter and unpalatable. The actual quantities you must learn by experience. Drink the liquid or use it as an astringent lotion on your skin, according to the herb you use. A *decoction* differs from an infusion in that you must boil the leaves of the herb, its root or seeds in water for twenty minutes to an hour in order to extract the goodness. Again depending on the herb, you may use this as a health-giving drink or face cleanser.

A *maceration* is made either by soaking herbs in pure alcohol or steeping them in warm fat.

An *enfleurage* is made by laying newly picked scented leaves and flowers on purified fat in a flat tin or tray. Leave them thus for two or three days, then remove the old flowers and add fresh ones. Repeat this process until the fat is thoroughly impregnated with the scent.

Herb shampoo and rinses

Make a strong infusion of rosemary leaves and add this to a good quality baby shampoo in the proportion of 1 to 3. After washing your hair, use any of the left-over infusion in the final rinsing water; this is a very good rinse for greasy hair. For rinsing blond hair, make an infusion of chamomile flowers and marigolds and add the juice of a lemon.

Grey hair can be tinted with a decoction of sage leaves. Put a handful of freshly picked sage leaves into an enamel saucepan and pour over 500ml/2 cups of water. Bring to the boil and then reduce the heat and simmer for 30 minutes. Strain into a clean bottle. Use the lotion in the final rinse after shampooing.

The Bay tree from Gerard's *Herball* (1633).

Herbal Eyewash

Infusions of raspberry or marshmallow leaves can be used as a soothing eyewash or compress. Soak some cotton wool in the mixture and lay it on your closed eyes as you rest.

Sage tooth powder

Dry fresh sage leaves and coarse cooking salt together in a slow oven. When the leaves are brittle, pound the mixture well until it will pass through a sieve. Use with a soft tooth brush instead of toothpaste.

Freckle remover

To get rid of freckles, make an infusion of parsley leaves and use this night and morning on the freckles. The freckles may only fade, but the infusion is astringent and will clean your skin. Horseradish is another good skin bleach: shred 30g/1oz of the root into 2 teaspoons borax and cover with boiling water. When cool, strain the lotion into a bottle; dab it on to the skin with cotton wool.

Thyme Linctus

Thyme used as an infusion was once considered a panacea for many ills.

To make a syrup for relieving coughs, take a handful of fresh or dried leaves and boil them in 500ml/2 cups water until the liquid is reduced by half. Then strain and add a tablespoon of honey. Allow to cool and take a large spoonful every hour, or when the cough becomes aggravating. This mixture also makes a good gargle for soothing a sore throat.

In the kitchen use thyme when cooking poultry and chopped into cream cheese.

Sachets for scenting bed linen

Dry the herbs in the usual way, crumble them and lightly fill small muslin bags to lay between bed sheets in the linen cupboard. The best herbs to help keep out moths are southernwood, rue, tansy and costmary.

To perfume the linen closet, fill more bags with fragrant leaves such as lavender, rosemary, lemon verbena, scented pelargoniums, meadowsweet, and eau-de-cologne mint. The traditional way to scent linen, as practised by Elizabethan housemaids, was to lay damp sheets and pillowcases along a hedge of lavender or rosemary bushes. But a more practical idea, for anyone with time to spare, is to make lavender, rose or rosemary water by infusion or decoction and use this in the final rinsing water when doing the laundry.

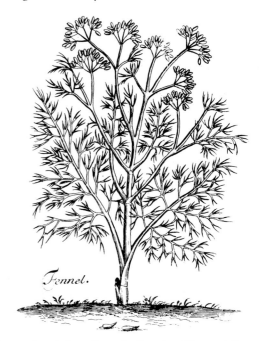

Sweet fennel from Pomet's *Compleat History of Drugs* (1725).

Basic furniture polish

I include this because the smell of ready-made furniture polish is anathema to me, but the genuine, home-made product is a delight to use and scents the room beautifully.

You will need 900g/1lb beeswax and 1.5L/6 cups turpentine. Melt the beeswax in a bowl over a saucepan of warm water. Remove from the heat and add the turpentine which should be at room temperature. Meanwhile boil four handfuls of lavender flowers in 1L/4 cups water for 30 minutes; strain to remove the flowers and add 60g/2oz soap, stirring until the soap melts. Allow both mixtures to cool to blood heat, then slowly add the soap mixture to the beeswax, adding only enough to obtain a creamy consistency. If the scent is not strong enough add a few drops of concentrated oil of lavender.

Herb vinegars

These add a fresh taste to salad dressings and are very simple to make. Start with a collection of screw-top or cork-stoppered bottles. As a bottle of herb vinegar is a welcome present, keep an eye out for attractive bottles that can be nicely labelled to make distinctive gifts.

You will need white and red wine vinegar; the amount depends upon the number of bottles to be filled.

In the summer, when the herbs are at their best, pick leaves of basil, parsley, sage, mint, tarragon, bay and chives – I like to include a few chive flowers. Wash these and dry them perfectly; this is important, for if the herbs are not properly dried, the vinegar will cloud. You can use the leaves either whole or chopped. Into each bottle put several teaspoonfuls of a single herb. Then fill the bottle with the wine vinegar, seal it tightly and add a label. One of my favourite flavours is made with lemon-scented geranium leaves and very thin slivers of lemon peel; if you twist the peel around the leaf as you put it into the bottle it will spiral around the geranium leaf and look most decorative. Purple basil will give a pleasant pink tinge to white wine vinegar.

Herb sugars

Herb sugars have many variations, but the principle is the same. Simply add any sweetly scented leaves such as rose geranium leaves, peppermint, lemon verbena, bergamot leaves or rose petals to fine white sugar. Put the mixture into a screw-top jar and store it in a cool dark cupboard for at least three weeks, by which time the leaves will have dried and their essential oils will be incorporated into the sugar. Use the sugar for decorating cakes and to sprinkle on to baked egg custards. Mint-flavoured sugar can be used to sweeten cool drinks in the summer.

Lavender from Gerard's *Herball* (1633).

Herb jelly

I would feel I had forgotten something important if the summer went by without my making a few jars of herb jelly. It is so simple to do and you can allow your culinary imagination plenty of scope.

First you must gather the earliest unripe apples as they will contain plenty of pectin. Wash and quarter the apples. Put them, seeds and all, into a pan, just cover them with water, and boil until they are reduced to a pulp. Strain this through a muslin jelly bag.

After 24 hours, measure the liquid and add 450g/2 cups sugar per 500ml/2 cups apple juice. Put this in a pan on the stove, and while it heats gather the herbs: mint, marjoram, lemon verbena, rosemary and tarragon. Keep them separate and chop each very finely. Put the herbs into clean glass jars and, when the apple jelly is at setting point, carefully fill each jar. You must stir the herbs into the jelly several times as it is setting so that they are evenly distributed throughout the jelly.

When it is cool, seal the jars and label them. These jellies make delicious accompaniments to meat and game dishes and are good on bread and butter.

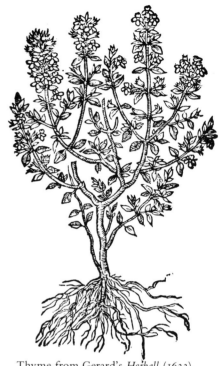

Thyme from Gerard's *Herball* (1633).

Eggs in moonshine

This is adapted from the Kirby Hall *Receipts* of about 1650. Make 500ml/2 cups rose water following the instructions given on page 42. Heat this in a shallow saucepan and add 250g/1 cup sugar. Boil to dissolve the sugar. Take eight eggs and separate the yolks from the whites. Poach the yolks in the rose water syrup until they are firm. Arrange them on a flat dish and pour the sweetened rose water over them. Cool in the refrigerator and serve with bread and butter with chopped lemon balm used as garnish.

Herb butter

For each 250g/1lb of butter prepare 4 tablespoons of chopped herbs; use either a single herb or a mixture of several. Soften the butter with a fork. Gradually add the chopped herbs and 1 teaspoon of lemon juice. Put the butter on a sheet of greaseproof or waxed paper, shape into a cylinder and then put it into the refrigerator to harden. Use as a garnish for grilled/broiled steaks or other meat.

Herb-flavoured oils

Flavoured oils are the perfect partners to fine wine vinegars in home-made salad dressings. Use only the best virgin olive oil or else a mild-flavoured oil such as safflower.

Clean a number of bottles, put a branch of fresh herbs into each and fill it up with oil.

Peppercorns, garlic cloves and whole dried chilies may be added if desired. Seal the bottles and put in a cool dark place to mature for several weeks before using.

A selection of herbal oils and vinegars, a jug of fruit punch flavoured with balm leaves and borage flowers, a neatly prepared bouquet garni and pungently flavoured seeds, such as dill and coriander, illustrate the many flavoursome uses of herbs.

Herb-flavoured punch

Herb-flavoured oil

Tarragon vinegar

Bouquet garni

Dill and coriander seeds

Shrubs, trees and climbers

The fragrance of fruit and flowers was the prime consideration of 17th-century gardens, a fact illustrated by the description in John Milton's poem *Paradise Lost* of the Garden of Eden where the Serpent first found Eve 'veil'd in a cloud of fragrance'. He then goes on to describe the temptation of Adam:

> . . . . . . in her hand
> A bough of fairest fruit, that downy smiled,
> New gathered, and ambrosial smell
>   diffused.

Long before Milton wrote his poem, scented shrubs and trees were being sought and transplanted from their native soils.

One of the first recorded plant-hunting expeditions is depicted on the walls of the temple at Karnak. In 1495 BC, the Egyptian queen Hatshepsut sent an expedition to the land of Punt, probably Somalia or Ethiopia, to find the incense tree. The specimens the expedition returned with were either a species of boswellia or *Commiphora myrrha*, it is not certain which. In the wall painting, slaves are seen carrying thirty-one trees slung between poles, their roots contained in soil in wicker baskets. The trees are shown being loaded on to the ships for transport to Egypt where they were planted in the garden of the temple of Amon at Thebes. The balm, or gum, from these trees is much prized as it holds its scent for a long time, and was one of the gifts given by the Queen of Sheba to King Solomon.

When the Romans conquered Britain, they imported many of their trees and plants, such as cherry, pear, damson, quince, peach and fig and, of course, the grape-vine. Most of these survived, as did some of the vegetables and herbs, but, interestingly, fifteen hundred years later, at the time of the dissolution of the English monasteries by Henry VIII in 1536–9, the emphasis was still more on fruit growing than on vegetables. The use of herbs for medicinal purposes had been kept alive by the expertise of the monks, but the routine cultivation of common vegetables, such as cabbages and carrots, known then as pot herbs, was less popular. Fruit trees were another matter. Once a fruit tree was established it would flourish and bear its crop without too much attention, nevertheless grafting and pruning had become a highly skilled and much practised art.

Shrubs clipped to form low fragrant hedges, climbers trained over arbours and trellis to fill the air with scent, and trees planted to provide perfumed shade are the backbone of the scented garden.

This print from *Le Jardinere du Pays-bas* (1681) by
J. van der Groen, gardener to William, Prince of
Orange, shows fruit trees growing in 'Versailles' tubs.

In 1578 the garden writer Thomas Hyll explains the most successful, simple, and I think fascinating, way to grow a quickset hedge, essential he says, because a garden must be enclosed to keep out wandering animals and marauders. 'Gather seeds found in the red berries of the biggest and highest Briars (which are called the wild Eglantine Briar), ripe seeds of the bramble and the white thorn, the berries of the gooseberry and barberry trees . . . mix and steepe for a time all the berries and seeds in the blending meal of tares, unto the thickness of honey; the same mixture lay diligently into old well or ship ropes . . . in such manner that the seeds couched within the soft hairs may be preserved from the cold unto the beginning of the spring . . . then dig in handsome manner two small furrows, two or three foot asunder, into which lay your ropes with the seeds, covering them workmanly with light earth . . . the seeds thus covered will appear within a month.'

The 'herber', or 'roosting place' as it was called in Tudor times, was an arbour erected 'for comfort and delight. The plants to run up and serve comeliest for the straight herber, ought to be those of a fragrant savour, and that grow or shoot up high . . . the which, the Rosemarie, the jasmine and red rose in many gardens beautifie an upright herber,' explained Thomas Hyll, who was clearly an admirer of scented plants.

The frame of the herber could be made with juniper poles for these 'may well endure for ten years'; willow, however, would only last for three years. Hyll continues to lay much stress on the fragrance of plants, the musk rose, damask rose and privet tree. Growing up the herber, these will not only defend the ladies from the heat of the sun, 'but yieldeth a delectable smell, much refreshing to the sitters under it.'

Hyll's successor Francis Bacon, in his essay *Of Gardens*, also makes much of the fragrance of flowers. He distinguishes between those which are 'fast flowers of their smells' and 'that which above all others, yields the sweetest smell in the air . . . the violet, especially the white double violet.' Of trees, shrubs and climbers, he loves daphne, almond, Sweet Brier, honeysuckle and lavender.

John Gerard and Parkinson both extolled the virtues of scent, and I have the feeling that the gardeners at that time were far more aware of its importance than were the men and women of the latter half of the 18th century, when formal gardens influenced by the French style were fashionable. (Gerard even suggests how to restore one's sense of smell: writing of the virtues of nigella, he says, 'The seed parched or dried at the fire, brought into powder and wrapped in a piece of fine lawn or sarcenet, cureth catarrhs, drieth the brain and restoreth the sense of smelling unto those which have lost it, being often smelled unto from day to day, and made warm at the fire when it is used.')

In the second half of the 17th century the three most celebrated writers in English on gardening practice were John Evelyn, John Rea and John Worlidge. All of them mention the importance of fragrance, and all were interested in the new plants which were becoming available for the pleasure garden. Evelyn's advice, when writing to commission plants and seeds to be brought from abroad, was: 'The seeds are best preserved in papers; their name written on them and put in a box. The trees in barrels their roots wrapped about in moss; the smaller the plants and trees the better . . . Some are of the opinion that plants or roots that come from abroad will be better preserved if they are rubbed over with honey before they are covered with moss.'

Worlidge in his *Art of Gardening* (1677) devotes several pages to 'gratefully odoriferous' shrubs and trees, and recommends that the white jasmine be grown up a wall or along a

Hamamelis virginiana,
from
*Traité des Arbres et
Arbustes*, Vol 1 (1755).

palisade, and commends the 'Syringa Pipe-tree or Lilac . . . affording you branches of fine white scented flowers in April and May.' The spring-flowering dwarf almond is also praised as 'a humble shrub, but deserves a place in your garden.' By humble I believe he means low in growth. 'The mezerion is one of the most hardy plants in nature, sending forth its pleasant, beautiful and odoriferous plants [flowers] in the coldest seasons of this northern climate. One of the most useful and necessary greens is the rosemary.'

John Rea writes, 'The best hedges for our country are those set with Pyracantha and Phyllirea. The hedges must be kept narrow and supported with stakes or laths on either side, and as they grow cut straight by a line on top, and even on the sides.' In other words, they should be formal and well trimmed. His recommendations for climbers, jasmine and honeysuckle are, in fact, no different from those of Tudor times, and for scent he advises planting the double white lilac *Syringa persica*. The common lilac, *S. vulgaris*, had been in cultivation since the 16th century, but the strongly fragrant *S. persica* was only introduced in 1640, so would have been a novelty. He also writes of Spanish broom, *Spartium junceum*, which had been grown by William Turner as early as 1548. It was probably introduced as a medicinal plant, but certainly warranted a place in any scented garden.

A character outstanding in the gardening scene of the late 17th century was Henry Compton, Bishop of London from 1675 to 1713. He was an ardent lover of plant rarities and, in his garden at Fulham Palace, he took great pride in growing all the most recent introductions from the Americas such as the tulip tree, the magnolia, the sassafras, aralia, hickory and *Arbutus unedo*. He sent the Rev. John Bannister as a missionary to North America with instructions to send seeds, as well as news of his missionary successes.

According to unromantic statistics 940 plants were introduced into Britain in the 17th century and nearly 9000 in the 18th. This clearly reflects the advance in communications between the continents. By the time Humphry Repton and John Claudius Loudon were advocating the use of plants near the house, there was a far greater range from which to choose, but I feel they must have been dazzled by the galaxy of colour and so forgotten about fragrance, for in their books I have found no references to scent comparable to those in the works of Hyll and Gerard. One cannot, without a smile, imagine a party of Victorian ladies admiring a stunning but gaudy array of carpet bedding, all on their hands and knees enjoying the scent of lobelias and echeverias.

Fortunately William Robinson, quickly followed by Gertrude Jekyll, rescued us and once more set gardeners back on the path to the natural and most easily achieved 'beautiful'. In his classic book, *The English Flower Garden*, Robinson devotes a chapter to 'Fragrance': 'A man who makes a garden should have a heart for plants that have the gift of sweetness as well as beauty of form and colour.' He mentions all the scented flowers and concludes with much affection, 'Many of these treasures have been shut out of our thoughts owing to the exclusion of everything that did not make showy colour.' In other words, carpet bedding! 'No one may be richer in fragrance than the wise man who plants hardy shrubs and flowering trees . . . families of fragrant things.'

To bring us well into this century, when gardening was once more able to take its legitimate place in our everyday life, Victoria Sackville West was writing to inspire gardeners. She was noticeably conscious of the scents around her and in the spring of 1954, wrote for the London *Observer* newspaper: 'Much depends also on the keenness of the nose, and also on the fact that not all scented plants give off their scent all the time. They may vary with the temperature, with the degree of moisture in the air, and even with the time of day. This capriciousness makes them perhaps more precious. One may catch an unexpected whiff as one passes a bush of wintersweet or witch hazel, not to be detected an hour ago, or of that vanilla-scented little tree *Azara microphylla*. And the scent of box in the sun, and the box clippings as you crush them underfoot. And a bed of warm wallflowers. And the night-scented stock, that lack-lustre annual which comes into its own after twilight.' These precepts were put into practice in her garden at Sissinghurst Castle, Kent where on a warm summer day, one can wander in and out of the 'rooms' of the garden, inhaling the delicious perfumes of the plants therein.

Named in honour of the American botanist Caspar Wistar, the hardy climber *Wisteria sinensis* is the most fragrant species of the genus. The white form, *alba*, is even more strongly scented than the purple, but it is rarely seen in gardens today.

The plants to grow

Acacia dealbata

Albizia julibrissin

Abeliophyllum distichum

Sometimes I wonder whether some plants fail to become popular because of their tongue-twisting names; could *Abeliophyllum distichum* be one of these? It came to the West in 1924 from Korea where it is known as white forsythia. Korea has harsh winters and quite hot summers, so to be sure of success the best place for it is on a south-facing wall. Then the honey-scented flowers should open in early spring to entice the bees away from their pollen gathering among the crocuses. Most good shrub nurseries have this species in their catalogues.

Of the many species of acacia, one of the most suitable for outdoor cultivation in cool climates is the silver wattle, or mimosa, *Acacia dealbata*. It is a tree worth the extra trouble for the fragrant yellow flowers smell of sweet violets and appear in time to relieve the dullness of winter's months. This mimosa, brought from Australia in 1820, is now cultivated in abundance in the south of France where the cheerful yellow feathers stand out marvellously against the azure sky. But where the climate is less favourable, it is a shrub which must be wintered in the conservatory, or grown against a wall and in winter swathed with bracken, as one friend does. I would like to grow it in a pot in a cool greenhouse to have ready to bring indoors for its fragrance when the flowers open with their conspicuous yellow stamens.

Albizia julibrissin, closely related to the acacia, is another of those desirable and fragrant small trees supposedly only hardy in the mildest climates. It will, in fact, stand a few degrees of frost, and with plenty of summer warmth can reach 10m/30ft. It was brought to Europe from the Near East and China, where it is known as the silk tree. The fragrant flowers appear in terminal clusters, their chief feature being thread-like pink stamens. Grown from seed in spring, it makes an attractive sub-tropical effect in summer bedding, but there are so many scented plants which will grow without difficulty that I prefer to leave the *Albizia* genus to places with a frost-free climate.

Shrubs of the genus *Buddleia*, being mostly vigorous and hardy, are too easy and accommodating to receive the attention that they deserve. The *B. davidii* varieties are especially valuable in new gardens for they will make up to 3m/10ft of growth between spring and summer. The shrub's name certainly conjures up thoughts of famous plant collectors. The Rev. Adam Buddle (in honour of whom the genus was named) was an early 18th-century botanist and Père Armand David (who gave his name to the species) was a French missionary in China who first discovered the shrub in 1869. But it is from seeds sent back to England by the plant collector E.H. Wilson between 1900 and 1908 that the present garden varieties are descended.

The most effective for the garden are the varieties 'Black Night' with long dark-violet trusses; 'Royal Red', a rich purple-red; 'Peace', the best white and 'Fascination', a very showy pink. Even more spectacular is 'Dartmoor' with lilac panicles as wide as they are long. They are all sweetly scented, honey being the prevalent aroma.

B. alternifolia makes a splendid tree. You

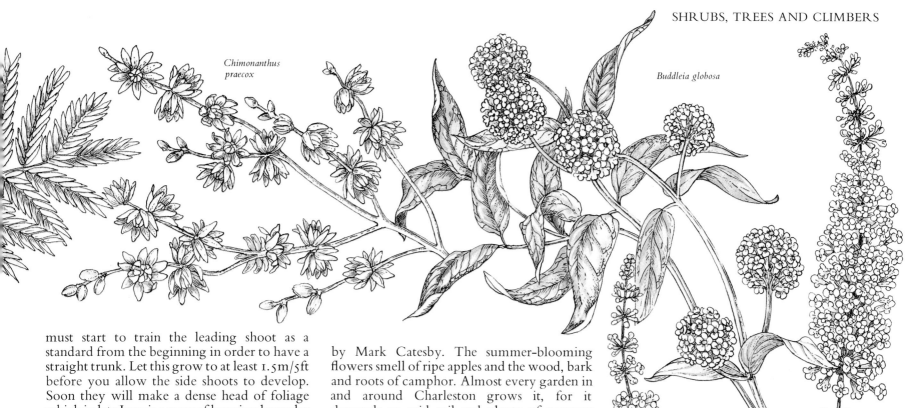

Chimonanthus praecox

Buddleia globosa

Buddleia davidii

must start to train the leading shoot as a standard from the beginning in order to have a straight trunk. Let this grow to at least 1.5m/5ft before you allow the side shoots to develop. Soon they will make a dense head of foliage which in late June is a mass of hanging lavender flower spikes, very strongly scented. *B. fallowiana* has white felted stems, the leaves are densely covered with hairs, giving the whole shrub a silvery tone. The flowers are lavender blue and very fragrant. The white-flowered form *alba*, is even more white and woolly. *B. crispa*, from the Himalayas, blooms in early summer; the flower panicles are lilac and each individual flower has a white eye. The variety which has been with us the longest is *B. globosa*, arriving in Europe from Peru in 1774. The bright yellow flower heads are the size and shape of ping-pong balls and there are usually four or five of these to each stem.

Pruning buddleias is important and easy. *B. alternifolia*, *crispa* and *globosa* must be pruned immediately after flowering. *B. davidii* and *fallowiana* require hard pruning in early spring.

B. colvilei was discovered in 1840 in Sikkim by Joseph Hooker who described it as 'the handsomest of all Himalayan shrubs' – it is just as attractively scented. It is not hardy when young, so has acquired a bad reputation, but it will live through a hard winter when it is mature. Planted against a wall, it is easily given extra protection. Annual pruning is unnecessary, cut back only enough to keep the shrub tidy. Seek a good form such as 'Kewensis'.

Calycanthus floridus, the Carolina allspice – an enticing name – was sent to England in 1726 by Mark Catesby. The summer-blooming flowers smell of ripe apples and the wood, bark and roots of camphor. Almost every garden in and around Charleston grows it, for it demands an acid soil and plenty of summer sunshine to ripen the wood and produce next year's flower buds. In cooler climates it needs a warm garden and sheltered site to prosper.

The hardy *Chimonanthus praecox*, wintersweet, is the Chinese counterpart of the North American allspice. It flowers during the winter, usually producing a few of its waxy yellow and purple flowers for my Christmas nosegay. You must have it near the house, preferably against a wall, so that its fragrance of jonquil and violet can filter indoors. The leaves are undistinguished, so a scented climber, such as sweet pea, growing through the branches will improve its looks in summer.

Pruning wintersweet is to me a problem, but the authorities say that one should shorten back the strongest twigs, then remove weak and overcrowded ones. My experience is not to delay this after the onset of spring or the following year's crop of flowers will suffer, for they appear on the axils of the old stems.

That great authority W.J. Bean says of the scented *C. virginicus*, the fringe-tree and a member of the olive family, 'there is nothing like it among flowering shrubs'. It is a native of the eastern United States and perfectly hardy in cool climates. The drooping racemes of white flowers will appear in summer, but it will never achieve quite the profusion of bloom elsewhere that it does in its native country.

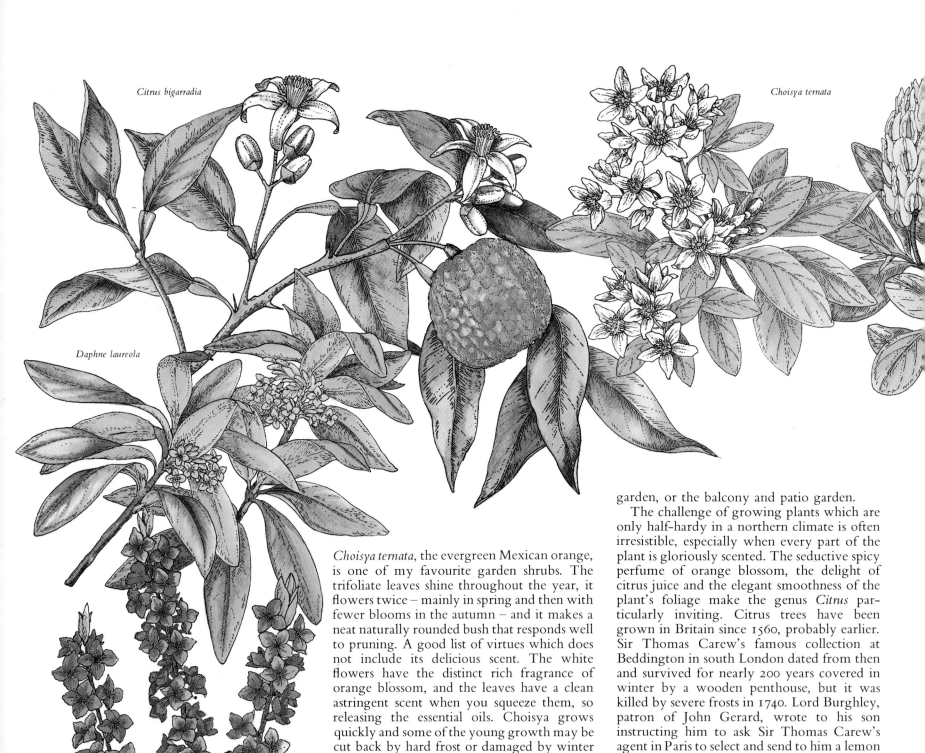

Citrus bigarradia

Choisya ternata

Daphne laureola

Daphne
mezereum

Choisya ternata, the evergreen Mexican orange, is one of my favourite garden shrubs. The trifoliate leaves shine throughout the year, it flowers twice – mainly in spring and then with fewer blooms in the autumn – and it makes a neat naturally rounded bush that responds well to pruning. A good list of virtues which does not include its delicious scent. The white flowers have the distinct rich fragrance of orange blossom, and the leaves have a clean astringent scent when you squeeze them, so releasing the essential oils. Choisya grows quickly and some of the young growth may be cut back by hard frost or damaged by winter winds but, so far, my fifteen-year-old bushes have not been destroyed. Prune any extra long or damaged shoots back to healthy wood and they will soon sprout again. Cuttings taken with young wood root very easily. I have seen the shrub most effectively trained against a south wall where there was no space for it to billow forward on to a path, and because of its tidy form it is a good subject for the small garden, or the balcony and patio garden.

The challenge of growing plants which are only half-hardy in a northern climate is often irresistible, especially when every part of the plant is gloriously scented. The seductive spicy perfume of orange blossom, the delight of citrus juice and the elegant smoothness of the plant's foliage make the genus *Citrus* particularly inviting. Citrus trees have been grown in Britain since 1560, probably earlier. Sir Thomas Carew's famous collection at Beddington in south London dated from then and survived for nearly 200 years covered in winter by a wooden penthouse, but it was killed by severe frosts in 1740. Lord Burghley, patron of John Gerard, wrote to his son instructing him to ask Sir Thomas Carew's agent in Paris to select and send to him a lemon and a pomegranate tree. The writer Thomas Hyll, a contemporary of Gerard, recommended that orange trees be planted in tubs which could 'be rolled hither and thither'. We do not know which varieties they grew.

The taxonomy of citrus species is confused and complicated. *C. aurantium* is the Seville or bitter orange from which marmalade is made. The blooms of its form bigarradia yield the

Cytisus battandieri

Clematis flammula

John Evelyn's advice to his gardener in the 17th century. Water them sparingly in winter and 'Never expose your oranges, limons and like tender trees, whatever season flatter, 'til the Mulberry puts forth its leafe, then bring them boldly out of the greenhouse; but for a fortnight let them stand in the shade of a hedge.'

Of the climbing plants, clematis is an international favourite. There are many attractive forms, admired for their fabulous flowers, elegant seed heads and, in some cases, quick growth. In the scented garden they can be extremely useful too. The robust evergreen climbing *Clematis cirrhosa* with strong rope-like stems covers tall trees in its native countries round the shores of the Mediterranean. Discovered by the Dutch botanist Clusius, it was first mentioned as growing in English gardens in 1590. In cool climates it is less vigorous but the honey-scented, white or greenish-yellow flowers are shaped like little drooping bells prettily covered with glossy down on the outside; the pale green buds are like small silken nuts. The flowers of *C. cirrhosa balearica* (syn. *C. calycina*), creamy-white freckled with reddish-purple on the outside, open just before Christmas and the pretty fern-like leaves turn an attractive bronze in winter. The flowers of this variety are also sweetly honey-scented. The pure white flowers of *C. flammula* open in late summer and have an almond or vanilla scent. Two other scented varieties are *C. rehderiana*, primrose yellow, and *C. jouiniana*, white opening to pale lilac blue. Both have a fresh fragrance and should be grown over an old tree trunk where they can indulge their climbing nature, or up the sides of garden steps where you can fully enjoy their scent. 'Alexander' and *wilsonii* are scented cultivars of *C. montana*.

Most species of *Clerodendron*, such as *C. capitatum* or *C. splendens*, are not hardy but make excellent plants for the conservatory. Hardy species for the garden are *C. bungei* and *C. trichotomum*. The flowers are sweetly scented but the leaves often have a noxious smell, probably to keep away grazing animals, for these shrubs are indigenous to tropical Africa.

If you have seen coronilla growing wild along the coast of the Mediterranean you will wish, as I do, to have it in your garden. The yellow pea flowers are only fragrant by day. *Coronilla glauca* and its variegated leaf form are best for cooler gardens. I have it in a raised bed in a warm corner where it thrives and is seldom out of flower, appreciating its situation on a well-drained soil, protected from the wind.

For three or four weeks in late spring *Crataegus oxyacantha*, the English hawthorn or May tree, smells deliciously of honeyed almonds. The double red form makes an attractive small tree, and is especially pretty if clipped to keep the head in a tidy round shape.

In summer, *Cytisus battandieri* is one of the joys of the scented garden. It has the reputation of being slightly tender, perhaps because of its common name Moroccan broom, but actually it is found wild high up in the Atlas mountains and is quite hardy. I planted my first specimen against the house and it very quickly shot up to the bedroom windows. This plant lived for eighteen years then, as a final bonus in its last summer, set and ripened several seed pods. From these I now have a new generation of plants in the garden. The young growth is attractively covered with silky down, and when in full flower the dense racemes of yellow spikes smell deliciously of pineapple.

You will find a suitable plant for every part of your garden out of the fifty or so daphnes described in Hillier's *Manual of Trees and Shrubs*, at least half of which have scented flowers. *Daphne cneorum* is one of the best lime-loving plants for the rock garden, flowering twice each year, but it is quite difficult to establish. *D. alpina* flowers in early summer, is dwarf, and a real gem.

If you find a patch of *D. blagayana* you may be sure the owner is a good gardener. This species likes partial shade and plenty of leaf mould, and the prostrate branches will root if pegged down. The white flowers start to open in spring and produce a wonderful rich scent. Two rather similar daphnes are *D. pontica* and *D. laureola*, the spurge laurel, which flowers in February; its dense clusters of yellow-green flowers are tucked under the thick shiny green leaves. Both grow to 60cm/24in, enjoy a shady site and release their perfume as light fades. The scent is elusive but firm and sweet, thrown out to attract moths to fertilize the flowers. The moths must be successful for you will always find a few seedlings around. *D. bholua*, a tall shrub from the Himalayas, only recently available, has marvellous large sweet-scented flowers, white when open and deep reddish-mauve in bud; *D. odora* has a powerful scent you can smell from a distance. The spring-flowering *D. mezereum*, a British native, is often seen growing up a cottage garden path in either its white or pink form.

essential oil of neroli, an ingredient of Eau de Cologne. Another ingredient is the oil extracted from the bergamot orange, *C. bergamia* grown in Calabria. The lemon tree *C. limon* and the sweet orange *C. sinensis* both flourish in Mediterranean countries and the delicious fragrance of their flowers can only be described as 'of orange blossom'. Crush the leaves and you will find they are fragrant too.

In cool climates lemon and orange trees must be grown in containers and overwintered indoors – think of the orangery at Versailles. For at least a dozen years I have had an orange and a lemon tree that winter in a greenhouse kept just frost free. The flower buds open from spring onwards and as these take a year to develop and ripen, flowers and fruits are often there together. Needless to say, the flowers scent the greenhouse wonderfully. I follow

Humulus lupulus

Plants of the genus *Datura* are a challenge for most as they must be kept frost free. I have a friend who has completely mastered the situation, and each summer, even during the most sunless, his plants are covered with bloom. He grows three species, *arborea*, *suaveolens* and *sanguinea*. He takes cuttings in early summer, pots these on into 25cm/10in pots, overwinters them in a frost-free but unheated greenhouse, prunes them if need be in April, then stands them outside in June, putting them either into large Versailles tubs or else planting in well manured ground. In a good summer they will soar to 3m/10ft and one year he counted 200 blooms on a single plant. After flowering and when cuttings have been taken, the plants are discarded. A lesson to learn from his experience is that one good plant is worth more than twenty bad ones. The scent is intoxicating – clouds of perfume reminiscent of narcissus and lilies.

D. suaveolens, Angel's Trumpets, has white flowers, *D. arborea* very pale yellow ones, while those of *D. sanguinea* are orange-red. These all die quite tidily, the flowers dropping as they fade, but the flowers of the double form, particularly of *D. cornigera* become brown and unattractive before they fall.

Red spider mite is the worst enemy of *D. suaveolens* but the other two species are immune because of their hairy leaves. The only sure remedy is constant spraying, even in winter. Watch out also for white fly.

It would take a lifetime to become an expert on the gum tree. I love the lemon-scented gum *Eucalyptus citriodora*, but that must be grown in the conservatory. I have grown *E. globulus* from seed and planted them in my garden but they died in a bad winter. Another seedling from this batch went to London where it quickly overtopped a three-storey house and then died of exhaustion. *E. gunnii* is one of the hardiest and in my garden has survived with 20 degrees of frost. The snow gum *E. niphophila*, has a beautiful trunk, patchworked green, grey and white and *E. perriniana* ought to be grown for its beautiful juvenile leaves which cling around the stem; you should coppice this variety to keep the young growth active. *E. parvifolia* is perhaps the hardiest species of all and will even tolerate a chalk soil. But as we are growing these for the scented leaves, perhaps in a small garden, I would choose either *E. coccifera* with extremely fragrant leaves, *E. gunnii* – prune this hard every spring, or *E. citriodora*, and keep it in a pot in a greenhouse except in a warm climate.

In 1578 Captain Winter reported that the bark of a shrub he found near the Straits of

Drimys winteri

Hamamelis mollis

Magellan was 'as a medicine very powerful against scurvy' for his seamen; this was *Drimys winteri*, and it is still known as Winter's bark. This shrub was not introduced to Britain until much later, and is only hardy there, and in similar climates, when grown against a sheltered wall. The white flowers have the scent of jasmine and the bark a strong aromatic smell, almost like myrrh. *D. lanceolata* (syn. *D. aromatica*), reputed to be tender, is from Tasmania. I have seen a large shrub of this growing against a house in Oxfordshire. The leaves have a pungent peppery taste and smell, and the dried fruits can be used as a substitute for pepper.

The ideal place to grow *Hamamelis mollis*, witch hazel, is a sunny site with a background of dark green yews or box so that on a sunny winter's day the tree can show off its delightful clusters of deep yellow, spidery flowers along the leafless stems. There is a lovely cultivar 'Pallida', with large sulphur-yellow flowers. To me their clean fresh smell signals that spring is not far off.

Helichrysum angustifolium, a native of southern Europe, should perhaps be used in the herb garden for the leaves make an excellent ingredient for pot pourri. It is a good edging plant, about 30cm/12in high, with pretty silvery foliage which emits a strong curry scent, especially after rain. Position this in the garden so that you will brush against it as you pass by: the scent will fill the air. There is a dwarf species *H. italicum*, with small, shining silver leaves, a neat habit of growth and an equally powerful scent. Crush the leaves to discover their scent; to me it has the astringent smell of eucalyptus.

Humulus lupulus, the common hop: who has not experienced the smell of this hardy herbaceous climber of a sunny summer's day? The fruits are used for brewing, but the form *H. lupulus aureus* makes a wonderful golden-leafed summer cover for an arbour or trellis. I have it growing over an arbour above a chamomile seat and on warm afternoons the scent of both is wonderful. The golden leaves show up in a spectacular way against the blue sky.

Hypericum calycinum, rose of Sharon, a dwarf shrub with large buttercup-yellow flowers in July, is a wonderful ground cover for a dry bank, a difficult corner, under trees or beside the driveway where car fumes can be a nuisance. Pruned to ground level in early spring it will quickly make fresh young leaves.

H. 'Hidcote' is the best variety for the shrub border or to use as a lax hedge. This semi-evergreen will grow to 2m/6½ft and make the same spread. Throughout late summer and autumn it is covered with yellow flowers.

H. × *moseranum*, a cross between the rose of Sharon and *H. patulum*, is midway in height between them, blooms all the summer and has conspicuous, attractive reddish anthers. The leaves of the species *H. androsaemum*, commonly known as tutsan, were once used to cover open wounds. *H. balearicum* has fragrant flowers, but requires a frost-free climate.

Datura suaveolens

Eucalyptus parvifolia

Hypericum 'Hidcote'

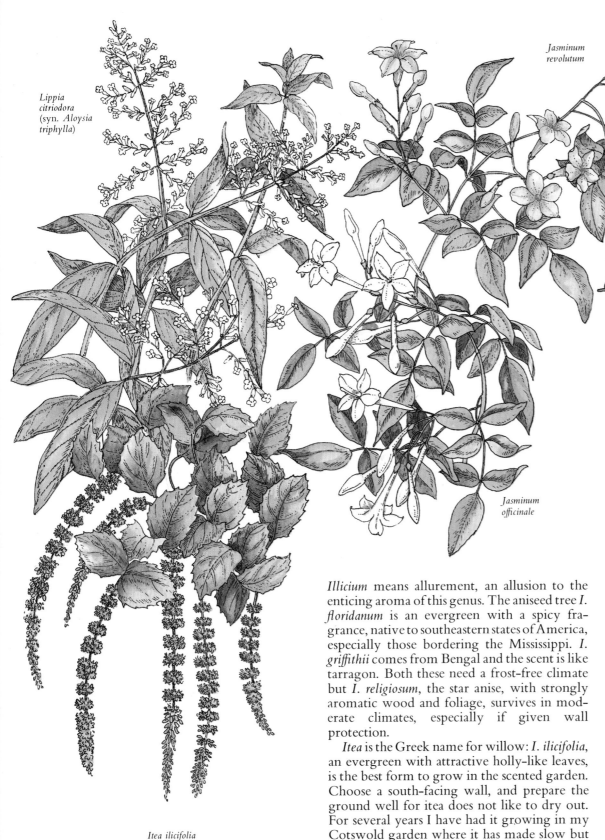

*Lippia
citriodora*
(syn. *Aloysia
triphylla*)

*Jasminum
revolutum*

*Jasminum
officinale*

Itea ilicifolia

steady progress, not suffering from hard winter frosts. It was only recently that I discovered the sweet honey scent of the flowers when an old, retired gardener told me how a few flower tassels would fill a whole room with their fragrance, but only in the evening.

Thomas Hyll, author of the earliest books on practical gardening, described in his *Gardener's Labyrinth* of 1577 the making of an arbour: 'The owner also may set the jasmine tree bearing a fragrant flowre, the muske rose, damask and privet tree in beds, to shoote up and spread over the herber . . . it yieldeth a delectable smell, much refreshing the sitters underneath it.' Certainly the common *Jasminum officinale* produces one of the best summer scents, very sweet and lingering. But do not grow it as I did, against the house; it is so strong it will raise the roof tiles or penetrate right into the walls! Amazing for such a seemingly gentle plant. Rather grow it over an arbour as Thomas Hyll recommends, and keep it in check by judicious pruning. If you do not feel brave enough to take on this climber but want the jasmine in your scented garden, *J. stephanense* has fragrant pink flowers and is not so vigorous.

I love *J. revolutum*, a hardy evergreen with angular stems and golden flowers carried in clusters. Against a wall it comes into flower early in summer, but I grow it also in a mixed border, planted with variegated honeysuckle which twines up the jasmine's strong stems. I prune both almost to the ground in early spring and by the end of summer the jasmine is in full

Illicium means allurement, an allusion to the enticing aroma of this genus. The aniseed tree *I. floridanum* is an evergreen with a spicy fragrance, native to southeastern states of America, especially those bordering the Mississippi. *I. griffithii* comes from Bengal and the scent is like tarragon. Both these need a frost-free climate but *I. religiosum*, the star anise, with strongly aromatic wood and foliage, survives in moderate climates, especially if given wall protection.

Itea is the Greek name for willow: *I. ilicifolia*, an evergreen with attractive holly-like leaves, is the best form to grow in the scented garden. Choose a south-facing wall, and prepare the ground well for itea does not like to dry out. For several years I have had it growing in my Cotswold garden where it has made slow but

Lonicera fragrantissima

Lonicera periclymenum

Magnolia × wieseneri

flower, wafting its scent for yards around.

J. polyanthum is one of the most satisfactory climbers for the cool greenhouse or sheltered patio. It is extremely free flowering, its pink buds opening to white in winter, and a few open panicles brought indoors will fill the room with perfume.

If you have a rock garden, or indeed a container-garden on a balcony, there is one species for you. This is *J. parkeri*, a dainty evergreen only 30cm/12in high, with pretty yellow, scented flowers that appear in summer.

In a warm corner of a cottage garden where I lived in 1942 there grew a marvellous lemon-scented verbena, *Lippia citriodora* (syn. *Aloysia triphylla*). It was 1.5m/5ft tall and just as wide. All through the year it gave me pleasure, for the bare stems are scented as well as the leaves. Several years later, wanting a plant, I called to ask for a cutting, but alas it had gone, removed to make way for a garage. I felt as though an old friend had died, wondering how anyone could have been so ruthless. This shrub is certainly hardy outside given a good position, and even if the top is cut by frost it will always shoot again from ground level. I grow it as a standard in tubs, and in the winter the plants are put under cover and kept quite dry, then in April I prune them and bring them back into growth. The lemon scent is sharp and refreshing, the leaves make a special contribution to pot pourri, and an interesting addition to china tea; a leaf in your pocket or pressed in a book will hold its scent for weeks.

The honeysuckle genus *Lonicera* plays a great part in the scented garden. For winter, *L. fragrantissima* from China starts to flower about Christmas time and its creamy white blooms go on for at least two months, scenting the air around. It is a robust bush and will do best in a north position away from direct sunshine.

The old-fashioned woodbine *L. periclymenum* 'Belgica', or early Dutch honeysuckle, flowers in early summer. Plant it to climb a trellis near a window so that the scent can waft inside on warm days. Later in the season it makes a mass of red berries, much enjoyed by sparrows and other small birds. The cultivar 'Serotina' or late Dutch, flowers from the end of summer through autumn with deep purple-red buds which open to yellow.

I planted *L. japonica* 'Halliana' against a sunny wall. It died, I believe through lack of moisture, but had already made its way to the north side where it has flourished ever since, freely scenting the air around.

The so-called bush honeysuckle, *L. syringantha*, also from China, has climbed 3.5m/12ft up the walls of my house, and flowers twice a year with very fragrant, delicate pink flowers. It is marvellous but untidy. The right place to grow it would be beside a three- to four-foot wall where it is free to sprawl unrestrained.

'Faint was the air with odorous breath of magnolia blossoms.' wrote William Wordsworth. You can achieve a scented magnolia – a

most elegant plant – in your garden in spring, summer and autumn! *Magnolia heptapeta* (syn. *M. denudata*) flowers in late spring, with large pure white flowers which glisten on sunny days and emit a gentle scent of violets. *M. kobus stellata*, the star magnolia, is the best for a small garden. It starts to bloom when only two years old and to quote E.A. Bowles: 'In 1912 I realized for the first time how strongly scented the flowers are; a delicious whiff of bean fields reached my nose and set me sniffing around to locate its origin, and I tracked it down to the magnolia. The bruised bark emits quite a different scent. One day, when sawing off a rather large bough I was struck by the resemblance of the scent of the wood to that peppery fragrance peculiar to wooden Japanese cabinets.'

The summer-flowering magnolias, *M. wilsonii* and *M. × wieseneri* (until recently named *M. × watsonii*) are small trees with white flowers. *Wilsonii* has pendant saucer-shaped flowers with conspicuous crimson anthers; *wieseneri*, upward facing and spicily fragrant flowers that have inner petals of ivory white set off with crimson stamens and outer petals tinged with rose.

The evergreen species *M. grandiflora*, has huge creamy flowers with a lemon scent. In cool climates plant it against a wall to protect its dark green glossy leaves that are covered underneath with a thick red brown felt.

Every plant has its special place in the garden and none more so than the winter-flowering shrubs. *Mahonia japonica* with stiff, stout stems, pinnate leaves and scented flower spikes, does well in a shady corner, but it must be in a place where you will often pass by to enjoy its refreshing lily of the valley scent. My specimen is much too far from the house and I regret not planting it near the west-facing front door.

The American plant collector Lawrence Johnston brought back seeds of *M. lomariifolia* from Yunnan in 1931, grew it first in the south of France and then took it to his garden at Hidcote in Gloucestershire. The flower spikes are almost erect as are the lemon-yellow racemes of the variety 'Charity'. The best named-clones of the cross between *M. japonica* and *M. lomariifolia* are 'Buckland', 'Lionel Fortescue', 'Charity' and 'Winter Sun'.

The classic myrtle *Myrtus communis*, sacred to Aphrodite the goddess of love, was worn at weddings in Mediterranean countries as a symbol of love and chastity. John Parkinson grew three sorts in his garden in 1629, but adds 'we keepe them in the countrey, with great care and diligence'. All parts are fragrant: the leaves (which retain their fragrance well when dry), the wood and the flowers which bloom in August (these are also quite tasty and can be used in salads and as a garnish). Myrtles will succumb in bad winters, but fortunately they are easy to root and are fast growing so can be replaced. The small leafed variety, *M. communis tarentina* is a delightful potted plant, and can be clipped into pyramids or balls. *M. luma* from China which grows to a 9m/30ft tree

has wonderful cinnamon-coloured bark; the flowers are white with green stamens.

Phillyrea decora has now been moved into the genus *Osmanthus*. This means that the erstwhile *Osmarea burkwoodii*, a cross between *Osmanthus delavayi* and *O. decorus*, is now known as *Osmanthus burkwoodii*. It is a wonderful spring flowering shrub, about 2m/6ft tall with dark evergreen leaves and intensely fragrant, small white flowers growing in clusters up the stems. It makes a good hedging plant as long as you do not want to keep it too well clipped.

O. heterophyllus (syn. *O. ilicifolius*) has prickly holly-like leaves and flowers in autumn. The rather tender *O. fragrans* flowers all through the winter and should be grown in a pot in the greenhouse to be brought indoors.

Philadelphus flowers are usually pure white, which is most often the colour of heavily scented flowers. *Philadelphus coronarius*, the European mock orange, has been grown in England since the 16th century, probably even earlier, for Gerard grew it in his London garden. The scent is so intense that a single branch of flowers brought into the house will perfume many rooms, and it is said that the heavy fragrance is capable of causing headaches – perhaps this is the origin of the description 'a heady scent'! I know that, without fail, it is in flower in my garden on 23 June. There are

Osmanthus burkwoodii

Myrtus communis

Mahonia japonica

many species and varieties to choose from. *P. microphyllus* with its delicate leaves and pineapple-scented flowers is good for a small garden. *P.* 'Belle Etoile' is a compact shrub whose white flowers are flushed with purple at their centres, and *P.* 'Burfordensis' has conspicuous yellow stamens. Recently I planted *P.* 'Sybille' for its beautiful arching branches and the characteristic orange-scented flowers. For a double-flowered variety my choice is 'Virginal'.

Some shrubs are especially suitable for certain conditions: those of the genus *Pittosporum* enjoy the salt sea breezes of warm temperate regions. *P. tenuifolium*, 'Garnettii' and 'Silver Queen' do well in cooler climates, although they usually need wall protection to succeed and they rarely flower. *P. tobira* from China has flowers scented of orange, and never looks better than when growing as a hedge in the south of France. *P. eugenioides* is native of Japan with honey-scented flowers – the leaves have an incense fragrance when you crush them. It can be hardy outdoors in cool climates given adequate care and protection.

Certain shrubs have special associations and for me *Poncirus trifoliata* recalls the evening in May when I first saw it. The scent was intoxicating, just like orange blossom, and never having seen it before I was amazed by its dark green, flattened branches with lethal spikes, so opposite to its delicate perfume.

There is a tree-like specimen at the Brooklyn Botanic Garden in New York which, when I saw it one autumn, was literally covered with fragrant yellow fruits. I was told to use them instead of lemon in China tea.

From the unusual to the ordinary: I turn to the common laurel, *Prunus laurocerasus*, which was very popular in 19th-century shrubberies. I am grateful to a past owner of my house who planted a single specimen – probably a hundred years ago! Now it is a full 6m/20ft tall and needs judicious pruning. It flowers each spring and the scent is tremendous, but fleetingly so, only for a day or two. A much more recently raised variety of this is 'Otto Luyken'. This has a horizontal habit of growth, dark, narrow shiny leaves and terminal racemes of honey-scented flowers. I have one growing in a mixed border and soon it will occupy too much space, spreading to 2m/6ft or more.

Out of the hundreds of species and hybrid rhododendrons you can find, there are several which are fragrant, but on the whole I would not call them a scented genus. All those with a scent have white or rather pale flowers.

One of the most fragrant species is the common *R. luteum*, the yellow azalea from the Caucasus, flowering in spring. A bush of this species spreads its perfume far and wide. *R. occidentale* is medium-sized with scented white flowers, and has become the parent to many garden hybrids. Also in spring *R. prinophyllum*

(syn. *R. roseum*) has strongly clove-scented flowers. *R. discolor*, introduced in 1900, is pink and flowers in summer.

R. edgeworthii (syn. *R. bullatum*) has a scent described as 'about the finest in the genus'. The flowers are white tinged with pink and the leaves have great attraction too. They are bright green on top, are deeply puckered and have ravishing saffron-coloured, felted undersides. This needs a mild area, but *R.* 'Princess Alice' (*R. edgeworthii* × *R. ciliatum*) has the same attractive leaves and scented flowers and has also inherited a greater hardiness from its *ciliatum* parent.

For a succession of bloom choose the early flowering hybrid, *R.* 'Fragrantissimum' which has puckered leaves (derived from its *edgeworthii* parent), white flushed rose flowers and is extremely fragrant; but it is only hardy in the mildest areas. Slightly later to flower is *R.* Loderi, considered to be the finest hybrid, with richly scented white to soft pink flowers. The clone 'King George' is perhaps even better. *R.* 'Midsummer Snow' is late flowering, as are *R.* 'Polar Bear' and *R.* 'July Fragrance'.

These are all more suitable for larger gardens, so if your garden is small, grow pots of *R. saluenense*, a small shrub with highly aromatic leaves – the scentless flowers are crimson. And for the connoisseur the 30cm/12in species *R. sargentianum* has leaves which are nicely fragrant when crushed.

Rhododendron luteum

Prunus laurocerasus 'Otto Luyken'

Ribes odoratum

Wisteria sinensis

Skimmia japonica

To most of us ribes means currants, and *Ribes sanguineum*, the popular flowering currant, with rosy-red flowers in spring. As a child I thought it quite wonderful; we had a tall hedge of it all the way up our long drive and I loved its musty scent. But now my nose has become more selective, I prefer the North American 'buffalo currant' *R. odoratum*, until recently named *R. aureum*, for its golden foliage, golden flowers and delicious clove scent. For some years I have wanted *R. laurifolium*, discovered and introduced by Wilson in 1908. This has yellow-green flowers in winter and a scent of spring to come. The evergreen leaves of *R. viburnifolium* have a turpentine scent.

The honey locust was one of the first American trees to reach Europe. Seeds were sent in 1601 to Jean Robin, founder of Les Jardins des Plantes in Paris. He believed it to be an acacia, the generic name of mimosa, and unfortunately acacia has stuck as a common name. Later Linnaeus called it *Robinia pseud-*

acacia in honour of Jean Robin. It is a fast-growing tree as was borne out by John Parkinson who wrote in his 1640 *Herbal* that Master Tradescant had a 'locust tree of exceeding height in his garden'. This was only thirty-nine years after the seeds reached Robin. There is a fine specimen, over 200 years old, at the Royal Botanic Gardens at Kew. Although recommended as a good avenue tree by John Evelyn in his famous *Sylva*, it did not become popular until the journalist William Cobbett wrote about it in the 1830s. He called it by its American name Locust, and had soon sold hundreds of seedlings of his own growing. I have a magnificent tree in my garden estimated to have been planted around 1840, and I know from happy experience how delicious the scent of this robinia can be. Every July it flowers profusely and spreads its vanilla fragrance around. Robinia blooms when quite young so do not feel depressed that the tree you plant will not flower for you. Recently the variety 'Frisia', from a Dutch nursery, has been planted extensively in domestic gardens for its striking golden leaves. It flowers well, too, and is a bonus for the scented garden.

The sweet box, *Sarcococca*, are dwarf evergreen, winter-flowering shrubs with heavily scented white or cream flowers. I grow *S. hookeriana digyna*, a native of China, which flowers in winter. I always keep a plant in a pot and bring it indoors for its particularly spicy scent. *S. ruscifolia* flowers all winter and makes an attractive 60cm/24in shrub.

Robinia pseudacacia

Spartium junceum

Viburnum × bodnantense

Skimmia had been rather a puzzle until the last volume of the eighth edition of W.J. Bean's *Trees and Shrubs Hardy in the British Isles* was published in 1980. It flowers in spring in terminal panicles and then, if you have done your homework and any necessary pollination, you will have a cheerful show of red berries in autumn. It likes a rich acid soil and will succeed in partial shade. For a small garden choose *S. reevesiana* 'Fortunei'. From China, it is hermaphrodite and self-fertile, free flowering and by autumn should be covered with crimson berries. *S. japonica* grows bigger – up to 120cm/48in or more – with male and female flowers on different plants, so you need at least one male and two females to make a handsome group. The flowers all have a powerful, lingering lily of the valley fragrance.

Spartium junceum, the Spanish broom, has a delicious and distinctively sweet scent which reminds me of oranges. (Do not confuse this with Spanish gorse which flowers in spring and smells faintly of ripe apples.) Always attracted by ripe seeds, I gathered some long seed pods from an unoccupied garden years ago, and from these I have had a small forest of Spanish broom growing behind a yew hedge. When the flowers are in full blow the scent always intrigues visitors, and they are often unbelieving of my diagnosis of the source of the scent. This broom grows tall and leggy so use it at the back of your border, and keep a supply of seedlings ready as replacements.

Many viburnums are fragrant and grow well on alkaline soil. My choice for the scented garden are *V. × bodnantense*, a hybrid between *V. fragrans* and *V. grandiflorum*, a lovely plant which blooms right through the winter with tightly packed, very fragrant flower clusters coloured pink, fading to white. *V. × burkwoodii* is a good choice for a town garden as it will tolerate a city atmosphere. *V. carlesii* is an old favourite with white flowers in spring. *V.* 'Anne Russell' is a cross between the last two and has scented pink flowers in spring. *V. × carlcephalum*, a hybrid from *V. carlesii*, is good for cold districts, fast growing and with rather stiff branches. I also grow *V. foetens* 'Koreana', a marvellous winter-flowering shrub with stout reddish stems and extra large leaves. The old *V. fragrans*, now called *V. farreri*, is alluded to by Reginald Farrer as 'this most glorious of shrubs'. It is indeed hard to better; robust, free with its blooms and scent, and unharmed by the hardest of winters. All these viburnums have a sweet honey scent and retain their fragrance when picked for indoors. I cannot find any vestige of scent in the *V. opulus* varieties nor in *V. tinus*.

Wisterias are all beautiful ornamental climbers, but for the best and strongest scent you should plant *W. sinensis*, 'the noblest hardy climber ever introduced', imported from China in 1816 and named in honour of Caspar Wistar of Pennsylvania who died in 1818. It flowers in spring before the leaves are fully expanded, so the racemes of mauve or lilac flowers are not hidden. I have it growing up the supports of my laburnum walk; I prune it very hard so it does not have the chance to throttle the laburnum with its tight twisting branches. The mauve flowers appear as a marvellous complement to the scentless yellow laburnum blossom and add a rich honey fragrance to the scene.

There is a white variety with a more delicate fragrance. Both of these can be grown as standards and so make lovely specimen trees for an important place.

Terraces and twilight

I am often asked the question, 'What should we plant on the patio?' Of course it will depend on which way it faces, how much wind it gets, and other conditions but generally, because of its intended purpose, a patio is well sheltered and has a south aspect. It is an area which must look good at all times of the year; you will want something special to enjoy during the cold months of the year, as well as treasures to show to your visitors. It should have an exotic aura and a pungent scent on warm summer evenings when you will be sitting outside to enjoy the last moments of the day. It may seem a great challenge, but your success will be satisfying. There can be a lot of showmanship about gardening, especially where space is limited.

Most patios are paved, so there will be plenty of space to stand pots and tubs that can be brought forward or moved around to give those which are in flower the most important positions. Perhaps there will be chinks between the stones into which you can slip small clumps of thyme and other perfumed creepers like pennyroyal.

Let us start with the wall; if your ground space is limited you must make the most of the height. When there is room, shrubs are invaluable and these should span every month with their scented flowers or fragrant leaves. *Acacia dealbata* and *Azara microphylla* will scent the air in winter and early spring. Early Dutch honeysuckle, *Lonicera* 'Belgica', prefers a sunny wall, and will flower for a good four weeks in early summer. On the shady wall you can put *Lonicera* × *tellmanniana*, which flowers in midsummer with copper-yellow, sweetly scented blooms. The evergreen climber *Decumaria sinensis* has deliciously honey-scented green and white flowers in spring. It needs ample support and enjoys twining through another shrub. It will probably be new to many of your guests, so remember to give it a label. *Trachelospermum asiaticum* – in my opinion hardier than *T. jasminoides*, the most frequently grown species – is a self-clinging evergreen with creamy white, scented, jasmine-like flowers in late summer.

The back door leading on to this patio garden is very nearly hidden by the flowering plants and climbers growing so lavishly in containers. This patio garden demonstrates two golden rules for success; every bit of space has been utilized and generously planted. Nothing looks worse than a few lonely plants dotted about an expanse of concrete paving.

No terrace would be complete without a climbing rose, and 'Zéphirine Drouhin' is ideal, as it is thornless, so will not catch hold of bare arms in summer. It has a wonderful perfume, and flowers continuously throughout the summer. 'Aimée Vibert' is another good choice, with dainty sprays of small white flowers, which open to display yellow stamens and show up well against a red brick wall. It is robust, fragrant and repeat flowering. 'Phyllis Bide', a climbing Polyantha rose with petals pale gold at their base becoming flushed with pink, blooms continuously throughout the summer.

You will need evergreen shrubs to give form in the winter and provide foliage for winter flower arrangements. You could choose myrtle for the sunny side and sarcococca and osmanthus for the shadier wall. I would put scented ground cover plants such as thyme, marjoram and peppermint round the base of all shrubs and roses. Small bulbs like *Iris reticulata* and the early flowering daffodils could be planted to grow through the ground cover. Larger bulbs would be inappropriate as they would create untidy moments while their leaves were dying down.

You must, of course, include shrubs with scented leaves. The old favourites of which one never tires, like rosemary and santolina, lavender and the curry-scented helichrysum, and southernwood are the best to use and they help to keep the flies away in summertime; rosemary and lavender will also attract honeybees. All these shrubs can be kept quite low and in control by pruning and shaping them in the spring.

A patio garden must have a wide variety of pots of all shapes and sizes, full to the brim with plants; wherever you see such a display of imaginatively selected and planted containers, you know immediately that the people living there must be flower lovers. In a village street in France I once saw six chimneypots, planted with all manner of herbs and scented flowers, standing at each side of an open window, while the windowsill was gay with ivy-leaf and scented pelargoniums; so much colour and fragrance in such a tiny space was absolutely stunning.

I think that there is nothing better than lilies for fragrance and elegance, and lilies grown in pots and tubs will lend an air of distinction to your terrace garden. With careful planning you can have them in bloom from summer until autumn. It is essential for lily bulbs to have good drainage so, whether you intend using pots or tubs, have enough broken crocks to make a layer 2.5cm/1in deep at the bottom of the container. Then add 2.5cm/1in well-rotted leaf mould and fill the pot with a mixture of good loam, leaf mould and coarse sand in the proportions 2:1:1, mixing in a handful each of bonemeal and wood ash. One bulb will be enough in a 20cm/8in pot; three will fit comfortably into a 30cm/12in pot. Personally I prefer using tubs; they are deeper and so better for the stem-rooting lilies. Container-grown lilies must be repotted each year, but in tubs you can leave them for two or even three years before disturbing them. Always allow at least 5cm/2in above the soil level, so you can add fresh compost to the pot as the stem-rooting varieties require it.

Choosing lilies for container growing can be confusing; they are all so lovely. A useful criterion is their order of flowering. In early summer the Asiatic hybrids such as 'Destiny', 'Enchantment' and 'Harmony' will make a brilliant show. Their colours are, respectively, lemon-yellow, orange-red and bright orange. The species lilies *L. candidum*, the Madonna lily, and *L. longiflorum*, come into flower in midsummer. The Madonna lily is the oldest lily in cultivation and produces satin-white flowers of outstanding fragrance. You must plant these bulbs the autumn before they are to flower. *L. longiflorum* from Formosa is a stem-rooting hybrid with a delicious sweet scent. *L. hansonii*, the yellow martagon lily, golden yellow with crimson spots, is a stately 120cm/48in tall and is also midsummer flowering. Nothing can better the pervading scent of

Using a collection of one type of container, in this case, a selection of earthenware crocks, glazed and unglazed, brings a unifying element to a patio garden, making widely dissimilar plants into a pleasing group.

Terraces and twilight 2

L. regale at the height of summer. The 120cm/48in stems carry large funnel-shaped flowers, pure white streaked pink inside, with golden yellow shading at the throat. *L.* 'Pink Perfection' and *L.* 'Golden Splendour' are trumpet hybrids, also stem-rooting, and highly fragrant. In late summer the *L. speciosum* hybrids, ranging in colour from pure white through to pink and crimson, are particularly remarkable for their lovely fragrance.

You must spare a space on the patio for the scented-leaf pelargoniums mentioned on pages 150–1. They all require protection in winter and an airing in the summer sunshine. The variation in the scent of their leaves is amazing, and due to the oil in the leaves they manage to survive colder nights than the zonals.

Freesias, lily of the valley, and *Gladiolus tristris* all make a fragrant contribution to the terrace garden, as will mignonette and standard lemon-scented verbena.

The evening garden

The garden in early morning, with the dew on the ground and the scent rising, has a magic only equalled by the garden in the evening, as the light fades and the warmth of the day's sun enhances the floral perfumes, and gently reflects in the flowers and foliage. This benison is something for which all gardeners who are confined during the day to city offices should be grateful, for if flowers were fragrant only by day, the weary worker would miss so much.

Colours change; in the morning light red shines out bright and clear and the blues merge into their surroundings, melting into the greens; but by evening the reds lose their piquancy, embracing a quieter tone and shifting toward the blues in the rainbow. Yellow flowers remain bright and white ones become luminous, shining like ghostly figures against a darkening green background. Grey-leaved plants assume more importance and the night-flying moths will guide you to the flowers which hold their scent till evening: to *Daphne laureola* in spring, honeysuckle and *Datura suaveolens* in summer, *Choisya ternata* in

Container-grown standard roses hold their fragrant blossoms high against the backdrop of a bay tree, while plantings of sweet-smelling lavender and thyme encircle tubs of colourful begonias and marigolds. Imagine this paved patio of a town garden without its fragrant floral dressing and you will understand how deprived our lives would be without the soothing effect of scented flowers and shrubs.

autumn and the winter-flowering hellebores.

I feel, therefore that when planning a scented garden thought should be given to allocating a patch especially for evening-scented plants. Consider where you spend the most time in the evening: sitting by an open patio door reading the papers, in the kitchen preparing a meal or reclining on your bed reading a book; a fragrant evening garden by the front door to welcome home the office worker would certainly be appreciated.

There are many plants suited to the purpose. I have the early Dutch honeysuckle and the climbing rose 'Albertine' growing round my bedroom window. The honey-bees live in the roof just above and share the honeysuckle's nectar with the night-flying moths.

You must be in your garden by about four o'clock in the afternoon to watch the Marvel of Peru, *Mirabilis jalapa*, open its flowers, for the opening mechanism is triggered off by a falling temperature. For several summers I have had pots of this standing on the southeast facing steps by the house. The sun moves off them by mid-afternoon and the flowers open – the rich fragrance of even one solitary flower announces its presence. This native of Peru, brought to Europe by the Spaniards in the 16th century, is easy to propagate, either from its hard black seeds the size of peppercorns or from its tubers. Leave the tubers in pots during the winter and keep them dry in a frost-proof frame. Repot them in spring and start them into new growth. In a frost-free climate they can be left in the ground and will reappear in spring.

Cestrum is another genus from South America which emits its scent as the temperature falls in the evening. In moderate climates it will succeed as a wall shrub, or even when growing up a pillar, and the climate in the southern United States suits it well. The species which do best for the evening garden are *C. parqui*, *C. aurantiacum* and *C. nocturnum*. *C. parqui*, from Chile, has unusual yellowish-green tubular flowers, so merging with the leaves that you may not notice them until you become aware of their fragrance. *C. aurantiacum* is a rambling shrub with bright orange flowers and certainly worth cultivating for its colour and evening scent, but in cool climates you must insure against losses by rooting a supply of cuttings each winter. *C. nocturnum* comes from the West Indies and its common name of night-blooming jessamine describes it admirably.

Colour plays a part in the scented evening garden, although the bright hues of plants like chieranthus fade with the sun. Therefore, it is necessary to bolster the

Heliotropium peruvianum is grown as a hedge in its native country Peru, and in warm climates an attempt could be made at growing this deliciously fragrant flower in this way. The tendency in Europe has been towards breeding as dark a flower as possible, which is unfortunate, as it is the paler varieties which produce the best scent. (Dark blue flowers do not usually have a strong scent. This must be becoming apparent as you study the scented plants mentioned in this book.) There is a white-flowered variety called 'White Lady', which, to my mind, is not so attractive as the pale mauves.

I class the lantanas, members of the verbena family, with heliotropes, no doubt because they are both associated with the sunshine in the south of France and with Victorian gardening books. For the most part lantana originated from the New World – Brazil and the West Indies – but *Lantana camara mutabilis* may now be seen growing vigorously in Mediterranean coastal gardens. Over the years I have

visual impact with companion plantings of purple-, blue- and white-petalled flowers as these are colours that display themselves best in the twilight.

brought cuttings back from there, and pots of lantana, with their intriguing colour mutations, adorn my garden. But since it needs to be propagated anew each year, the old plants are neglected and the frost kills them.

I associate a heavy evening scent with exotic flowers which are only half-hardy, such as the ginger plant, *Hedychium gardnerianum*, *Jasminum polyanthum*, datura and *Hoya carnosa*. All require greenhouse treatment.

There are many hardy bedding plants which reserve their scent for the evening. The annual *Matthiola bicornis* is a straggling little plant which, as is obvious by its common name of night-scented stock, comes into its own in the evening; the flowers perk up and produce a strong fragrance of honey. Most of the dianthus are also more strongly scented in the evening. The well-known tobacco plant, *Nicotiana alata* (syn. *N. affinis*) will flower continuously from midsummer until the first autumn frosts. The pale colours produce the best scent and these are the colours – white and pale rose-pink – that show up best in the evening light. I feel I must always apologise for my *N. sylvestris* when a visitor bends to smell them in the daytime.

The white and pale mauve dame's violets, *Hesperis matronalis*, mingled with the evening primrose, *Oenothera biennis*, in a wild or secret part of the garden, add an air of mystery with the pale flowers lighting up against a dark background. Both smell sweetly in the evening and are good companions, as the hesperis flowers in spring and the oenothera blooms later. Several species of the latter are native to North America: the delightful *O. missouriensis*, a low perennial with buttercup-yellow flowers opening in late afternoon; *O. californica* and *O. caespitosa eximia*, both good for rockeries.

Another flower which shows up well in the evening light, and looks almost ghost-like, is the white-flowered californian tree poppy, *Romneya coulteri*. It hates to be disturbed, but once established will romp away, so choose the right home for it, near a wall or at the edge of the garden. The grey leaves add an air of distinction to the overall appearance and the crinkly white flowers give off an exotic perfume – but only in the evening.

Hemerocallis flava, the day lily, and its hybrids, bear flowers of varying shades of yellow which have a rich honeysuckle scent in the evening. Try planting it in a shady corner into which the sun does not penetrate at all – the same sort of situation that you would choose for ferns.

Nearly all phlox smell good, but for the evening garden I would certainly choose the white and very pale cultivars of *P. maculata* and *P. paniculata*, both for their scent and for their luminosity in the evening light.

Thinking of flowering shrubs for the evening garden, we come back to white yet again. Philadelphus and viburnum, syringa and elaeagnus, clethra and osmanthus all have white flowers and are among the most sweetly scented of flowering shrubs. Certainly they are fragrant by day, but their evening scent is more pronounced.

Scented screens

In my garden the prevailing wind comes from the west. Thankfully, it is a fairly gentle wind and carries with it the smell of new-mown hay and green pastures. But this did not prevent me, twenty years ago, planting a boundary hedge of beech. How I wish that I had been more imaginative and used a scented shrub. By now it would be well established, wafting its fragrance into the garden. A scented hedge would be a useful and welcome addition to most gardens, providing a fragrant backdrop to containers on a patio, isolating a secluded

A tall hedge of *Thuya plicata* and a scented climber, weaving its way through a wooden screen, ensure privacy in a secluded part of the garden.

corner of the garden, or simply serving to mark property boundaries.

The plants that you choose for this purpose should have the following characteristics: they should be tough; tall enough to offer protection from the wind; tidy and defined, and able to be clipped without sacrificing the flowers which provide the scent. Quite a difficult choice – but not impossible.

Berberis julianae would be suitable as it is evergreen, dense, 3m/10ft tall at maturity, utterly hardy, and, when in flower in late spring, it produces an amazingly sweet scent for such a thorny, abrasive shrub.

Of course, box hedges have a scent, but planting them is planting for posterity as they take their time, and longevity is the virtue of their slow growth. The box hedges in my garden, over 100 years old and 2.5m/8ft high, were planted by a far-sighted 19th-century clergyman. Obviously, do not choose box if your problem is immediate.

A shrub used by the Romans in the gardens of their villas, and whose praises I wish to sing, is phillyrea, particularly *P. angustifolia* and *P. latifolia*. The former is at least 3m/10ft high at maturity and the latter can become a small tree, but both can be clipped for hedges. The small white flowers appear in summer and have a sweet honey-like fragrance. Phillyrea is reputedly very hardy; to be evergreen is a virtue for hedges and to be scented is an added attraction.

A scented windbreak could well be planted to become as colourful as a tapestry by using together berberis, phillyrea, *Thuya plicata* (which has the scent of ripe apples and parsley), golden privet, osmanthus and *Escallonia rubra macrantha*, one of the best hedging shrubs to withstand sea gales.

There is a subtle difference between hedging and screening. To make a quick screen to hide, say, an oil tank in your own garden I suggest putting up a wooden trellis and covering it with several honeysuckles, among them the semi-evergreen *Lonicera americana*, vigorous and well scented, and flowering in midsummer; *L. japonica* 'Halliana' and the early and late Dutch honeysuckles. Between them the tank should soon disappear.

If the object you wish to screen is in your neighbour's garden, you should use a small tree such as *Eucalyptus gunnii*, kept trimmed to the required height. *Crataegus monogyna*, a flowering cherry or crab, or *Clerodendron trichotomum*

Balcony gardens often suffer from over-exposure to the sun. A fragrant solution to the problem is to build a pergola over one end of the balcony and clothe it with a dense-growing climber. Be sure to use a deciduous climber as an evergreen will block out the warmth of the sun's rays during winter.

are suitable alternatives. The leaves of the latter have an unpleasant smell if crushed, but the flowers in late summer have a surprisingly pleasant fragrance.

If you want to blot out an ugly building in the distance, and your garden is large enough, there are three poplars the leaves of which are aromatic as they unfurl in spring. These are *Populus × acuminata, P. balsamifera* and the fastest-growing of all balsam poplars, the 'Black Cottonwood', *P. trichocarpa*, all of which are native to North America. On a wet day with the wind blowing gently through these trees, the scent is medicinal, resinous and exciting.

There often comes a special moment when visitors to my garden remark on the different aromas that reach them. One such is when they walk along the rosemary hedge surrounding the knot garden which is clipped twice a year, and past the hedge made of *Rosa rugosa*. This was originally planted as a windbreak and has now become a fragrant feature of the garden.

This, too, is regularly clipped to keep it neat and compact, as otherwise the flowers would only bloom on unattractive, tall lanky shoots that would be too high to smell.

Around the corner is a long edging of southernwood, the most easily cultivated of the artemisias. Clipped as often as you wish, it will still make new growth but – and most importantly – it is essential to cut it almost to ground level in early spring. In my garden southernwood acts as a deterrent to greenfly and to black spot on nearby rose bushes.

Any aromatic grey shrub will make a wonderful low hedge to edge pathways or create a new atmosphere in the garden layout. Lavender, of course, should be used in all its varieties, pink, dark mauve and the paler mauve 'Dwarf Munstead'. The curry plant, *Helichrysum serotinum* (syn. *H. angustifolium*), with small yellow flowers, and *H. italicum*, the dwarf form, always have a strong scent, but especially so after a shower of rain.

Winter wonders

One day last January I had a visitor from Wisconsin in the United States. Although it was still winter, he was entranced by the sheer number of different flowers already in bloom in my garden. He explained, I think somewhat ruefully, that the harsh winters would not permit him such a splendid show in his own garden at that time of the year. Yet with thoughtful planning and careful protection for the plants, he could manage a pleasing display a month or two later, after the thaw set in. Like me, he feels that the extra trouble is repaid by the charm of seeing the first flowers emerge.

The best site for winter-flowering plants is near the house, where you can see and enjoy them without having to make a sortie to the end of the garden on a cold winter's day. Several of the gardens which I admire most have groups, or even entire beds, of winter plants between the house and the front gate. So let us imagine we are creating a garden like this in an area around the driveway. The first thing is to define your bed with a low wall to prevent cars driving on to it.

If you have space for a small tree, give it a position at the back, in the corner, at least 1.8m/6ft away from the boundary fence or wall. *Prunus mume*, the Japanese apricot, a native of China, is a delightful small tree with single, almond-scented pink flowers that generally open in late winter. This could be underplanted with early bulbs, such as dark blue grape hyacinths or a carpet of *Chionodoxa luciliae* 'Pink Giant'. Although growing at the back of the border, they will be blooming and in view before the deciduous shrubs form their leaves. I like to have a mixture of evergreens with deciduous shrubs. The evergreens provide form and shape where the shape of the shrubs has to be sacrificed in pruning to produce the maximum number of flowers.

The two evergreens I would choose for shade are mahonia and skimmia. Try to buy a well-developed specimen of mahonia; the bush is a slow starter, but once established will not look back. *Mahonia lomariifolia*, reaching an ultimate height of 3m/10ft, starts flowering in midwinter and continues producing superbly scented flowers for at least ten weeks. I have *M. japonica* against a northwest-facing wall and

Some of the summer's most sweetly scented flowers assume an important role in the winter garden. The flowers of the *Skimmia japonica* in the foreground have developed into clusters of bright red berries.

Oh, how good the
snapping and the
crackle
Of the frost that daily
grows more keen!
Laden with its dazzling
icy roses,
The white-flaming bush
is forced to lean
Anna Akhamatova

The last rose of summer,
caught by the first frosts,
heralds the onset of
winter, when flowers and
plants especially chosen
for their beauty and
fragrance at this time of
year come into their
own.

from January right through until March it
sends out its lily of the valley fragrance for
yards around; I prefer its scent out of doors to in
the house. The leaves are very prickly so do not
plant it in a position where it will be brushed
against. For half-shade choose skimmia. If you
have space for only one plant then probably
'Foremanii' or *S. reevesiana* would be most
suitable. Both should give you plenty of
sweetly scented white flowers in spring, and
the berries are a brilliant red, adding colour on
winter days. With more space you can plant
both a male and a female plant to ensure a mass
of berries on the female. Put generous clumps
of yellow crocus under the mahonia and white
ones under and around the skimmia.

Daphne laureola also likes a little shade –
think of its common name, daphne of the
woods. The habit is most appealing, with
leathery dark green leaves growing in well-
organized rosettes, and green flowers deliciously scented in the evening. For a bonus you
will always find seedlings around, as you will
with *D. mezereum* in its pink or more unusual
white form. I wish my garden had some
pockets of acid soil so that I could grow a few
of the lime-hating plants. I have tried *D. odora*
and it survived for four years, during which
time it gave enormous pleasure, its rich scent
permeating the air. The variety with a gold-
edged leaf is the prettiest when not in flower,
and also the toughest.

If the bed is large enough I suggest you use
shrubs with coloured stems – not scented, you
will say – but the red stems of *Cornus* 'Sibirica'
show up well against the evergreens. In the
sunnier part of the bed plant *Chimonanthus
fragrans*, at the back since it looks a bit coarse in
the summer. Two or three viburnums could
span the winter months, *V. farreri* and
V. × bodnantense for midwinter blooms and
V. × burkwoodii and *V. carlesii* for late winter to
early spring. A shrub which gives me endless
pleasure is *Hebe* 'Mrs Winder'. The narrow
leaves enable it to put up with much harder
frost than some of the speciosa hybrids. It is a
bush which is in flower almost every month of
the year as long as you find time to dead-head it.
The leaves have a very attractive plum-purple
tinge which is particularly noticeable in winter,
and the scent of the darkish blue flowers is
remarkable. Underplant it with *Iris reticulata*.

The whole of the front of this border I
would fill with violets, winter-flowering pansies, *Helleborus orientalis*, primroses and dwarf
narcissi, violas and cyclamen, and a clump of
Iris unguicularis, giving it plenty of grit in the
soil for good drainage.

Do not forget the leaf scents: lavender,
santolina, artemisia, eucalyptus clipped to keep
it low, rosemary and the sticky-leafed *Cistus
ladanifer*. The shape and form of the garden in
winter is almost more important than it is in the
summer; it can raise your spirits by its beauty,
or make you long for the summer by its
barrenness.

Fragrant exotica

Gardeners have always been tempted by the lure of unusual plants, and have provided the objects of their affection with elaborately constructed glasshouses, in an effort to create a climate conducive to unhindered and happy growth.

The Romans knew that if grape-vines were protected the fruit could be ripened out of season, and the Emperor Tiberius, prescribed a cucumber a day for his health, housed the plants in special growing frames: pits filled with rotted dung and covered with translucent sheets of mica.

In 1550 a special house was built at the botanic garden in Padua for overwintering tender plants and later, in 1620, Salomon de Caus designed a movable wooden structure to cover 400 orange trees at Heidelberg. In England also the concern was for protecting citrus fruits, rather than tender ornamental plants, and it was John Evelyn who first used the term 'greenhouse' to describe the building which housed 'greens' – plants without winter flowers. And the 'conservatory' was, literally, to conserve plants. John Rea, writing in 1676, directed that tender plants which grew in greenhouses during winter should, 'on fairer days be acquainted with the sun and air'. In 1700 Mary, first Duchess of Beaufort, had a stove-house constructed at Badminton to house her collection of rare plants and succulents from South Africa.

As the popularity of gardening as a pastime increased, plants were more frequently grown for the sake of their beauty than for their practical uses. Eventually by the early 19th century, gardening authorities, such as John Loudon and Walter Nicol, were advocating the cultivation of exotic plants, and insisting on sound methods of conservatory and greenhouse gardening. They decreed that a glasshouse was an essential feature of a gentleman's home. In 1845 the tax on glass in Britain was removed. As you can imagine, this had an immediate effect on the number of glasshouses constructed. In order to have rose blooms all through the year, special houses for growing roses became popular.

Humphry Repton, who in the last years of the 18th century did much to return flowers to gardens, suggested that the smell of the earth in the glasshouse might be stronger than the scent of the flowers, but he was clearly proved wrong. Conservatories were built to adjoin ladies' boudoirs, so that they could walk among the exotic and scented plants at any time of the day, without going out of doors. Mrs Loudon, and later Shirley Hibberd, wrote especially for ladies. Keeping abreast of recent introductions, they included among their favourite plants mignonette, pelargoniums, aloysia, fuchsias, mimosa, bouvardia, jasmine, balsam, climbing lapagerias, verbena, datura and many ornamental bulbs.

The 19th century was the age of invention and spectacular feats of architectural engineering created some of the most fabulous greenhouses ever seen. In 1836 Joseph Paxton designed and started construction of the Great Conservatory at Chatsworth, seat of the Duke of Devonshire. This breath-taking structure served as a model for the Crystal Palace built in 1851 for the Great Exhibition in London. Several years before this, in 1848, the Palm House at the Royal Botanic Gardens, Kew was constructed and fifty years later a replica of it was built in the grounds of the New York Botanical Garden.

With Victorian attention to detail and pre-occupation with 'modern engineering', the fuelling systems in these glasshouses were so designed that no unpleasant sights would reach the eyes of visitors, and unobtrusive flues carried the smoke well away from the buildings. There were hidden doors so that the gardeners could slip away unnoticed when the owners or visitors arrived.

Shirley Hibberd wrote, 'A conservatory should be a garden under glass, and a place for frequent resort, agreeable at all seasons,' and although it is unlikely that the clock will be put back to the Victorian days of cheap fuel and labour, our modern technology has provided small efficient greenhouses, easy to maintain. Plastic covering, double glazing, mist propagation, soil heating cables, automatic ventilation and clever devices for watering all help to put greenhouse gardening and, consequently, the marvels of exotic flowers and plants, within the reach of most keen gardeners. For those without gardens, floor-to-ceiling glass doors and windows leading on to patios and balconies are a boon. I am always impressed with the good health of plants grown in front of such large expanses of glass. If scented shrubs and climbers are planted immediately outside, on summer evenings the scent will waft deliciously into the room, while inside the sweetly scented *Hoya carnosa*, *Humea elegans*, stephanotis and scented pelargoniums will perfume the room.

In the 19th century no garden was considered complete without a conservatory, and the cultivation of exotic flowering plants became a popular pastime.

Delicate climbing roses like 'Maréchal Niel' and other scented climbers were trained up the walls of the conservatories and fragrant plants such as heliotrope were grown in pots so that they could be easily moved into the house. The engraving, *far left*, from Cassell's *Family Magazine* of 1891 shows that conservatory gardening was a respectable family affair.

It is known that the ancient Chinese were skilled horticulturalists and that the royal gardens of the emperors surpassed any in Europe during the 10th and 11th centuries.

Tender plants were carefully cultivated and their flowers used to make restrained yet elaborate floral arrangements such as that shown, *left*, in a 19th-century scroll painting.

The plants to grow

Aponogeton distachyus, the water hawthorn, although indigenous to the Cape of Good Hope and Australia, is quite hardy in cool climates. Once established, it is a long-lived plant: I know of one specimen that has been growing in a garden pool for over half a century.

It is an interesting and attractive plant for a small patio pool. It will also do well in a tub, which brings its delicate fragrance closer to appreciative noses. Plant the tuberous rhizomes in mud 25cm/10in below the water surface, so that the strap-shaped leaves lie flat on the water. If your pond is not as deep as this, do not worry, water hawthorn is most accommodating and will manage in much shallower water. The vanilla-scented flowers are pure white and stand on forked stems above the surface of the water, appearing regularly from spring through to autumn, if mild days continue. There are two points to remember. The plants love clean water, so if you plant them in tubs, add a can of rain water daily to float dust and dirt over the sides. This, I am told, is like a tonic to them. Secondly they do not combine well with water snails, so do not think that these will do the cleansing job for you – the snails will eat the young shoots.

Although you need to possess a stove house, or else live in the temperate zone, to be able to grow your own frankincense and myrrh, the valuable gifts given to the infant Christ in Bethlehem, it is, nevertheless, interesting to know their provenance.

Boswellia carteri, an evergreen tree from Arabia and East Africa produces a gum, bled from its trunk, which is an ingredient of frankincense.

Myrrh comes from *Commiphora myrrha*, a small shrub or tree native to Arabia and Ethiopia. The aromatic resin is taken from the stems and young shoots and used in incense. The very best resin or balm is squeezed from the green berries.

Balm of Gilead, the common name given to *Cedronella triphylla*, a member of the labiate family, is a half-hardy herb. It is well worth growing in a pot for its leaves smell strongly and pleasantly of camphor mixed with turpentine. It is easy to cultivate and should be treated as any other half-hardy shrub; take cuttings in the autumn, overwinter these under glass and repot them in spring, ready to be placed outdoors on the patio. During the winter the plant can be kept on a warm windowsill,

perhaps in the bathroom. In a frost-free place the Balm of Gilead will reach a height of 150cm/60in.

When times were more leisurely and labour and heating less costly, bouvardia was a popular flower for bouquets and buttonholes; a perfect way to enjoy the marvellous fragrance – a blend of jasmine and honey. It is a native of Mexico and South America and so must be kept comfortably warm during winter (minimum temperature 18°C/65°F). The white species, *Bouvardia longiflora*; *B. jasminiflora* and *B. humboldtii corymbiflora* are all especially fragrant and make splendid potted plants. When in flower the plants may be moved outside to a warm patio. Bouvardia must be hard pruned in the autumn to encourage new growth, as it flowers on young wood.

Seeds of *Dregia sinensis* – I call it wattakaka, a more resonant name – were given to me some years ago by a friend who lives in Malta and has a resplendent plant growing up her garden wall. The seeds germinated and the plants flourished almost embarrassingly in my cool greenhouse, and I have since given many away. The story is always the same from satisfied

Eucharis grandiflora

Aponogeton distachyus

recipients: *D. sinensis* romps away in summer, would take over the greenhouse if given the chance, and blooms profusely, its highly scented white flowers filling the greenhouse with fragrance. It should be cut hard back in the autumn, leaving only a few new green shoots; then, as the spring days come, the shoots will lengthen, needing daily attention to keep them twined and trained. A friend of mine keeps European tree frogs in her greenhouse. The frogs love the nectar from the white flowers as it attracts flies, the frogs' main diet. I have seen

the plant growing outdoors in southwestern England on a sheltered south wall, protected from winter frosts by bracken round its roots and lowest shoots.

Having seen and smelled *Eucharis grandiflora*, the Amazon lily, growing in a Kenyan garden, I long to have a few bulbs to grow in a pot. They need the same treatment as hippeastrums, with plenty of moisture when in growth and a drier period after flowering. The flower stems are each 45cm/18in long with four to five narcissus-like white flowers, faintly tinted

green. This lily is still only a dream in my Cotswold garden, but then this to me is the joy of gardening: there is always something to look forward to.

I have no experience of growing gardenias, just a happy childhood memory of their velvet petals and luxurious fragrance, for they were the fashionable flowers of my mother's time. Sadly, they are now only associated with warm greenhouse cultivation. *Gardenia jasminoides* has bright, glossy green leaves and white flowers which open in late summer and autumn. Given the right conditions it is very free flowering, requiring a lime-free compost and plenty of light – but not direct sunlight. The plants must never dry out or be allowed to stand in water, and they like only rain water. Flower buds will not develop unless the minimum temperature is at least 16°C/60°F, and they are apt to drop if the temperature fluctuates or the watering programme is not consistent. When in their natural surroundings, gardenias bloom for months on end and form decorative evergreen bushes. In the south of France in summer you can see them growing in pots on terraces; they are overwintered under glass or otherwise very well protected. However, in cooler climates they are best kept always indoors. Young plants are more floriferous than old specimens, and there is no difficulty in taking cuttings.

Then, with the falling of dusk,
The scent of Mignonette and Musk
Will all the air enshroud.

There are many plants that will provide a gracious perfume at sunset and some of them make ideal potted plants because they require the special attention that indoor cultivation

Gardenia jasminoides

Bouvardia longiflora

allows. I was given large potted plants of *Hedychium gardnerianum* and *Hoya carnosa* on the same day at least twelve years ago.

My usual treatment of hedychium is to over-winter it in a frost-free greenhouse, keeping it dry. By spring its ration of water is increased and soon new, stout shoots appear from the rhizomes. The plants are placed outside from spring onwards, grow quite quickly, and by midsummer the flower buds show at the ends of the thick, reed-like stems, 1.2–1.5m/4–5ft long. The lemon-yellow flowers have bright scarlet filaments, and hedychium makes an exciting impact as a special plant standing on the patio. The fragrance is sweet, heavy and all-pervading. Indeed, two flower spikes standing indoors overnight will probably cause half the household to wake up with a headache – something I learned the hard way – but out of doors the scent is more dispersed and altogether more pleasant. Hedychium is very easy to increase by division of the rhizomes in early spring, which is also the best time for repotting to provide good drainage and a rich compost.

Hoya carnosa, the wax flower, is a vigorous climber from Queensland, Australia and from China, and a subject for the cool greenhouse. Its long shoots are made heavy by thick, oval, fleshy leaves, but it is one of the easiest plants to train as it seems impossible to break the stems, however much you twist and turn them. You can either train them along the roof of the greenhouse, or else make a framework of bamboo in a large pot and twine the long stems firmly around this. There is an obvious right and wrong side to each shoot; the leaves face you, the right way or turn their backs, the wrong way. If you train them right sides facing, then the heavily scented flowers will tend to hang toward you too.

Each pink flower bud is shaped like a five-pointed star, opening from the centre as though each petal were the flap of an envelope. The flowers are white inside and, as the day goes on, large drops of nectar develop, enticing insects to aid pollination. My hoya has never set any seed so presumably the right insects do not live in Britain. The flowers are in umbels on a stout stalk or stump; this you must never remove or you will be robbing yourself of future flowers. Each year the stump gets a little longer. Hoya tends to flower best with a restricted root run. Water the plants sparingly in winter, increase the amount as the days get longer, and feed them regularly during the summer.

H. bella is easier to accommodate but I find it more difficult to get it to flower. It is a dwarf shrub with pendant branches about 30cm/12in long, and has small clusters of exquisite rose-crimson flowers with a dark centre and a scent like honey. It needs plenty of moisture, so is a good little plant for the bathroom or the kitchen windowsill.

Humea elegans has an unmistakable aroma of incense; every part of the plant is scented, and in late summer the scent is intoxicating. So why is the plant so seldom seen? *H. elegans* is admittedly not the easiest of plants to grow and for advice I approached William Taylor, head gardener at Shute House in Dorset, who is noted for his success with humea, and this is what he told me. Sow the seed, which must be fresh, in early winter, covering it with a very thin layer of sand. Water sparingly and there-after keep seeds and seedlings out of a damp situation. The seed is very tiny and will take

three to four weeks to germinate in a temperature of 16°C/60°F.

As seedlings grow, the temperature may be slightly reduced. When they are about 5cm/2in high with four leaves, pot on in a garden compost, taking care to provide good drainage in the pots. At the final potting, add a layer of rotted manure above the drainage. Never stand these plants outside until early summer, and then they should be staked and protected from wind. A warning: the leaves of humea bring some people out in a rash.

Jasminum polyanthum is one of the joys of my greenhouse and one of my favourite plants. I firmly believe that, as with all good things, you can acquire an especially good strain of this jasmine. I saw it growing in a pot, so covered with bloom that you could scarcely see the leaves. I took cuttings, and from this beginning I now have a stock plant which grows in a pot and is trained over a trellis in the greenhouse. After it flowers in the spring, I clip it hard back to its support, then during the summer it has regular feeding to encourage new side growths, which will carry next year's flower trusses. The flower buds are pale pink, opening white, but it is the rich, luxurious scent which counts. This variety grows wonderfully outdoors in gardens in warm Mediterranean countries, but in cool climates older plants can be trained round bamboo or hoops.

I love *J. mesnyi* (syn. *J. primulinum*) too, with its pretty yellow, delicately scented flowers on stiff stems. In cool climates it is almost hardy

Nymphaea odorata

Hoya carnosa

but needs some warmth during winter.

Although every reference to *Nerium oleander* warns you how poisonous all parts of it are, I still enjoy the faint but sweet perfume of the white and pink blooms. These appear in summer and autumn on my pot-grown plants, which have all come from cuttings taken on holidays in Italy and France, where the oleander flowers in profusion; cuttings root so easily –even in a glass of water. After potting, pinch out any too-vigorous shoots to achieve a well-shaped bush. Oleander needs plenty of moisture and responds to a tonic of foliar feed given during the warmer months of the year.

Hardy water-lilies are the aristocrats of the aquatic garden, displaying their elegant blooms from early summer until the first autumn frost, opening in the morning and closing up in the late afternoon or evening, according to the amount of sunshine. Although several varieties of *Nymphaea odorata* have a sweet scent, this does not always carry well on the air, and may go unnoticed. However, the flowers can be

Hedychium gardnerianum

Nerium oleander

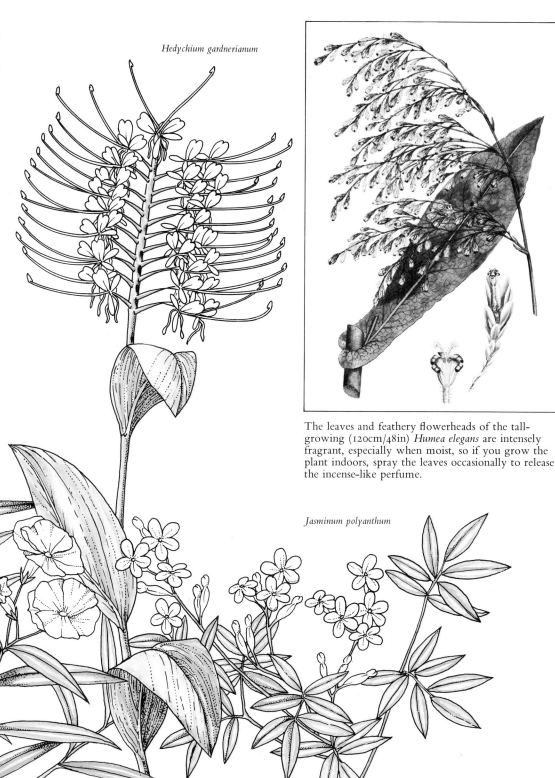

The leaves and feathery flowerheads of the tall-growing (120cm/48in) *Humea elegans* are intensely fragrant, especially when moist, so if you grow the plant indoors, spray the leaves occasionally to release the incense-like perfume.

Jasminum polyanthum

picked, and a bloom floating in a flat bowl indoors brings the refreshing scent well within reach. Scented water-lilies have either white, pale to dark pink or yellow flowers, and you can choose between a large-flowered variety with 25cm/10in blooms, or a miniature for a tiny pool. All of these are perennial; their leaves and stems completely disappear in the winter. They love sunshine and still water and must be planted in the correct depth of water.

You should plant water-lily roots in the spring, just as they are starting into growth. Put them in soil, either at the bottom of a natural pond, or in boxes or baskets in an artificial pond. Plastic baskets are inexpensive and preferable to natural fibre baskets as they last for years and very soon become hidden. Fill the container with soil to within 5cm/2in of the basket top. Put the root into the soil, leaving the crown uncovered. Add a final layer of gravel or small stones to keep the soil from floating away – then all is ready to lower into the pond.

Mature leaves die back and are quickly replaced by new growth. If possible, it is a good thing to cut off the dead flower heads and leaves before they sink to the bottom of your pond and cause an accumulation of decaying vegetable matter.

It is easiest to classify the various water-lilies according to colour. There is one scented hardy yellow, *N. odorata sulphurea grandiflora*, with deep yellow flowers standing well up above the water surface. It has long, pointed petals and the leaves are attractively mottled with chocolate-brown. This lily needs at least 60cm/24in of water, preferably more.

If you have a really deep pool then the best white to choose is *N. alba*, which will grow in 3m/10ft of water; it is quite unsuitable for small pools. The star-shaped flowers are richly scented. *N. marliacea* 'Albida' is a very reliable hybrid and will grow in even deeper water. The best white for a small pool is the strongly fragrant *N. caroliniana nivea* which will manage with only 30cm/12in of water. *N. odorata alba* is happy in similar conditions, while the white *N. odorata minor* needs only 15–20cm/6–8in, so it is the most suitable for a trough in the patio garden.

There is also a range of pale and blush pinks suitable for shallow water: *N. odorata* 'Luciana' and 'Rosea', pearly pink with a strong scent; *N. odorata* 'W.B. Shaw' is very like 'Rosea' but larger and it will do well in only 45cm/18in of

water. For a pool 60cm/24in deep choose *N. caroliniana rosea* with lovely flesh-pink flowers and coppery foliage.

For a deeper pink flower you should choose *N.* 'Laydekeri Rosea' or *N.* 'Rose Arey'; both need 30cm/12in of water, or more, and have a delicious scent. *N. odorata* 'Helen Fowler' has large, perfectly shaped flowers coloured deep rose and a strong perfume.

Although most of the tropical lilies prefer warmth throughout their growing season, they may be grown outside if started in a warm greenhouse during winter. They can then be placed outside in large, waterproof tubs in summer, when they will flower. If you have a conservatory or a warm, sheltered garden, you could grow one of the scented varieties, such as *N. caerulea*, the blue lotus of the Nile.

When one thinks of exotic plants, orchids immediately spring to mind. But they are not difficult to grow indoors if the right conditions are provided. One of the best species for the purpose is *Odontoglossum grande*, a native of Guatemala. The flowers are very large, up to 12cm/5in across, richly fragrant and coloured yellow with chocolate markings. A healthy plant will produce up to five flowers on one stem.

The plant comes into growth in late spring and should be regularly watered throughout summer. When the flowers appear, give the plant plenty of light, but do not put it in too warm a spot as it prefers a cool atmosphere.

Growing scented-leaf pelargoniums can provide tremendous pleasure. Although they need protection from frost, they take up little space in the cool greenhouse and make excellent foliage houseplants. They put up with central heating and are quite at home in the bathroom or on the kitchen windowsill, provided they have enough light. Stand them outside on the patio in the summer or bed them out, and they will appreciate it. The more robust varieties such as *P. graveolens* and *P. tomentosum* will make large specimens 60cm/24in wide and equally as tall by the autumn, if planted in a border, and will probably be too large to pot up again! So remember to take your cuttings in late summer, because the most difficult time to propagate geranium cuttings is during the short winter days, when they are likely to damp off before roots have grown.

My favourite is 'Mabel Grey' with a strong citrus smell. Put one of the softly textured leaves in your pocket to carry the scent around

with you. 'Mabel Grey' likes only rain water; she has a positive dislike of hard, limy chlorinated tap water. Now that I know this, I get on better with her. Second choice is *P. graveolens*, one of the most useful for its marvellous ability to survive and reproduce itself – as well as for its deliciously orange-scented leaves, a necessary ingredient for pot pourri. The cream and green variegated form of this is called 'Lady Plymouth' and has a definite rose scent, so lovely in a pot close to hand. *P. radula* has leaves that should be used for flavouring sponge cakes and custard. It is easily distinguished by its narrow, divided leaves and a lemony-rose fragrance. The spicy leaves of *P. quercifolium* are dark green with a darker marking in the centre and are shaped like those of an oak. I like the scent for its mossy, pungent quality.

Polianthes tuberosa

For association, I must have 'Clorinda', with large rose-pink flowers and a surprising cedar-like perfume.

Then there is *P. fragrans* and its variegated form, both with white flowers and a clean pine scent. There are many more: 'Prince of Orange', 'Joy Lucille' and 'Attar of Roses' to name a few; it would be so easy to become an enthusiast with a comprehensive collection. But my final choice, and perhaps almost as good as 'Mabel Grey', is *P. tomentosum*, with lovely velvety leaves and peppermint smell.

Unfortunately *Plumeria* needs hot-house conditions to prosper, but visitors to tropical countries have repeatedly been impressed by its delicious jasmine-like perfume. Known commonly as frangipani, this small tree seems to be in flower all through the year. The blossoms are white, pink and deep rose, and each flower keeps its scent long after it is picked.

Polianthes tuberosa is a native of Mexico which bears scented flowers in racemes at the ends of leafy stalks. It was the source of the decidedly Victorian perfume 'Tuberose' and, according to Shelley, it was 'the sweetest flower for scent that blows'. Plant the bulbs in March in pots with bottom heat.

One of my favourite springtime scents is that of *Prostanthera sieberi*, the Australian mint bush. The slender shoots of this plant have small but strongly perfumed leaves which release a sweet mint scent when crushed. The purple flowers are scented too. It is a small, almost hardy bush, and I grow it in a large pot which can be put under cover if frost persists.

I was fortunate to see the Queen of the Night, *Selenicereus grandiflora*, in bloom one still evening by the Mediterranean. It was wonderful to gaze upon and the scent was intoxicating. It was an old plant, full of buds ready to open on successive nights. But this night-flowering cactus only survives if the minimum temperature is 10°C/50°F.

I envy my friends who have succeeded with *Stephanotis floribunda*. This fragrant beauty with waxy flowers needs plenty of space for root growth, a lot of sunshine and warmth, enough water in summer and less in winter, and trellis or canes to twine around. Old plants flower better than young ones.

Trachelospermum is an evergreen climber, hardy in warm gardens; the Cape Jasmine, *T. jasminoides*, has fragrant white flowers in the autumn.

Selenicereus grandiflora

Stephanotis floribunda

Odontoglossum grande

Pelargonium 'Clorinda'

Perfume with a view

A keen gardener whose verdant 'sward' happens to be the balcony of a town apartment can achieve, with a little imagination, as much as another person would in a fair-sized garden. Designing a balcony garden is rather like arranging a stage set: success lies in getting the maximum use from the minimum of space. Props are all important, and must be chosen carefully. For example, the railings of the balcony, if painted, should be either black or white; use a colour and you run the risk of unsightly clashes – imagine trying to choose a green that would suit the many shades of foliage. Also, everything will be seen at close quarters and must be perfect; in this respect the maintenance of a praiseworthy balcony garden is as intensive as that of a show garden open to the public. The plant supports and containers must be well cared for and the plants well tended: no dead flowerheads allowed!

Balcony gardens usually have quite a lot of wall space, so begin by putting well-made trellises on to every spare space on the wall; you will not want climbers flopping over you.

Provide a means to grow hanging plants. If there is no overhang to take hooks and baskets, brackets on walls or railings are a good alternative. It is wise to put as much on the walls as possible since you thereby reduce the weight and stress on the balcony itself. If you are at all concerned about how much weight the balcony can take, you would be wise to contact the architect or owner of the building.

Do not use containers just because you already have them. Remember that this is your special garden and deserves the best you can afford – would you decorate a room with left-over odds and ends of paint, just because you had some in the cupboard? Rectangular containers fit neatly together, and enough should be acquired to go around the base of the railings. Different levels should be created by using some containers that are taller than others. If the containers are made of wood, make sure they are soundly constructed and treated with a wood preservative of the type that will not harm plants. Troughs made of composition material are lighter in weight and can be so well disguised that you cannot distinguish them from the real thing.

On a small balcony a judicious use of trellis, troughs and tubs will provide the interested gardener with the space to grow a variety of scented plants which will, in summer when the windows are open, fill the room with their fragrance.

Make quite sure that all the containers have adequate drainage; on no account must water be allowed to lie stagnant at the bottom of the containers, as this will drown the roots and kill the plants.

Most of the plants we buy nowadays are growing in a peat-based compost, with no soil. They do very well in this until they have used up all the available nutrients, then they have nothing left to live on. It will be the same if you buy a peat-based potting compost to fill the containers on your balcony. Good garden compost may be purchased from gardening centres, but this can be an expensive way to fill a large number of containers; it would be better to use good garden soil mixed as follows: two parts soil to one part peat and one part coarse sand or grit. Fertilizers should be added and I recommend that you use the slow release type which will continue to feed the plants for three months, but must then be renewed. To give plants an extra boost, buy a bottle of foliar feed and use it according to the manufacturer's instructions. Remember that foliar feed is an instant tonic, absorbed through the leaves, whereas a granular fertilizer is absorbed through the roots and takes longer to benefit the plant.

Put the containers in position on the balcony, cover the drainage holes with clean pebbles or broken pottery crocks. Half fill them with soil and then put the plants you have chosen into their prospective home. Stand back and consider whether you have selected the right position for containers and plants. Will climbers have adequate support? Can the sun reach the sun-loving plants? Are any plants creating shade where you do not wish it? Ask yourself these questions and consider your scheme carefully. When you have reached the right balance, complete the planting.

With a limited space you must keep the plants well trimmed, and when they have done their best for you, they should be discarded in favour of new ones. Every day of the year you must tend the plants, seeing they are kept free of aphids and other insect pests and do not suffer from lack of moisture or food. For convenience and for the welfare of the plants, a tap with a hosepipe on the balcony is almost essential. Water the plants regularly in summer and on really hot days spray the foliage and also soak the outside of the pots. Above all do not forget to feed the plants regularly, especially in the growing season.

A vertical herb garden was the answer for this gardener who found that it is not necessary to have a plot of land to grow the plants desired. Imagination and creativity are as much a part of gardening as seeds and soil. If you are seriously interested in growing plants, allow these qualities to assert themselves and you should be able to overcome what might, at first, seem a problem.

Heightened scents

Often the scent we wish to enjoy is at our feet – spring violets or primroses nestling under shrubs or in the hedgerow, and the scented cyclamen in the woods. If you bring these delicious fragrances into your garden why not plant them so you can delight in their perfume without having to get down on your knees?

There are several practical ways that this can be achieved. You can make a raised bed with local stone or brick, or even build one from old railway sleepers laid on edge. It is essential to keep your eyes open for material that would otherwise be thrown on to a dump; if you have no use for it today – then store it away until inspiration comes to you tomorrow.

Wide raised beds should be free-standing so that you can walk all around them to tend and enjoy the plants. But where beds are built up against an existing high wall, they should be no wider than you can reach across – 1.2m/4ft is quite wide enough.

Then there are the old stone watering troughs, hard to come by these days but worth their weight in gold when you find them. Often they are rather shallow, so only suitable for shallow-rooting and drought-resistant plants. Old enamel/porcelain kitchen sinks (replaced by modern stainless steel) are becoming rare, but may be found at demolition sites and builders' yards. If you find one, snap it up; you can cover the outside surface in the following way, and texture it to resemble stone.

Wash the sink to remove any trace of grease and paint it over with a mixture of 1 part ceramic tile adhesive and 1 part water. It should then have a matt finish. Mix 2 parts clean sand to 1 part peat and 1 part cement. Put about one-third of this mixture into the remaining adhesive and add water until the mixture is wet enough not to crumble, but dry enough not to slip off the smooth surface of the sink. A flat

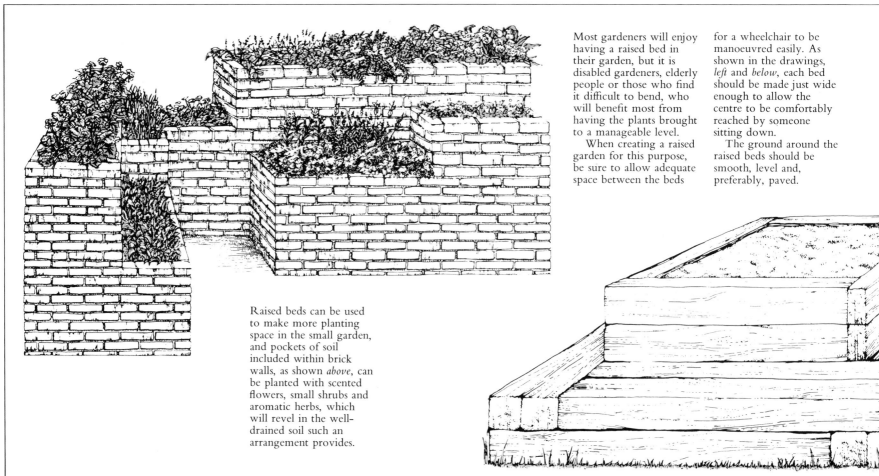

Raised beds can be used to make more planting space in the small garden, and pockets of soil included within brick walls, as shown *above*, can be planted with scented flowers, small shrubs and aromatic herbs, which will revel in the well-drained soil such an arrangement provides.

Most gardeners will enjoy having a raised bed in their garden, but it is disabled gardeners, elderly people or those who find it difficult to bend, who will benefit most from having the plants brought to a manageable level.

When creating a raised garden for this purpose, be sure to allow adequate space between the beds for a wheelchair to be manoeuvred easily. As shown in the drawings, *left* and *below*, each bed should be made just wide enough to allow the centre to be comfortably reached by someone sitting down.

The ground around the raised beds should be smooth, level and, preferably, paved.

piece of wood is the best tool to use for applying the mixture. Start at the top at a corner and work downwards; the mixture dries quickly, so you must work fast. When it is dry pat it over with a mixture of composted manure and milk; this will encourage lichens and moss to grow.

You can use a different soil mixture in each trough or raised bed to accommodate lime-loving and acid-loving plants separately; or, as a friend has proved in his exciting garden full of alpine plants, you can just use plain pea gravel with an initial handful of bonemeal.

One of the most exciting plants for the limy trough will be *Daphne cneorum eximia*, which likes a well-nourished soil and full sun. The stems are almost prostrate, the flowers larger and deeper pink than in the more common *mezereum*; the form with the leaf edged by a narrow band of gold adds year-long interest. These and the sweet-smelling *D. retusa* love the

good drainage of raised beds. But *D. blagayana*, a creeping species that rambles about when happily situated – pegged down with stones and given plenty of leaf mould – would be totally unhappy in a raised bed.

Leontopodium haplolhylloide, the well-known edelweiss, is strongly scented of lemon and revels in dry conditions, when its woolly white stars will bloom to perfection as they do when the plant is growing in the wild on a sunny mountainside.

Petrocallis pyrenaica, rock beauty, which has 5cm/2in high pale lilac or white flowers with a distinct smell of honey, is also a lover of sunshine and good drainage; as is *Coronilla valentina*, a dwarf version of the more usual *C. glauca*, whose pea-like yellow flowers smell most sweetly at night.

Do not forget the more common treasures just because you have already grown them elsewhere in the garden. The wonderful *Prim-*

ula auricula, with clear yellow flowers and rosettes of leathery leaves dusted with gold, has a delicious fragrance. The variety 'Dusty Miller' goes back in my memory to the days when I first realized the excitement of gardening: there it was with its distinctive covering of golden 'meal', growing in the top of a wall. These lovely auriculas, which like a peaty well-drained soil, have now been developed to produce, in cultivation, a wide range of subtle colours, from blues to a dark red.

Lavandula stoechas and *L. dentata*, with good drainage and a bit of protection, will survive cold winters; and all the thymes make superb plants for raised beds.

Mentha requienii, the tiny Corsican mint, is a gem for a raised bed. It has a powerful, minty scent and minute leaves and flowers, but will make a dense, evergreen mat provided you allow it enough moisture and some shade. *Satureia subspicata* is an intriguing dwarf

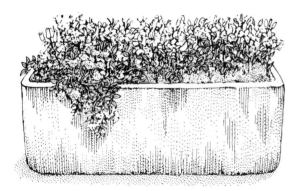

Alpine plants, if not grown in special rock gardens, do well in old stone sinks or troughs as shown *left*, and a small raised bed such as this is ideal for a balcony garden.

The construction, *left*, of wooden railway ties and stout planks of wood that have been treated with a wood preservative, is both a garden seat and a raised bed, where scented alpine plants and similar fragrant flowers may be planted to enjoy at close quarters.

Fragrant jasmine and climbing roses, trained over a cupola, shelter a garden seat, *right*, planted with creeping thyme and chamomile that release their scent when touched. Fragrant benches such as this were once a popular feature, especially in Elizabethan gardens.

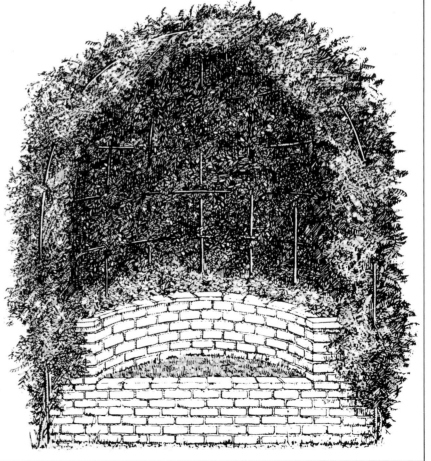

Heightened scents 2

The ancient Egyptians associated the water-lily with Osiris, the god of the dead, who represented reincarnation and eternal life, because the flowers of some species of water-lily withdraw under the water at sunset to re-emerge at dawn in the first rays of the rising sun.

ing *Santolina chamaecyparissus* 'Weston', only 15cm/6in high at its tallest, is a mass of shining silver-white filigree leaves. Touch them and their scent will stay on your fingers for a long while.

A marvellously fragrant sub-shrub for the back of the raised bed with a wall behind it is *Escholtzia stauntonii*. It is semi-woody but dies back almost completely in the winter, sending up new downy shoots with aromatic leaves in the spring and pink flower spikes in the autumn. It is an unusual plant but well worth searching for. Having found it, it is not difficult to propogate using semi-ripe shoots in late summer.

My final thought on raised beds and troughs is that when you have finished your planting you should add a layer of chipped stone or pea gravel. Not only does this help to retain the moisture, but it keeps the soil cool on blazing summer days, and keeps the flowers from being splashed on really wet ones.

If you have a small garden or a patio and an urge to grow water-lilies, then a raised tank or raised tiny pool would be a good idea, provided it is in full sun. For the patio garden this could be quite small, only a square metre/yard, and still contain a water-lily and one or two other small plants, which should all be scented. In a larger pool, three or four types of scented water-lily could be grown.

Two varieties from which to choose are *Nymphea odorata alba* and *N. odorata minor*. Both have distinctive circular leaves with a purplish tinge when they are young, becoming greener as they mature. *N. odorata minor* comes from the shallow marshes of New Jersey and

savory, only 20cm/8in high, with aromatic leaves and flowers opening in the autumn; and then there is the even smaller *Origanum amanum*, only 15cm/6in high, with tubular pink flowers and aromatic leaves.

Most of the large dianthus tribe will thrive in well-drained and sunny raised beds: 'Mrs Sinkins', 'Pike's Pink', 'Waithman's Beauty' and 'Constance Finnis', with a lovely single flower, crimson dappled with white. The double salmon-pink, 15cm/6in high 'Emile Paré' flowers over a long period, and you must include some of the self-coloured, clove-scented varieties 'Lustre Clove', 'Lavender Clove' and 'Glynde Clove'; they will scent the air deliciously for you.

From the Faulkland Islands comes the scen-

ted *Sisyrinchium filifolium*, 15cm/6in tall, with elegant, nodding, scented white bells, lightly traced with faint red lines.

It always surprises me when I squeeze the leaves of the low-growing *Dimorphotheca barberiae compacta* and rediscover how strongly scented it is. The daisy flowers are pink with a darker centre and, given plenty of sunshine, continue to appear throughout the summer. Another fragrant treasure is *Dionysia aretiodides*, which makes a 7.5cm/3in hummock of grey foliage, covered in spring with primrose-scented yellow flowers. It likes lime and plenty of grit, but will only succeed if protected from winter rain.

The resinous quality of the scent of dwarf conifers is especially appealing and the charm-

has abundantly produced, fragrant, star-shaped flowers only 8cm/3in across. For a pink flower you could plant the strongly scented *N. caroliniana* with slender, soft-pink petals and conspicuous yellow stamens – it is a plant of great merit both for its fragrance and performance. A recently introduced cultivar is 'Dorothy Lamour', raised in the United States in 1960. It has small yellow blooms with a greenish flush. You will certainly enjoy this water-lily in a waist-high pool as not only are the yellow flowers fragrant, but the oval leaves which float on the water's surface are curiously variable. The top of the leaves is olive green with crimson flecks, but turn them over and you will see the leaves are much paler on their undersides and have bold red markings. Then look under the water, for the submerged leaves are arrow-shaped, more yellow than green and have maroon blotches.

These are suggestions for white, pink or yellow water-lilies to grow in a patio pool, but my advice is to keep your choice to one colour as you will not want to overcrowd a tiny pool, and you must leave space for other plants.

Before leaving the subject of water-lilies, I must mention the exciting pigmy varieties which you can easily grow in a bowl or half-barrel tub, either indoors or out. The most accommodating are *N. pygmea alba* and *N. pygmea helvola*, a pretty pale primrose. Find a bowl at least 30cm/12in across and 18cm/7in deep, put in 5–7cm/2–3in of soil, and firmly plant one lily. Add a layer of pebbles and fill the bowl with water. This could provide you with a succession of blooms from midsummer until Christmas time.

Water was an important part of early gardens: it was used to create fountains and channels which supplied the irrigation system that watered the garden.

Today, water gardens are usually decorative and can take the shape of a formal pool, *right*, or barrels and tubs, *left*, on a patio. Both arrangements make attractive settings for scented aquatic plants.

Appendix

Plants with scented leaves

Acacia dealbata
Achillea filipendulina
Achillea millefolium
Acorus calamus
Allium spp.
Althaea officinalis
Anethum graveolens (syn.
   Peucedanum graveolens)
Angelica archangelica
Anthemis nobilis (syn.
   Chamaemelum nobile)
Anthriscus cerefolium
Artemisia abrotanum
Artemisia absinthium
Artemisia camphorata
Artemisia dracunculus
Asperula odorata
   (syn. Galium odoratum)
Borago officinalis
Boswellia carteri
Calamintha grandiflora
Calendula officinalis
Calycanthus floridus
Carum carvi
Cedronella triphylla
Choisya ternata
Chimonanthus praecox
   (syn. C. fragrans)
Chrysanthemum balsamita
   (syn. Balsamita major)
Chrysanthemum balsamita
   tanacetoides (syn.
   Balsamita major
   tanacetoides)
Chrysanthemum parthenium
   (syn. Tanacetum
   parthenium)
Cistus ladanifer
Citrus spp.
Commiphora myrrha
Dictamnus albus
   (syn. D. fraxinella)
Dracocephalum moldavicum
Dracocephalum sibiricum
   (syn. Nepeta sibirica)
Drimys lanceolata
   (syn. D. aromatica)
Elsholtzia stauntonii
Escallonia rubra macrantha
Eucalyptus spp.
Filipendula ulmaria
Foeniculum vulgare
Helichrysum angustifolium
Helichrysum italicum
Humea elegans
Humulus lupulus
Hypericum: most spp.
Hysoppus officinalis
Illicium floridanum
Illicium griffithii
Illicium religiosum
Lavandula spp.
Levisticum officinale
Lippia citriodora (syn.
   Aloysia triphylla)

Melissa officinalis
Mentha spp.
Monarda didyma
Monarda fistulosa
Myrrhis odorata
Myrtus spp.
Ocimum spp.
Origanum spp.
Osmanthus fragrans
Pelargonium 'Clorinda'
Pelargonium fragrans
Pelargonium graveolens
Pelargonium 'Mabel Grey'
Pelargonium quercifolium
Pelargonium radula
Pelargonium tomentosum
Petroselinum crispum
Petroselinum sativum
Phuopsis stylosa
Pittosporum eugenioides
Populus acuminata
Populus balsamifera
Populus trichocarpa
Prostanthera sieberi
Ribes viburnifolium
Rosa eglanteria
   (syn. R. rubiginosa)
Rosmarinus spp.
Ruta graveolens 'Jackman's
   Blue'
Salvia spp.
Sanguisorba minor (syn.
   Poterium sanguisorba)
Santolina chamaecyparissus
Santolina incana
Saponaria officinalis
Satureia spp.
Tagetes spp.
Tanacetum vulgare
Teucrium chamaedrys
Thuya plicata
Thymus spp.

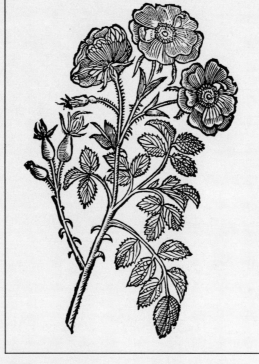

Plants with scented flowers

Abeliophyllum distichum
Acacia dealbata
Achillea millefolium
Acidanthera bicolor
Acorus calamus
Albizia julibrissin
Allium spp.
Alyssum maritimum (syn.
   Lobularia maritimum)
Amaryllis belladonna
Anthericum liliago
Aponogeton distachyus
Arbutus unedo
Asperula orientalis
   (syn. A. azurea setosa)
Azara microphylla
Berberis julianae
Borago officinalis
Boswellia carteri
Bouvardia humboldtii
   corymbiflora
Bouvardia jasminiflora
Bouvardia longiflora
Brompton stock
Buddleia spp.
Calamintha grandiflora
Calendula officinalis
Calycanthus floridus
Centaurea imperialis
Centaurea moschata
Cestrum aurantiacum
Cestrum parqui
Cheiranthus cheiri

Chimonanthus praecox
   (syn. C. fragrans)
Chionanthus virginicus
Chionodoxa luciliae
Choisya ternata
Cistus ladanifer
Citrus spp.
Clematis cirrhosa
Clematis cirrhosa balearica
   (syn. C. calycina)
Clematis flammula
Clematis jouiniana
Clematis macropetala
Clematis montana
Clematis rehderiana
Clerodendron bungei
Clerodendron capitatum
Clerodendron splendens
Clerodendron trichotomum
Convallaria majalis
Coronilla glauca
Coronilla valentina
Corydalis bulbosa
   (syn. C. cava)
Corydalis lutea
Crambe cordifolia
Crataegus monogyna
Crataegus oxyacantha
Crinum moorei
Crinum × powellii
Crocus spp.
Cyclamen spp.
Cytisus battandieri
Daphne spp.
Datura spp.

Decumaria sinensis
Dianthus spp.
Dictamnus albus
   (syn. D. fraxinella)
Dimorphotheca barberae
   compacta
Dionysia aretioides
Dracocephalum
   moldavicum
Dracocephalum sibiricum
   (syn. Nepeta sibirica)
Dregia sinensis
Drimys lanceolata
   (syn. D. aromatica)
Drimys winteri
Echinopsis multiplex
Elaeagnus spp.
Escallonia rubra
   macrantha
Eucharis grandiflora
Filipendula hexapetala
Filipendula ulmaria
Freesia × kewensis
   (F. × hybrida)
Fritillaria imperialis
Galtonia candicans
Galanthus spp.
Gardenia jasminoides
Gladiolus alatus
Gladiolus carinatus
Gladiolus gracilis
Gladiolus tristis
Hamamelis mollis
Heliotropium peruvianum
Hemerocallis flava
Hesperis matronalis
Hesperis tristis
Hoya bella
Hoya carnosa
Humea elegans
Humulus lupulus
Hypericum androsaemum
Hypericum balearicum
Illicium floridanum
Illicium griffithii
Illicium religiosum
Iris spp.
Itea ilicifolia
Jasminum spp.
Lantana camara mutabilis
Lathyrus odoratus
Laurus nobilis
Lavandula spp.
Leontopodium
   haplolhylloides
Lilium spp.
Limnanthes douglasii
Lonicera spp.
Lupinus arboreus
Lupinus polyphyllus
Magnolia spp.
Mahonia japonica
Mahonia lomariifolia
Matthiola bicornis
Mirabilis jalapa
Monarda didyma
Monarda fistulosa

Muscari spp.
Muscarimia moschatum
   (syn. Muscari
   moschatum)
Myosotis spp.
Narcissus albus plenus
   odoratus
Narcissus areissus triandus
Narcissus canaliculatus
Narcissus jonquilla
Narcissus poeticus
Narcissus poeticus recurvus
Narcissus pseudonarcissus
Narcissus tazetta
Nemesia floribunda
Nepeta mussinii
   (Nepeta × faassenii)
Nerium oleander
Nicotiana alata (syn.
   Nicotiana affinis)
Nicotiana suaveolens
Nicotiana sylvestris
Nymphaea alba
Nymphaea caerulea
Nymphaea caroliniana
Nymphaea marliacea
   'Albida'
Nymphaea odorata vars.
Nymphaea pygmea alba
Nymphaea pygmea helvola
Oenothera spp.
Origanum marjorana
Origanum vulgare
Osmanthus fragrans
Osmanthus heterophyllus
   (syn. O. ilicifolius)
Osmaria burkwoodii
   (formerly Osmanthus
   burkwoodii)
Oxalis enneaphylla
Paeonia emodi
Paeonia lactiflora
Paeonia mlokosewitschii
Paeonia officinalis
Petasites fragrans
Petrocallis pyrenaica
Philadelphus spp.
Phillyrea angustifolia
Phillyrea latifolia
Phlox maculata
Phlox paniculata
Pittosporum spp.
Plumeria spp.
Polianthes tuberosa
Polyanthus (Primula
   vulgaris × P. veris)
Polygonatum multiflorum
   (P. × hybridum)
Poncirus trifoliata
Primula spp.
Prostanthera sieberi
Prunus laurocerasus
Puschkinia libanotica
Reseda odorata
Rhododendron discolor
Rhododendron edgeworthii
   (syn. R. bullatum)

Rhododendron
  'Fragrantissimum'
Rhododendron 'July
  Fragrance'
Rhododendron Loderi
Rhododendron luteum
Rhododendron
  'Midsummer Snow'
Rhododendron occidentale
Ribes aureum
Ribes laurifolium
Ribes odoratum
Ribes sanguineum
Robinia pseudacacia
Romenya coulteri
Rosa: most vars.
Ruta graveolens 'Jackman's
  Blue'
Saponaria officinalis
Sarcococca hookeriana
  digyna
Sarcococca ruscifolia
Satureia subspicata
Scilla spp.
Sedum spectabile
Selenicereus grandiflora
Sisyrinchium filifolium
Skimmia japonica
Skimmia reevesiana
Smilacina racemosa
Spartium junceum
Stephanotis floribunda
Syringa spp.
Tagetes spp.
Trachelospermum asiaticum
Trachelospermum
  jasminoides
Tropaeolum majus
Tulipa celsiana
  (syn. T. persica)
Tulipa gesneriana
Tulipa sylvestris
Verbena × hybrida
Viburnum spp.
Viola canina
Viola cornuta
Viola odorata
Wisteria sinensis

Scented plants for spring

Abeliophyllum distichum
Acacia dealbata
Acidanthera bicolor
Allium schoenoprasum
Anthericum liliago
Aponogeton distachyus
Azara microphylla
Berberis julianae
Brompton stock
Buddleia crispa
Buddleia globosa
Cheiranthus cheiri
Chionodoxa luciliae
Choisya ternata
Clematis cirrhosa
Clematis cirrhosa balearica
  (syn. C. calycina)
Clematis montana
Convallaria majalis
Coronilla glauca
Coronilla valentina
Corydalis bulbosa
  (syn. C. cava)
Crataegus monogyna
Crataegus oxyacantha
Crocus ancyrensis
Crocus chrysanthus
Crocus susianus
  (syn. C. angustifolia)
Crocus tomasinianus
Cyclamen balearicum
Cyclamen creticum
Cyclamen hederifolium
  (syn. C. neapolitanum)
Cyclamen persicum
Daphne spp.
Decumaria sinensis
Dionysia aretioides
Drimys winteri
Freesia × kewensis
  (F. × hybrida)
Fritillaria imperialis
Galanthus elwesii
Galanthus nivalis
Gladiolus gracilis
Hamamelis mollis
Hebe 'Mrs. Winder'
Iris florentina
Iris germanica
Iris graminea
Iris histrioides
Iris reticulata
Iris unguicularis
  (syn. I. stylosa)
Jasminum mesnyi
  (syn. J. primulinum)
Lonicera fragrantissima
Lonicera syringantha
Magnolia heptapeta
  (syn. M. denudata)
Magnolia kobia stellata
Mahonia japonica
Mentha spicata
Muscari armeniacum
Muscari botryoides

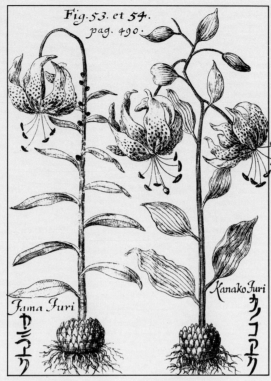

Fig. 53. et 54.
pag. 490.

Fama Juri

Kanako Juri

Muscarimia moschatum
  (syn. Muscari
  moschatum)
Myosotis spp.
Narcissus: scented spp.
Osmanthus fragrans
Osmaria burkwoodii
  (formerly Osmanthus
  burkwoodii)
Paeonia officinalis
Pelargonium 'Clorinda'
Pelargonium graveolens
Pelargonium fragrans
Pelargonium 'Mabel Grey'
Pelargonium quercifolium
Pelargonium radula
Pelargonium tomentosum
Petasites fragrans
Philadelphus microphyllus
Phillyrea angustifolia
Phillyrea latifolia
Pittosporum tenuifolium
Polygonatum multiflorum
  (P. × hybridum)
Poncirus trifoliata
Populus acuminata
Populus balsamifera
Populus trichocarpa
Primula auricula vars.
Primula denticulata
Primula florindae
Primula involucrata
Primula veris
Primula vulgaris
Prostanthera sieberi

Prunus laurocerasus 'Otto
  Luyken'
Puschkinia libanotica
Rhododendron
  'Princess Alice'
Rhododendron prinophyllum
  (syn. R. roseum)
Rhododendron edgeworthii
  (syn. R. bullatum)
Rhododendron
  'Fragrantissimum'
Rhododendron luteum
Rhododendron occidentale
Ribes aureum
Ribes laurifolium
Ribes odoratum
Ribes sanguineum
Rosa primula
Sarcococca hookeriana
  dignya
Sarcococca ruscifolia
Scilla nutans (syn.
  Endymion non-scriptus)
Scilla sibirica
Skimmia japonica
Skimmia reevesiana
Smilacina racemosa
Syringa spp.
Tulipa gesneriana
Tulipa sylvestris
Viburnum 'Anne Russell'
Viburnum × burkwoodii
Viburnum × bodnantense
Viburnum carlcephalum
Viburnum carlesii

Viburnum fragrans
  (syn. V. farreri)
Viola canina
Viola cornuta
Viola odorata
Wisteria sinensis

Scented plants for summer

Achillea filipendulina
Achillea millefolium
Acorus calamus
Albizia julibrissin
Allium cepa proliferum
Allium fistulosum
Allium sativum
Alyssum maritimum (syn.
  Lobularia maritimum)
Aponogeton distachyus
Artemisia dracunculus
Asperula orientalis
  (syn. A. azurea setosa)
Borago officinalis
Bouvardia humboldtii
  corymbiflora
Bouvardia jasminiflora
Bouvardia longiflora
Brompton stock
Buddleia alternifolia
Buddleia colvilei
Buddleia crispa
Buddleia davidii
Buddleia fallowiana
Buddleia globosa
Calendula officinalis
Calycanthus floridus
Centaurea imperialis
Centaurea moschata
Cestrum aurantiacum
Cestrum nocturnum
Cestrum parqui
Cheiranthus cheiri
Chionanthus virginicus
Citrus spp.
Clematis flammula
Clematis jouiniana
Clematis macropetala
Clematis montana
Clematis rehderiana
Clerodendron capitatum
Convalleria majalis
Coronilla glauca
Coronilla valentina
Corydalis bulbosa
  (syn. C. cava)
Corydalis lutea
Crambe cordifolia
Cyclamen creticum
Cyclamen europaeum
Cytisus battandieri
Daphne alpina
Datura spp.
Dianthus spp.
Dictamnus albus
  (syn. D. fraxinella)
Dracocephalum
  moldavicum

Dracocephalum sibiricum
  (syn. Nepeta sibirica)
Dregia sinensis
Echinopsis multiplex
Escallonia rubra macrantha
Filipendula hexapetala
Freesia × kewensis
  (F. × hybrida)
Galtonia candicans
Gardenia jasminoides
Gladiolus alatus
Gladiolus carinatus
Gladiolus gracilis
Gladiolus tristis
Helichrysum angustifolium
Helichrysum italicum
Heliotropium peruvianum
Hemerocallis flava
Hesperis matronalis
Hesperis tristis
Hoya bella
Hoya carnosa
Humea elegans
Hypericum spp.
Iris pallida dalmatica
Itea ilicifolia
Jasminum officinale
Jasminum parkeri
Jasminum polyanthum
Jasminum stephanense
Lantana camara mutabilis
Lathyrus odoratus
Lavandula spp.
Lilium auratum
Lilium candidum
Lilium hansonii
Lilium henryi
Lilium longiflorum
Lilium regale
Limnanthes douglasii
Lonicera americana
Lonicera japonica
Lonicera periclymenum
Lonicera × tellmanniana
Lupinus arboreus
Lupinus polyphyllus
Magnolia grandiflora
Magnolia × wieseneri
  (formerly
  M. × watsonii)
Magnolia wilsonii
Matthiola bicornis
Mentha spp.
Monarda didyma
Monarda fistulosa
Myosotis spp.
Myrtus communis
Myrtus luma
Nemesia floribunda
Nepeta mussinii
  (N. × faassenii)
Nerium oleander
Nicotiana alata
  (syn. N. affinis)
Nicotiana suaveolens
Nymphaea alba
Nymphaea caerulea

Nymphaea caroliniana
Nymphaea marliacea
 'Albida'
Nymphaea odorata vars.
Nymphaea pygmea alba
Nymphaea pygmea helvola
Oenothera biennis
Oenothera caespitosa
Oenothera missouriensis
Osmanthus fragrans
Oxalis enneaphylla
Paeonia emodi
Paeonia lactiflora
Paeonia mlokosewitschii
Pelargonium 'Clorinda'
Pelargonium fragrans
Pelargonium graveolens
Pelargonium 'Mabel Grey'
Pelargonium quercifolium
Pelargonium radula
Pelargonium tomentosum
Philadelphus coronarius
Phillyrea angustifolia
Phillyrea latifolia
Phlox maculata
Phlox paniculata
Phuopsis stylosa
Pittosporum tobira
Polianthes tuberosa
Polyanthus (Primula
 vulgaris × P. veris)
Primula veris
Reseda odorata
Rhododendron discolor
Rhododendron
 'Fragrantissimum'
Rhododendron 'July
 Fragrance'
Rhododendron Loderi
Rhododendron
 'Midsummer Snow'
Rhododendron 'Polar Bear'
Robinia pseudacacia
Romenya coulteri
Rosa: most spp.
Salvia sclarea
Spartium junceum
Stephanotis floribunda
Tagetes spp.
Trachelospermum asiaticum
Trachelospermum
 jasminoides
Tropaeolum majus
Tulipa celsiana
 (syn. *Tulipa persica*)
Verbena × hybrida
Viola cornuta

Scented plants for autumn

Allium schoenoprasum
Alyssum maritimum (syn.
 Lobularia maritimum)
Amaryllis belladonna
Artemisia dracunculus
Aponogeton distachyus
Azara microphylla
Buddleia alternifolia
Buddleia davidii
Calendula officinalis
Centaurea imperialis
Centaurea moschata
Choisya ternata
Clematis flammula
Clematis jouiniana
Clematis rehderiana
Clerodendron bungei
Clerodendron capitatum
Clerodendron trichotomum
Coronilla glauca
Coronilla valentina
Corydalis lutea
Crinum moorei
Crinum × powellii
Crocus longiflorus
Crocus speciosus
Cyclamen alpinum
Cyclamen cilicium
Cyclamen europaeum
Cyclamen hederifolium
 (syn. *C. neapolitanum*)
Daphne cneorum
Dianthus barbatus
Escallonia rubra
 macrantha
Galanthus nivalis reginae-
 olgae
Gardenia jasminoides
Jasminum officinale
Jasminum parkeri
Jasminum polyanthum
Jasminum stephanense
Lantana camara mutabilis
Lilium candidum
Lilium henryi
Lilium speciosum
Lonicera japonica
Lonicera periclymenum
Mentha spp.
Nerium oleander
Nicotiana alata
 (syn. *N. affinis*)
Oenothera biennis
Osmanthus heterophyllus
 (syn. *O. ilicifolius*)
Paeonia officinalis
Pelargonium 'Clorinda'
Pelargonium fragrans
Pelargonium graveolens
Pelargonium 'Mabel Grey'
Pelargonium quercifolium
Pelargonium radula
Pelargonium tomentosum
Phlox paniculata
Rosa chinensis

Rosa damescena bifera
 (syn. *R. d. semperflorens*)
Rosa rugosa rubra
Roses:
 'Blanc Double de
 Coubert'
 'Boule de Neige'
 'Buff Beauty'
 'Cornelia'
 'Gloire de Dijon'
 'Kathleen Harrop'
 'Mme Alfred Carrière'
 'Mme Isaac Pereire'
 'Mme Pierre Oger'
 'Moonlight'
 'Prosperity'
 'Roseraie de l'Hay'
 'Stanwell Perpetual'
Satureia subscripta
Sedum spectabile
Spartium junceum
Stephanotis floribunda
Verbena × hybrida
Viburnum fragrans
 (syn. *V. farreri*)

Scented plants for winter

Abeliophyllum distichum
Acacia dealbata
Anthriscus cerefolium
Azara microphylla
Chimonanthus praecox
 (syn. *C. fragrans*)
Coronilla glauca
Crocus laevigatus fontenayi
Cyclamen hederifolium
 (syn. *C. neapolitanum*)
Freesia × kewensis
 (*F. × hybrida*)
Galanthus nivalis
Hamamelis mollis
Iris histrioides
Iris unguicularis
 (syn. *I. stylosa*)
Lonicera fragrantissima
Mahonia japonica
Origanum marjorana
Origanum vulgare
Osmanthus fragrans
Pelargonium 'Clorinda'
Pelargonium fragrans
Pelargonium graveolens
Pelargonium 'Mabel Grey'
Pelargonium quercifolium
Pelargonium radula
Pelargonium tomentosum
Petroselinum crispum

Puschkinia libanotica
Ribes laurifolium
Rosmarinus lavandulaceus
Rosmarinus officinalis
Salvia rutilans
Sarcococca hookeriana
 digyna
Sarcococca ruscifolia
Scilla mischtschenkoana
 'Tubergeniana'
Scilla sibirica
Thymus × citriodorus
Viburnum × bodnantense
Viburnum foetens
Viburnum fragrans
 (syn. *V. farreri*)
Viola odorata

Scented plants for evening and night

Cestrum aurantiacum
Cestrum nocturnum
Cestrum parqui
Daphne laureola
Daphne pontica
Datura spp.
Echinopsis multiplex
Gladiolus tristis
Hemerocallis flava
Hesperis matronalis
Hesperis tristis
Hoya bella
Hoya carnosa
Mahonia lomariifolia
Matthiola bicornis
Nicotiana alata
 (syn. *N. affinis*)
Nicotiana suaveolens
Nicotiana sylvestris
Oenothera biennis
Oenothera caespitosa
Petasites fragrans
Phuopsis stylosa
Selenicereus grandiflora
Viola cornuta

Scented plants for culinary uses

Acorus calamus
Allium cepa proliferum
Allium fistulosa
Allium sativum
Allium schoenoprasum
Althaea officinalis
Anethum graveolens
 (syn. *P. graveolens*)
Angelica archangelica
Anthemis nobilis (syn.
 Chamaemelum nobile)
Anthriscus cerefolium
Artemisia dracunculus
Borago officinalis
Calamintha grandiflora
Calendula officinalis
Carum carvi
Coriandrum sativum
Crocus sativus
Drimys lanceolata
 (syn. *D. aromatica*)
Foeniculum vulgare
Humulus lupulus
Hyssopus officinalis
Laurus nobilis
Levisticum officinale
Lippia citriodora
 (syn. *Aloysia triphylla*)
Mentha × piperita citrata
Mentha × piperita officinalis
Mentha spicata
Mentha × suaveolens
 (syn. *M. rotundifolia*)
Mentha × villosa
 alopecuroides
Myrrhis odorata
Myrtus communis
Ocimum basilicum
Ocimum minimum
Origanum marjorana
Origanum vulgare
Petroselinum crispum
Petroselinum sativum
Poncirus trifoliata
Primula veris
Rosmarinus lavandulaceus
Rosmarinus officinalis
Salvia officinalis
Salvia rutilans
Salvia sclarea
Sanguisorba minor (syn.
 Poterium sanguisorba)
Satureia hortensis
Satureia montana
Thymus × citriodorus
Thymus herbabarona
Thymus serpyllum
Thymus vulgaris
Tropaeolum majus
Viola odorata

Scented plants for cutting

Abeliophyllum distichum
Acacia dealbata
Achillea millefolia
Acidanthera bicolor
Alyssum maritimum (syn.
    Lobularia maritimum)
Buddleia spp.
Calendula officinalis
Centaurea imperialis
Centaurea moschata
Cheiranthus cheiri
Choisya ternata
Chimonanthus praecox
    (syn. C. fragrans)
Citrus spp.
Clematis cirrhosa
Clematis cirrhosa balearica
    (syn. C. calycina)
Clematis flammula
Clematis jouiniana
Clematis macropetala
Clematis montana
Clematis rehderiana
Convallaria majalis
Daphne spp.
Dianthus spp.
Eucharis grandiflora
Freesia × kewensis
    (F. × hybrida)
Galtonia candicans
Galtonia elwesii
Galtonia nivalis
Gardenia jasminoides
Gladiolus tristis
Hamamelis mollis
Heliotropium peruvianum
Hesperis matronalis
Iris graminea
Iris pallida dalmatica
Iris reticulata
Iris unguicularis
    (syn. I. stylosa)
Itea ilicifolia
Jasminum polyanthum
Lathyrus odoratus
Lavandula spp.
Lonicera fragrantissima
Lonicera japonica
Lonicera periclymenum
Lonicera × tellmanniana
Lupinus arboreus
Lupinus polyphyllus
Matthiola bicornis
Mentha × villosa
    alopecuroides
Monarda didyma
Monarda fistulosa
Muscari armeniacum
Muscari botryoides
Muscarimia moschatum
    (syn. Muscari
    moschatum)
Myosotis spp.
Narcissus albus plenus
    odoratus
Narcissus areissus triandus
Narcissus canaliculatus
Narcissus jonquilla
Narcissus poeticus
Narcissus poeticus recurvus
Narcissus tazetta
Nepeta mussinii
    (N. × faassenii)
Nerium oleander
Nicotiana alata
    (syn. N. affinis)
Nymphaea alba
Nymphaea caerulea
Nymphaea caroliniana
Nymphaea marliacea
    'Albida'
Nymphaea odorata vars.
Nymphaea pygmea vars.
Osmaria burkwoodii
    (formerly Osmanthus
    burkwoodii)
Paeonia emodi
Paeonia lactiflora
Paeonia mlokosewitschii
Paeonia officinalis
Philadelphus spp.
Phlox maculata
Phlox paniculata
Polianthes tuberosa
Polyanthus (Primula
    vulgaris × P. veris)
Primula auricula vars.
Primula veris
Primula vulgaris
Puschkinia libanotica
Scilla mischtschenkoana
    'Tubergeniana'
Scilla nutans (syn.
    Endymion non-scriptus)
Scilla sibirica
Stephanotis floribunda
Thymus herbabarona
Thymus serpyllum
Thymus vulgaris
Tropaeolum majus
Verbena × hybrida
Viburnum 'Anne Russell'
Viburnum × bodnantense
Viburnum × burkwoodii
Viburnum carlcephalum
Viburnum carlesii
Viburnum foetens
Viola odorata

Scented plants for growing indoors

Acacia dealbata
Albizia julibrissin
Artemisia dracunculus
Bouvardia humboldtii
    corymbiflora
Bouvardia jasminiflora
Bouvardia longiflora
Cedronella triphylla
Centaurea imperialis
Centaurea moschata
Clerodendron bungei
Clerodendron capitatum
Clerodendron splendens
Clerodendron trichotomum
Commiphora myrrha
Crocus chrysanthus
Crocus longiflorus
Crocus speciosus
Cyclamen balearicum
Cyclamen creticum
Cyclamen persicum
Dregia sinensis
Echinopsis multiplex
Eucharis grandiflora
Freesia × kewensis
    (F. × hybrida)
Gardenia jasminoides
Gladiolus alatus
Gladiolus carinatus
Gladiolus gracilis
Hesperis tristis
Hoya bella
Hoya carnosa
Humea elegans
Iris reticulata
Jasminum mesnyi
    (syn. J. primulinum)
Jasminum officinale
Jasminum polyanthum
Jasminum stephanense
Myrtus communis tarentina
Narcissus jonquilla
Narcissus poeticus
Narcissus poeticus recurvus
Narcissus tazetta
Nerium oleander
Ocimum basilicum
Ocimum minimum
Osmanthus fragrans
Pelargonium 'Clorinda'
Pelargonium fragrans
Pelargonium graveolens
Pelargonium 'Mabel Grey'
Pelargonium quercifolium
Pelargonium radula
Pelargonium tomentosum
Plumeria spp.
Polianthes tuberosa
Polyanthus (Primula
    vulgaris × P. veris)
Primula auricula vars.
Prostanthera sieberi

Salvia rutilans
Sarcococca hookeriana
    digyna
Sarcococca ruscifolia
Scilla sibirica
Selenicereus grandiflora
Stephanotis floribunda
Trachelospermum asiaticum
Trachelospermum
    jasminoides

Scented plants for outdoor tubs

Acidanthera bicolor
Bouvardia humboldtii
    corymbiflora
Bouvardia jasminiflora
Bouvardia longiflora
Cedronella triphylla
Cheiranthus cheiri
Choisya ternata
Citrus spp.
Coronilla glauca
Coronilla valentina
Crocus chrysanthus
Crocus longiflorus
Cyclamen cilicium
Cyclamen hederifolium
    (syn. C. neapolitanum)
Cyclamen persicum
Daphne alpina
Daphne bholia
Daphne cneorum
Daphne laureola
Daphne mezereum
Daphne odora
Daphne pontica
Daphne retusa
Datura spp.
Dianthus spp.
Dimorphotheca barberae
    compacta
Elsholtzia stauntonii
Eucalyptus citriodora
Freesia × kewensis
    (F. × hybrida)
Fritillaria imperialis
Galanthus nivalis
Gardenia jasminoides
Heliotropium peruvianum
Iris histrioides
Iris reticulata
Jasminum parkeri
Lavandula spp.
Laurus nobilis
Leontopodium
    haplolhylloides
Lilium auratum
Lilium candidum
Lippia citriodora (syn.
    Aloysia triphylla)
Mentha requienii
Muscari spp.
Myrtus communis tarentina
Narcissus albus plenus
    odoratus
Narcissus canaliculatus
Narcissus jonquilla
Narcissus poeticus
Narcissus poeticus recurvus
Narcissus pseudonarcissus
Narcissus tazetta
Nicotiana suaveolens
Nymphaea caroliniana
Nymphaea odorata minor
Nymphaea pygmea alba
Nymphaea pygmea helvola
Ocimum basilicum
Ocimum minimum
Origanum amanum
Osmaria burkwoodii
    (formerly Osmanthus
    burkwoodii)
Oxalis enneaphylla
Pelargonium 'Clorinda'
Pelargonium fragrans
Pelargonium graveolens
Pelargonium 'Mabel Grey'
Pelargonium quercifolium
Pelargonium radula
Pelargonium tomentosum
Petrocallis pyrenaica
Polyanthus (Primula
    vulgaris × P. veris)
Primula auricula vars.
Prostanthera sieberi
Puschkinia libanotica
Reseda odorata
Rosa chinensis
Ruta graveolens 'Jackman's
    Blue'
Salvia officinalis
Santolina chamaecyparissus
Satureia subspicata
Scilla sibirica
Sisyrinchium filifolium
Tagetes spp.
Thymus spp.
Verbena × hybrida
Viola odorata

Addresses

Should you experience any difficulty in obtaining some of the plants mentioned in *The Scented Garden*, it is possible to purchase them from nurseries outside the United States, but you must first obtain a personal import permit from the Plant Protection and Quarantine Programs. These are issued by the Permit Unit, Plant Protection and Quarantine Programs, Animal and Plant Health Inspection Service, USDA, Federal Building, Hyattsville, MD 20782, or local offices which are listed in the telephone directories. Certain plants are prohibited, but there are exceptions and other plants are restricted, again with exceptions; conditions for importing plants are clearly laid out – they must be free of soil etc. All necessary information is provided by the above office.

It is advisable first to contact the foreign nursery and establish whether or not they will export plants and what their conditions of sale are, as some require a minimum order for export sales. This particular condition can be complied with by several gardeners placing one order together. Of the UK nurseries listed here, those marked with a ● will export to the United States.

Also, information about old-fashioned and shrub roses may be had from the American Heritage Rose Society, c/o Mrs Leone Bell, 101 Cedar Grove Rd., Conshohocken, PA 19428.

UK

Allwood Brothers
Clayton Nurseries
Hassocks
West Sussex BN6 9LX
Hardy border carnations and dianthus (will export seeds)

Barnsley House Gardens
Barnsley House
Barnsley
nr. Cirencester
Gloucestershire GL7 5EE
Trees, shrubs, herbs, herbaceous plants

● Peter Beales
Intwood Nurseries
Swardeston
Norwich NR14 8EA
Roses

● Bees Ltd.
Sealand
Chester CH1 6BA
Trees, shrubs, hardy plants, bulbs, annuals, biennials

Blue Gums
Lamberhurst
Tunbridge Wells
Kent TN3 8AL
Eucalyptus (will export seeds)

Broadleigh Gardens
Barr House
Bishops Hull
Taunton
Somerset TA4 1AE
Bulbs, corms, tubers

● Beth Chatto Gardens
White Barn House
Elmstead Market
Colchester CO7 7DB
Unusual herbaceous plants

● R. Harkness & Co., Ltd.
The Rose Gardens
Hitchin
Hertfordshire SG4 0JT
Roses

● Hillier Nurseries
Ampfield House
Ampfield
nr. Romsey
Hampshire SO5 9PA
Trees, shrubs, roses, alpines

● Notcutts Nurseries Ltd.
Woodbridge
Suffolk IP12 4AF
Trees, shrubs, roses, perennials

● Peveril Nurseries
Derril
nr. Holsworthy
Devon
Clematis

Sherrard's
Garden Centre Ltd.
Wantage Rd.
Donnington
Newbury
Berkshire
Trees, shrubs, roses, perennials

Stoke Lacey Herb Farm
Bromyard
Herefordshire
Herbs (will export seeds)

● Suffolk Herbs
Sawyers Farm
Little Cornard
Sudbury
Suffolk
Herb seeds

● Van Tubergen
304a Upper Richmond Rd. West
London SW14 7JG
Bulbs, corms, tubers

Wells and Winter Ltd.
Mere House
Mereworth
Maidstone
Kent ME18 5NB
Herbs, alpines

USA

Armstrong Nurseries
Ontario
California 91761
Roses

W. Atlee-Burpee Co
Warminster
Pennsylvania 18974
General seed

Bluestone Perennials
Madison
Ohio 44057
Perennials

Carrol Gardens
Westminster
Maryland 21157
Herbs, perennials, shrubs

Jackson and Perkins
Medford
Oregon 97501
Roses

Lauray of Salisbury
Salisbury
Connecticut 06068
Container and indoor plants

Logee's Greenhouses
Danielson
Connecticut 06239
Herbs, container and indoor plants

George W. Park Seed Co
Greenwood
South Carolina 29647
General seed

William Tricker & Sons
Saddle River
New Jersey 07458
Waterlilies

Wayside Gardens
Hodges
South Carolina 29695
Perennials, trees and shrubs

White Flower Farm
Litchfield
Connecticut 06759
Perennials, annuals, biennials

During the late 16th and 17th centuries a group of French Huguenot refugees arrived in England. These people were specialist gardeners and became known as Florists. They concentrated on breeding and propagating hardy perennials such as dianthus and auriculas, and bulbs like tulips and hyacinths, in an effort to create perfect blooms, the best colour and the finest scent.

We are indebted to the Florists, for the results of their labours may be seen in the diversity of colour and form in many of the plants we grow today.

Index

Bibliography

Barber, Angus C. *Annual Flowers*. 1954
Bedichek, Roy *The Sense of Smell*. 1960
Blunt, Wilfred *The Art of Botanical Illustration*. 1950
Blunt, Wilfred and Raphael, Sandra *The Illustrated Herbal*. 1979
Bunyard, Edward A. *Old Garden Roses*. 1936
Coats, Peter *Roses*. 1962
Doerflinger, Fredric *The Bulb Book*. 1973
Fairchild, Thomas *The City Gardener*. 1722
Fletcher, H.L.V. *The Fragrant Garden*. 1965
Foster, Gertrude B. *Herbs for Every Garden*. 1976
Freeman, Margaret B. *The Unicorn Tapestries*. 1976
Furber, Robert *The Flower-Garden Displayed*. 1734 (1st ed. 1732)
Gardiner, Richard *Profitable instructions for the Manuring, Sowing and Planting of Kitchen Gardens*. 1603 (1st ed. 1599)
Garland, Sarah *The Herb and Spice Book*. 1979
Genders, Roy *Scented Flora of the World*. 1977
Gerard, John *The Herball or General Historie of Plantes*. 1597
Gerard, John (ibid.) *very much enlarged and amended by Thomas Johnson*. 1633
Gorer, Richard *The Flower Garden in England*. 1975
Grieve, M.A. *A Modern Herbal*. 1980 (1st ed. 1931)
Hampton, F.A. *Flower Scent*. 1925
Harkness, Jack *The Rose*. 1978
Hibberd, Shirley *Rustic Adornments for Homes of Taste*. 1870
Huxley, Anthony *Plant and Planet*. 1974
Hyll, Thomas *The Proffitable Art of Gardening*. 1568
Hyll, Thomas (Didymus Montaine) *The Gardener's Labyrinth*. 1578
Jekyll, Gertrude *Colour Schemes for the Flower Garden*. 1908 (1st ed. 1896)
Justice William S., and Ritchie Bell, C. *Wild Flowers of North Carolina*. 1968
Kent, Elizabeth *Flora Domestica*. 1823
Lawson, William *The Countrie Huswife's Garden*. 1618
Markham, Gervase *La Maison Rustique*. 1616
Mathews, Brian *Dwarf Bulbs*. 1973
Mathews, Brian *The Larger Bulbs*. 1978
McDonald, Donald *Sweet Scented Flowers and Fragrant Leaves*. 1895
Parkinson, John *Paradisi in sole paradisus terrestris*. 1629
Paul, William *The Rose Garden*. 1848
Rea, John *Flora: seu, de florum cultura*. 1676 (1st ed. 1665)
Robinson, W. *The English Flower Garden*. 1902 (8th ed.)
Salisbury, E.J. *The Living Garden*. 1935
Switzer, Stephan *Ichnographia Rustica: or the Nobleman, Gentleman and Gardener's Recreation*. 1718
Thomas, Graham Stuart *The Old Shrub Roses*. 1955
Thomas, Graham Stuart *Perennial Garden Plants or the Modern Florilegium*. 1976
Turner, William *A newe herball*. 1551
Turner, William *The Second parte of William Turner's herball*. 1562
Tusser, Thomas *Five Hundred Pointes of Good Husbandrie*. 1573
Twamley, Louisa Anne *The Romance of Nature*. 1836 (2nd ed.)
Wilder, Louise Beebe *The Fragrant Garden*. 1974
Wilson, Helen Van Pelt and Bell, Leonie *The Fragrant Year*. 1971
Wirt, Mrs *Flora's Dictionary*. 1855
Worlidge, John *Systema Horti-culturae: or the art of gardening*. 1683 (1st ed. 1677)